Praise for *Diamonds and Dust*

'It is a tale spattered with joy and grief in chronicling one of the great life histories in WA.' *West Weekend Magazine*

'Her story is an epic saga of life in one of the toughest and most beautiful terrains in Australia – a story of hardship, drought, joy and triumph.' *Gold Coast Mail*

'*Diamonds and Dust* tells a remarkable story of strength, courage and love that truly captures the spirit of the Territory.' *Sunday Territorian*

'This is a really inspiring read.' *Good Reading*

'This is the story of an unsung heroine.' *Albany Weekender*.

'While much of the book captures the deep love McCorry has for the diamond-sharp sunsets of the Kimberley, it is the dust of despair that blows across her life. She pulls no punches in this at times brutally frank and astringent book.' *Courier Mail*

'Move over Sara Henderson, here comes Sheryl ... What makes this story so fascinating is its transcending ordinariness.' *Weekend Gold Coast Bulletin*

DIAMONDS
AND
DUST

SHERYL McCORRY

PAN
Pan Macmillan Australia

First published 2007 in Macmillan by Pan Macmillan Australia Pty Limited
This Pan edition published in 2009 by Pan Macmillan Australia Pty Ltd
1 Market Street, Sydney

Reprinted 2009 (four times), 2010 (twice), 2011

National Library of Australia
Cataloguing-in-Publication data:

McCorry, Sheryl.
Diamonds and dust / Sheryl McCorry.

ISBN: 978 0 33042 469 1

1. McCorry, Sheryl. 2. Ranch managers –
Western Australia – Kimberley – Biography.
3. Ranches – Western Australia – Kimberley
– Management.

636.01092

Typeset in 11.5 Janson Text by Midland Typesetters, Australia
Printed in Australia by McPherson's Printing Group

Papers used by Pan Macmillan Australia Pty Ltd are natural, recyclable products made from wood grown in sustainable forests. The manufacturing processes conform to the environmental regulations of the country of origin.

For Kelly

CONTENTS

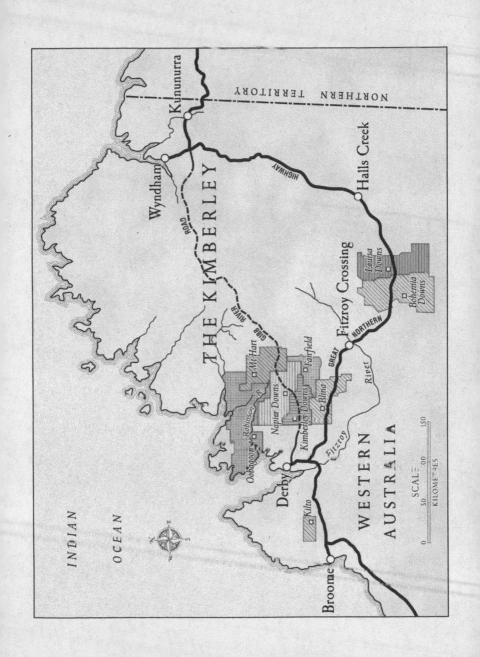

Introduction

Sitting on the back veranda of my farmhouse, I am watching the evening sun fade behind the Porongurup Range near Mount Barker. Their soft curves outlined against the sky, the hills turn different shades of mauve and purple as they dim. In the foreground I see stands of jarrah trees amid grassy paddocks catching the last golden rays of another day. My cattle – black, fleshy Angus – dot the fields. Faintly I can smell woodsmoke.

But in my mind I am not seeing miles, but years. My view stretches across the fields and back in time. I love these foothills so much because they remind me of the King Leopold Ranges, thousands of kilometres up north, which overlooked the great cattle stations where I lived and worked. The names come back: Louisa Downs, Bohemia Downs, Blina, Kilto, Kimberley Downs, Napier Downs, Fairfield. The cattle weren't these glossy well-fed Angus, but tough shorthorns, kicking up bulldust in their tens of thousands. And the sniff of woodsmoke takes me 40 years back, to the crackling glow of a stock-camp fire in the Kimberley.

I am content, this evening, on my small farm in the south-west of Western Australia – but as I look out over the land I travel back through layers of pain, chaos, heartbreaking loss and triumph, right back to when I was 'Yumun', or 'Boss Missus', as an Aboriginal elder would name me, of a million acres.

As a teenager I used to write letters to my grandfather in London. Bruce Watson Wallis had once been editor of the *West Australian*, the only daily metropolitan newspaper in Perth, and was a descendant of the great Scottish warrior William Wallace. My grandfather Wallis encouraged me to write letters and keep diaries, which I did, never dreaming that I would one day be writing the story of my life.

In my letters to him I wrote enthusiastically of the outback: its isolation, the smells and creatures, the parched earth the colour of oxblood. I told my grandfather about daily events and my wild ambitions. I told him how the Kimberley could be romantic and poetic, and how at times I had to abandon all civilised ways.

My grandfather died, and I met a man with a swag and two dogs, much older than me and seemingly unattainable. I remember how he made me forget all my fears and helped me navigate my way through the Kimberley. My 20 years with him were filled with extremes of happiness and tragedy.

Since those early letters to my grandfather, I have always written to heal myself, to cry away sadness as much as relate my encounters with the outback. Now I have lived the life that I barely thought possible when I was a girl writing to grandfather Wallis. I lived it, and I have written it. This is my story.

CHAPTER 1

Fresh Water Rapid Creek

I'll never forget the day Gran burned her bum on the toilet seat. It was 1955 and I was turning six the next day. Gran was taking a quick break from baking my birthday cake.

The house we lived in was perched on the banks of Fresh Water Rapid Creek, a little over 30 kilometres south-east of Darwin. Spear grass and pandanus grew robustly during the wet season, bending and folding during the dry. The house seems huge in my memory. Built of unpainted timber with a plain corrugated-iron roof, it was full of louvres that looked out in every direction. Its centre was a kitchen shared by my mother and grandmother – our two families lived in separate parts of the house on either side of the kitchen, and Mum would feed the children early, before the adults came together in the kitchen for their meal.

Ours was a big, happy, ramshackle household. My mother and father, my four brothers and I lived with Gran and Grandpa Bond, my maternal grandparents. Sometimes my mum's brother Iva lived there too, as well as Uncle Jaffa, a Thursday Islander who was the right-hand man in the road-construction gang of which Grandpa was the foreman.

Grandpa Bond spent the war years in Darwin, keeping the roads and airstrips operational.

The homestead was big enough for all of us. It had accommodated RAAF officers as a dormitory for their Darwin base during the Second World War, and as a result had six 'burning furies' all standing in a row: the toilets. The 'burning furies' were unpredictable and temperamental contraptions, constructed from 44-gallon drums with the bottom cut out and a hole in the top. You would dig a hole and sink half the drum into the ground, leaving enough out for the user to be reasonably comfortable sitting on the thing.

A 44 dug into the earth was not the cleanest device, so a chimney pipe was set into the back of the drum for burning. We would screw up old papers or cardboard, add some kindling and a good dose of diesel fuel, drop in a match, and the burning fury would come to life, the flames chasing spiders and crows as the smoke rattled up through the chimney. The fires cleaned the toilets, and also kept out the redback spiders. I thought we were quite well off having so many toilets, and in between the burning days my brothers and I would have one each: what a luxury!

This particular morning, Gran had asked Uncle Jaffa to light up the furies before she went down to the Aboriginal camp. The homestead was on a slight rise, and the camp was on a black soil flat about 200 metres down the hill, sheltered snugly among pandanus palms. There were usually 15 to 20 people living in the camp, some of them transient, some working in the house. When houses were built at that time, Aborigines who were already camping in the area were usually left alone or asked if they wanted to work at the house. Sometimes they moved away. When the RAAF were there the Aborigines on the property had moved, either to Darwin or to a government reserve 6 kilometres away, but since we'd been living there they had gradually re-established themselves. I always remember smelling and seeing the soft smoky haze from their camp fires hanging over the humpies. Something was bothering Gran, I could tell: probably trouble in the camp.

Something else was bothering her more when she came out of the fury – she was rubbing her hands frantically across her burning backside and yelling at everyone in sight. This was something to behold, as Gran was normally rather regal and imperious, but she had an immediate problem. Her worries about the camp must have made her absent-minded. She'd gone to the toilet and forgotten that the furies were alight.

The sight of her red and swollen backside scattered the old crows from their usual perch above the 44-gallon drums. Uncle Jaffa and I thought it best to keep out of sight; besides, we were laughing so hard we wouldn't have been able to help anyway.

My Grandpa Bond was English, a gentle, quiet man who carved decorative picture frames in his spare time. During the Depression, he had become an itinerant road worker because that was the only way he could support his large extended family. Gran, meanwhile, was Australian-born and lucky to be alive, considering what had happened to her grandmother, Fanny Wannery.

Born in 1852, Fanny was the daughter of an Aboriginal woman and an English stockman from a sheep station in south-west Western Australia. Fanny's mother was working in the station's farmhouse when she fell pregnant to the stockman. Knowing that the baby would be picked up by the English station couple, Fanny's mother left her close to the homestead, covered with leaves under a low scrubby salt bush.

The couple who found Fanny reared her as their own. She grew up as an English girl, well spoken and educated, and later, in 1870, married an English gentleman named Ben Mason in

Albany, south of Perth. Ben's mother had worked in Buckingham Palace as a kitchen maid and as a boy he had played with Queen Victoria's son, the future Edward VII. Arriving in Australia, Ben had jumped ship and changed his name to John.

He and Fanny would have four children, the third of whom, Dinah, was my great-grandmother. Born in 1879, Dinah married a wealthy Adelaide farmer, Patrick Coleman. Patrick and his twin brother Daniel had brought the first draught horses across the Nullarbor to Perth. Along the way they met the Mason family on Balladonia station, near the South Australian–West Australian border. Patrick and Daniel married Dinah and her elder sister Harriet. Dinah and Patrick settled in coastal south-west Western Australia, living mainly in Hopetown and Ravensthorpe, where my gran, Eva Coleman, and my mother were born.

At the end of that eventful day when Gran burned her bum, Mother put me into my old wire stretcher bed, pushed up the shutter to let in the breeze, kissed me goodnight on the cheek and went back to the kitchen where Gran, recovering from her injury, was putting the final touches to my baby doll cake.

A pretty dark-haired doll stood in the centre, and the cake was her ball gown, the most beautiful I had ever seen. I was too thrilled to sleep; tomorrow was my birthday and I could touch the doll on my cake!

Soon, the gentle breeze carried some camp fire smoke in through my window. I could hear the distant sound of sticks beating time with the vibrating hum of a didgeridoo. The barking of a dog underscored yells from camp children my own age. The excitement sent cold shivers through my body; nothing could keep me in bed. The smell of smoke and the continuous sounds pulsating from the didgeridoo were calling out to me: *Come . . . come . . . come . . .*

I was sharing the bedroom with my three younger brothers – Bruce, Darryl and baby Eric. They were sleeping soundly. I slipped out through the open shutter and let myself fall a metre or so to the ground. I had done this many times during the day, so I was used to it, although this was the first time I had done it at night. Once on the ground, I hugged the shadows and sneaked down towards the corrugated-iron shower enclosure. Staying there to catch my breath and hope like hell Mum wouldn't miss me, I gathered courage to creep down the slope to a stand of pandanus palms. I wove through the spiked and jagged leaves, giving no thought to the snakes or to the cuts I was copping.

My steps crackled and crunched on the dry pandanus leaves, seeming to echo into the night. Had anyone heard me? Quivering, I crouched low, poking leaves out of my way to see what was going on.

The camp was a collection of rough-hewn huts, made of bark and bushes layered up against a centre pole. Fires burned outside each hut. The moon was trying to shine through the smoky haze. Camp kids were running about and playing with the dogs. The gentle clapping of sticks underlined the didgeridoo's hum. I could see some of the adult men being painted with the white and red ochre. I knew what this meant: there would be a corroboree tonight.

Crouching among the pandanus leaves, I could hear the odd rustle. I told myself to stay calm. No matter what it was, it would not hurt me. Suddenly the sticks were playing louder; the heavy throb of the didgeridoo was building, and the people were starting to dance around the largest fire. The dance went on and on, but it didn't feel peaceful, like those I had seen before. The men danced, stopped and shouted, and went around again. Their bodies were glistening in the heat of the fire. They began dancing harder, the didgeridoo belting out louder and louder, faster and faster. There were no women in sight, and the dogs and camp kids had disappeared. I felt very alone.

The men were dancing at a wilder pace now, the didgeridoo cranking them up. Something was wrong – with no women or children in sight I realised I had better get out of there. I worked my way slowly backwards out of the pandanus, frightened, not wanting to be caught watching.

Next morning we discovered that Mary Larrikai, the woman who helped Gran around the house and kept an eye on me for my mother, had run away that night. I began to cry. I wanted her back. She was part of the family, a second mother, my friend and teacher of bush culture. My birthday seemed ruined, and not even Gran's beautiful cake could cheer me up.

After a day of endless questions from me, Gran sat me down and explained that Mary had had the bone pointed at her. This meant, under Aboriginal law, that she was to be punished. It might have been a death sentence, administered by a deadly bush potion slipped into her food. After having had the bone pointed at them, some people died without even being poisoned and others lingered on like the walking dead – the ritual was punishment enough. But what had Mary done? I was told she had been promised to a much older man, but she preferred a younger man from the wrong tribal group.

In the weeks afterwards, life seemed to go on as usual, but one day Mum and Gran seemed to be overprotective of Gran's bedroom. I sneaked inside and discovered Mary hidden under Gran's bed. Gran had protected Mary; there was no way she could return to her people, who would surely have speared her. To this day I don't know how Gran found her, but she certainly didn't look like our Mary. She looked like a very sick, old woman, thin and gaunt, barely able to move. She looked like she was going to die and there were days when she very nearly did. Grandpa said this was the only time he ever had a woman camp under his bed, and I'm sure he felt uneasy about the situation. Gran moved Mary to the safety of the Bagot Compound, a government reserve about 10 kilometres away, which had a doctor and nursing staff. Mary never looked well again, but she survived, living out her final years in and around the compound. Never being allowed to go home to her family was, to my young ears, a very confusing and frightening story.

One reason we lived with Gran and Grandpa Bond was that Dad was often away working. He was known as Snowy, because of his head of thick blond hair, and from an early age he loved the rugged and warm northern atmosphere of the outback. He had grown up in Cottesloe, Perth, but as a young man in 1939 he travelled north of Derby with a shearing team. He worked the shearing sheds moving across the Kimberley from Liveringa, Ellendale, Paradise and Blina stations, followed by stints in the sheds at Gascoyne as he returned home. After shearing he moved to Darwin and became one of the first long-haul owner-drivers, running his Leyland Hippo truck between Alice Springs and Darwin. They were long days and lonely nights with only a bottle of rum for company – Dad would later say that a little nip of OP rum in the evenings kept him driving throughout the night on the long and isolated Stuart Highway.

Between trips carting freight, he went buffalo hunting and crocodile shooting to supplement his income. Dad sailed with his mate 'Noondy' Harritos on barges around the treacherous Top-End coastline, delivering food, stores and fuel to coastal mission stations. Dad survived the wreck of the *Tiki* – a boat which already had a hell of a reputation from gun-running in the northern waters and getting involved in the New Guinea uprising. When Dad was aboard, one night the pilot fell asleep and the ship was wrecked 64 kilometres off Goulburn Island.

It was in Darwin that my parents met, in 1945. Three years later they married in the quaint little Church of England cathedral. My mother, named Eva after my gran, had a sister, Alvis, and twin brothers, Iva and Ian. Eva, the quiet and sheltered daughter of the foreman of a road construction team, had been a seamstress in Perth before meeting Dad in Darwin. Her favourite pastime, embroidery, kept us in beautiful tablecloths and doilies. Being a seamstress was very handy: she would whip up clothes for my brothers and herself in no time. She later began to collect seashells, amassing one of the largest collections I have seen.

I was their first born, in 1949, followed by Bruce, Darryl, Eric and finally Michael. Bruce and I, being seventeen months apart, were close as kids. Darryl was born two years after Bruce, followed by Eric three years later, and then Michael three years later again. I don't remember any fighting, physical or verbal. We grew up as good mates. This was extremely lucky, given the isolation of some of the places we lived.

A few weeks after my sixth birthday, Dad mustered and loaded us all into the cab of his old truck and we were off, heading south of Darwin to visit friends and deliver their tractor and their wet season's stores, enough tinned food and drums of flour to see them through the rainy period if the road became boggy and the rivers flooded. Dad was often doing favours for isolated friends, as he had one of the rare reliable, sizable trucks coming out of Darwin.

The track to Elsey was long and dusty, and the heat coming off the engine didn't seem to help. My beautiful blonde ringlets that Mum had so painstakingly put in after breakfast that morning were now standing on end. Bruce seemed half asleep, swaying gently in an upright position. I've always looked up to Bruce as if he was an elder brother. He was strong and calm, he made our billycarts and tin canoes, and he was there to throw us up trees when we were charged by angry buffalo, and to pull us down later.

Darryl, who was three years old, hadn't a care in the world, curled up like a kitten with his thumb glued in his mouth. Eric was home with Mum and Gran on the Fresh Water Rapid Creek block.

'What have we got here?' called Dad.

All three tired young bodies came alive. 'It's Elsey, Dad!' we yelled back to him. Dad shifted down a gear as we neared the homestead. Young Aboriginal kids, thin as whippets, came running out, arms waving madly, the camp dogs barking in tune with the children's cheers. The wet season's stores had arrived.

Uncle Harry, who was not a real uncle but a family friend, would have heard us coming for miles and was already organising the station boys to take over the truck. Uncle Harry was a large happy-go-lucky fellow, greeting the boys and myself with massive bear hugs and nearly smothering us to death. He gave Dad a handshake and a pat on the back.

'Follow me for a bite to eat,' he said and took us into the kitchen, where he produced his special – large corned-beef sandwiches and giant fried scones.

Between bites of the food and mouthfuls of sweet black tea, I could see movement under an old antique sideboard. Leaving the kitchen table and crouching down on my belly, I crab-crawled my way to a better view.

'If you catch it you can have it, girl,' Uncle Harry bellowed. 'It's a feral kitten.' The kitten had moved in to escape the camp kids and their dogs. What a sight: ginger in colour and all her fur standing on end. Every move I made, she spat and hissed and lashed out with a paw tipped with razor-sharp claws, scratching red angry welts into my hands. I was wondering if she really was worth rescuing. Dad found me a piece of old sheet and suggested I throw it over her and save myself from further mauling. Success! After chasing her from one end of the sideboard to the other, I was now the proud owner of Ginger the feral kitten . . . for approximately five minutes. Before I knew it, she hit the ground in full flight and shot through the kitchen door in an orange flash. I never saw her again.

CHAPTER 2

School Days in Fannie Bay

*W*hen I was nine years old, my mother and father decided it was time we had a house of our own. The boys and I were growing up and in need of education, so we moved to Fannie Bay, a township just west of Darwin that was gradually developing into a clifftop suburb of the expanding city. We were close to the new Parap Primary School and only a short bus trip from Darwin's only high school.

The move was at first an exciting adventure. After being in the outback, we were now 200 metres or so from the sea. Some days it roared as it pounded the cliff, sending fine spray high into the air. But Gran and Grandpa were not with us, and the house felt rather empty without them. This was a new beginning, but I wasn't sure if I liked it.

I was also missing our dog, Puppy. A mix of bull terrier and blue heeler, he was too large and savage to bring to a built-up area, so we'd had to leave him behind with a butcher 32 kilometres away who needed a guard dog to alert him to cattle duffers who were stealing the odd killer (a steer that had been put aside for butchering).

Our new house was fibro with a corrugated-iron roof and, wonder of wonders, a flush toilet, although I rather missed the excitement of the furies. Not as flash as Gran's house, I thought. Only one toilet!

Next door was the largest tree I had ever seen, a banyan tree. The canopy seemed to take up the whole block. The boys and I took one look around the house and we were off, in no time hauling lengths of timber up into the tree, plank by plank, until we completed our cubby house. This was our home away from home.

Dad was now working for the Department of Water Resources, gauging the rise and fall of rivers in the Top End. He was away working in the outback for weeks on end, and when he returned, he would have a drink with his mates Noondy Harritos and Nick Paspaley at the Fannie Bay Hotel, then come home and pull out the new record player and give us a good burst of Mario Lanza's amazing voice. Dad has a good voice and would joyfully join him. We would scuttle up into the cubby and listen.

The tree house had other uses. If one of us was in trouble, or wanted to get out of doing our chores, this was the place to come. At times you'd have to book to get in, as the cubby became very popular with the other kids in the neighbourhood. The boys and I saw a Tarzan movie at the Parap picture theatre. Johnny Weissmuller played Tarzan, and Maureen O'Hara was his Jane. I couldn't wait to swing from the banyan tree, it looked so easy! Bruce found a long rope in the shed and up the banyan we went. About 6 metres from the ground was the ideal, horizontal branch. I worked my way slowly along it, pushing the rope ahead of me. About halfway out, I wound the rope around the trunk and tied it securely. Grabbing hold of the end, without a second thought, letting out the cry of 'Tarzan!', I sailed towards the ground. Instead of swinging out gracefully I smashed straight into the earth, flat-out like a skinned dingo, stars and all. I had terrible trouble trying to breathe. I wasn't too sure whether I was dead or alive. I was lucky I came out without a broken bone, but was sore all over. Later we measured the rope; it was way too long.

About 11 pm one Sunday weeks after the move, in the middle of a wild electrical storm, we thought we were hearing things. Some mad animal was trying to claw down our front door. Dad was away working. With lightning strikes and rolls of thunder rattling every louvre in the house, we huddled together. As the storm eased, we could hear the mad animal's heavy claws grinding into the wooden front door. The howling wasn't going to stop; I wished Puppy was there to protect us. With the boys and me clinging to her, the noise from outside like nothing we'd ever heard before, Mum moved towards the door. Trembling and crying, I begged her to stay inside. Suddenly the howling stopped and in its place excited barking started. It was Puppy! How on earth did he ever find his way so many kilometres to our new house? There was no way the boys and I would let him go again, and after his miraculous journey we were allowed to keep him.

As time went on we made some very good friends, especially Shirley and Trevor Fong, whose parents owned a large house just over the road. Mrs Fong had to be the best fried-rice cook in the Territory, and anytime we visited she would make sure we had a huge plate.

Each morning and afternoon we would catch the school bus. Bruce, Darryl and I raced each other home, dumped our school bags, had a quick cup of tea and a biscuit, threw on our swimming costumes, then ran over the road to collect Shirley and Trevor and take off to the nearby Fannie Bay cliffs. The excitement was always on when we had a king tide. The sea would hammer the cliffs, draw out as if to gain breath, then pound them again. On king tides the swell would hit about halfway up the cliffs. Bruce, Shirley, Trevor and I climbed down the cliff face and dived into the foaming sea as it retreated. When we surfaced, it would throw us back at the cliff face. We were young daredevils; we enjoyed any challenge with an element of danger, and of course we never told our parents.

We were never alone for all the years that we swam in that area. Our friend Percy the manta ray would always swim and fish near us. We would cheer his arrival, then continue diving and swimming, feeling that Percy was there to protect us from any danger in the sea. Percy swam with us right up to the time Dad moved our family to Arnhem Land.

Between king tides, Bruce, Darryl, the Fongs and I ventured further around the coast to East Point, sneaking out and leaving our younger brothers home with Mum. We were excited about our secret venture, but unsure whether Mum and Dad would be quite so enthusiastic; we agreed to keep quiet about it until we were ready to float our new dugout canoe.

East Point was our jungle, a canopy of poinciana trees blazing red and shading the narrow bitumen road that wound its way to the old lighthouse. After trekking through the jungle for what seemed like hours, with the humidity high and the sweat trickling down our bodies, insects moving in for the kill, we all agreed that a huge cottonwood tree was the one. Each of us in turn wrapped our arms around the tree and decided we would be able to build our dugout from it. Also in its favour was that we were less than a hundred metres from the water's edge. Bruce marked the tree around the base and, a week later, after much chopping and hacking, down she came in a graceful fall, the cry of 'Timbaaaa!' echoing through the bush. But standing on the tree and having a good look at the situation, I was starting to wonder if we'd bitten off more than we could chew.

Bruce became our leader and worked harder than any of us. Eric took his turn on the axe, and Michael, being younger, played in the bush. Our idea was to build a canoe like those of the Aboriginal fishermen in the bay, who had given us some pointers and told us what type of tree to use.

Approximately six weeks later, the blisters on our hands having turned into tough calluses, we had completed our canoe. Throwing our hands in the air, cheering and yelling with excitement, we began wondering how to transport the dugout to the water's edge.

Bruce, Darryl and Trevor decided to bring their billycarts down to the point, put one under each end of the dugout and move it slowly to the cliff's edge. We would then roll the canoe over the cliff on a low tide so it would land on the sand. Then we would wait for an incoming tide and – hurray! – test-float our dugout at last.

Yes, it floated, after Bruce and his axe wrought a few minor changes to help with the balance. We were all very proud of ourselves, and naturally each of us wanted to be a crew member for the first trip, a little over a kilometre from East Point across to the Fannie Bay cliffs.

I insisted on being aboard. Darryl, Puppy and I hopped in. Bruce pushed us out into waist-deep water, and then climbed on. There was a bit of a wobble while we fought to balance the thing.

Puppy wasn't helping much – he started to whine and tremble with fright.

As we tentatively dipped our paddles into the clear blue water of the bay, Bruce and I synchronised our paddling, ignoring Puppy as we glided along. I could see the flashes of silver fish shoot past in the water. It seemed a very long way to the cliffs.

We were more than halfway across the bay when Puppy started barking hysterically. I glanced out across the water from the left to the right and spotted a huge dark shadow. Trying to stay calm, I yelled at Puppy to lie down and shut up. Darryl was having a terrible time as he tried to control Puppy. Bruce had also seen the shadow and told us to keep paddling and stay calm – pretty hard to do with a huge shark following us! It looked to be the same length as the canoe. One minute we'd see it, and the next it would disappear. By now Puppy was really upset. He knew this intruder meant danger. With his growling and barking and trying to pull away from Darryl's grip, the canoe had a very dangerous roll, oscillating from side to side and taking water each time.

Bruce was baling vigorously with a jam tin and seemed quite calm, as he always did when we got ourselves into these predicaments.

The sight of the huge dorsal fin became too much for Puppy. He fought Darryl, clawed his front paws over the side of the canoe, and over he went into the heaving sea to attack the predator and protect us. In a flash, our dog disappeared into the deep. Soon there were dark stains in the water; it had to be blood from Puppy. Once he looked like he was coming to the surface. There was turmoil all around us, the canoe rolling from side to side. Again we were taking in water. Terrified, we began to cry out for help, but of course no-one could hear us. There was nothing we could do. The monster moved in again and just as silently disappeared. We were trying to keep the canoe upright, trying to paddle and at the same time look out for Puppy and the shark. But we didn't see Puppy again. I wanted to be sick. My stomach was churning and I was trembling and crying.

Darryl and Bruce had gone silent and the three of us were furiously paddling for shore and hoping like hell that we would make it. Out of nowhere came a loud gunshot; we raised our tear-stained faces towards the sound. Dad was waving from the cliffs. He'd seen the shark circling our canoe. We were less than 50 metres from the beach now. I took one quick look over my shoulder to see if we were still being followed, then turned to paddle for all I was worth.

We beached the canoe. Dad was pulling us out and re-assuring us that we were now safe and that Puppy had been extremely brave. I believe Dad was so caught up with relief to have us on shore safely and all together that he forgot the real reason he went looking for us – to tell us we were in trouble. Mum had found out about the canoe and told him, and he'd come out to make sure that we never took the canoe into deep water!

Back at the house, Mother was acting calm. Although she kept her feelings close to her heart, I'm not sure she fully understood the distress we had come through.

Not long afterwards, Dad said he had a surprise for me. He pointed to a cut-down 44-gallon drum which was partly filled with murky water. I raced over to it and in went my hand. Wham! Something bloody sharp had hold of me. Shocked, I let out a blood-curdling scream, pulling back my hand a darn sight faster than it went in. A baby Johnston River crocodile was hanging onto my poor fingers with all its might. Once over the initial shock, with tears in my eyes and my heart beating overtime, I wasn't sure whether to be happy with this present or not. In fact I felt angry inside, but I was the eldest and had to be brave. Dad released the crocodile from my fingers and gave me a quick lesson on how to handle and feed my seven – seven! – new pets. Once a week I'd haul the little fellas out of the drum one by one, grabbing each at the back of its head, then pry open the top jaw and gently poke a little ball of fish down its throat. That was feeding time procedure until they got old enough to change their diet.

Over the next couple of years I would take one or two crocs to school to show the teachers and my schoolmates. Needless to say, the teachers treated me very well on those days.

A couple of years later my father suggested that he return them to the river. By this time I think they were wearing out their welcome in Mum's eyes. I'd moved them into her fish pond, which was full of beautiful guppies. I still don't believe they could possibly have devoured the whole lot overnight. There were hundreds of guppies, but by morning they were all gone.

This was one of the times I realised Mum wasn't too pleased with me: no yelling or shouting, just a slight change in her expression. To top it off, one of our larger pet crocs, over a metre long, escaped often and one day ended up walking through the house, frightening the hell out of Mum's lady friends, who left their morning tea behind in their rush to get out the front door. Bruce and I didn't mind, because we shared the visitors' abandoned cake. But as the crocs were now taking themselves for walks, I agreed with Dad that it was time to say goodbye. Off to the Alligator River they went.

CHAPTER 3

Arnhem Land

*I*n 1964 my father returned home from Gove Peninsula with a new job very similar to his last, only this time working with the sea, recording swell and sand movement for the mining company Gominco. This meant the family would be uprooting from Fannie Bay and moving as far east of Darwin as you could travel without falling into the Gulf of Carpenteria. The Yirrkala Mission was at Rocky Bay and our new residence was about 5 kilometres from it, perched on a bauxite plateau.

Mum seemed keen on the move, having taken up shell-collecting as a hobby. Her only worry was the boys' education, but this wasn't the boys' worry – they were raring to go. I was 15 years old, and three months earlier had dropped out of high school to take on a hairdressing apprenticeship. I wasn't too keen to leave. So before the family moved to Gove, Dad arranged accommodation for me in Darwin with his friend Silent Bill and his wife June, who was Matron of the Darwin Hospital.

Some months later Dad arrived in Darwin and told me to pack my gear: I was to join the family in Arnhem Land. He'd been told I had a Greek boyfriend. It wasn't true – all I'd done was go to the movies with a Greek girlfriend. I wasn't interested in men at this stage and was far too busy with study and night school. But Dad was worried for my welfare all alone in Darwin, and so I was on a plane to Arnhem Land, a flight to the outback that would change my life's direction. Aside from MacRobertson Miller Airlines' DC3 doing its kangaroo hop around the coastal mission stations, the only way in and out of Yirrkala was Noondy Harritos' coastal barge, which arrived once in a blue moon. The barge brought our wet season's bulk stores. The mail came via the DC3 every fortnight. Its landings during the wet season were as exciting as any flying I've done since, including mustering cattle in a chopper. The more times I landed in the aisle with luggage piled on top of me, the more I enjoyed the trips. Maybe I should have applied to become an airline stewardess.

Sunday was walkabout day and my Aboriginal friends had walked from Yirrkala Mission to our camp on top of the bauxite escarpment. Betty, Junie and I were roughly the same age and I looked forward to their company for walks through the bush. I was especially excited one Sunday as we were heading to Melville Bay, 28 kilometres west of our camp.

Distance never meant much and, girls being girls, we always had heaps to talk about. Betty and Junie were promised to quite elderly men in their tribe and the ceremony was getting closer. Under their tribal law, a young woman was promised to an older man so she would hunt for him and look after him, while a young man was promised to an older woman, to hunt and look after her.

In her broken English Junie asked, 'Who you promised man?' If they were promised, why wasn't I? As far as Betty and Junie were concerned, I was a girl about the same age as they were. They couldn't understand why I wasn't promised, and said I ought to think about it.

We were full of enthusiasm as we left the two-wheel dirt track the missionaries and my family used. Talking, laughing, we would yell 'Galka!', then run and hide. 'Galka' meant something like 'madman' or 'mad bushman', I was never really sure. All I knew was that if he was out there he wasn't meant to catch us. Of course the more we yelled 'Galka', the more we spooked ourselves.

We were heading in the direction of a claypan flat when we heard a low droning sound in the distance. Someone yelled 'Galka!' and in no time we were huddled behind the nearest anthill. I said to Betty and Junie that we should stop the game, as we were frightening ourselves. But the droning kept coming closer. I realised it was a light aircraft of some kind. We ran out from the shadow of the anthill, confident again.

We headed into the open country and started across another claypan flat. My silent thought was about the danger of lone buffalo bulls, now that we were walking further out from any decent trees and anthills to hide behind. But we were in a happy mood, knowing that once we arrived at Melville Bay we would swim, dig up turtle eggs, collect oysters as large as saucers and refresh ourselves with a drink of fresh water from Macassar's Soak.

Out in the middle of the flat we stopped, silent for a minute, listening. There was that droning sound again, heading in our direction. We spotted the aircraft and, clinging to each other, kept on walking. It circled the flat and came in at us, only this time much lower. What the hell was going on? I never expected a plane so close in the middle of the Never Never. This was Arnhem Land, where you'd expect a mail plane once a fortnight.

My heart was fairly pounding. The aircraft was circling the claypan and coming in once more, this time at treetop level. Now we really had something to panic about. We grabbed each other and huddled on the ground while the aircraft dived towards us. Turning my head skywards I imagined that the pilot hadn't seen us and for some unknown reason was going to land in the middle of this claypan flat, or possibly on us.

Screaming, I jumped up, Betty and Junie with me. Running as fast as our skinny legs would carry us, we headed towards a belt of timber on the edge of the claypan. The aircraft banked and approached again, directly at us. We fell in a heap once more. By now my heart was in my throat and I was having trouble believing that this was really happening. What was wrong with this bloody idiot? We ran towards the timber again. Junie went down, screaming in her own language that she had twisted her ankle. Betty and I grabbed an arm each, and without looking to see if anything was broken, we dragged Junie between us, still heading for the timber.

Once under shelter, we decided to head back to the billabong at the foot of the bauxite plateau, near home base. Too much had happened today and we decided to leave our walk to Melville Bay for another time. We were all too frightened to go on now and I thought Mum should look at Junie's ankle, which was swelling. We eventually made it home to find Bruce, Darryl, Eric and Michael having a good laugh. It turned out that the pilot had mistaken me for an albino Aboriginal girl, out walking with her friends. It probably did seem funny when he landed at my father's camp and they helped him out of his plane, babbling about this amazing find. But somehow I never quite got the joke.

At the foot of 'our' plateau was one of the largest and deepest freshwater billabongs in the north-east corner of Arnhem Land. This massive open span of water, dotted with islands covered in pandanus palms, flowed gently through the reeds and sandhills, then emptied into the beautiful blue sea by Yirrkala Mission. One of the Aboriginal elders was kind enough to give my brothers and myself a dugout canoe. Bruce, Darryl, Eric, Michael and I just couldn't wait to get the dugout down the side of the plateau and into the billabong. This was quite an exercise in itself, considering that we were only strong enough to roll it down sideways and the dugout was longer than the width of the track.

We persevered, rolling it over and over, every so often hitting a tree and having to pull the dugout back on track. At times the four of us just sat on it and talked about the good times we would have once we got the thing launched.

The boys had already constructed a jetty from gum saplings which they had tied together with bush twine. Each afternoon after school the boys would head off over the plateau to work on their project. I would stay behind only long enough to help prepare the evening meal or bake a huge cake. I was interested in cooking good solid meals, not the fancy stuff, and learned plenty from Mum. Ours wasn't a traditional household – our living quarters were 100 metres or so from the cook house. The men's quarters, office and workshop were each separate buildings. Mum had settled in well at the camp, although she battled most days trying to get the boys to put school lessons ahead of wild adventures.

Once we had the canoe in the water, we all piled in, got our balance and paddled out to a pandanus island. From island to island we floated, gazing down into the clear, crystal water and gawking in wonder at these huge dark areas that looked like caves' mouths. We found out later the dark patches were algae lifting from the bottom of the billabong.

On one of our many fishing trips we found an old yellow life jacket on an isolated beach. I decided that we should teach Michael, who was five, to swim. After making sure that it would carry his weight in the water, we tied a length of rope to the jacket, dropped Michael in the water behind the canoe and paddled off, with me sitting in the dugout holding the rope while the boys paddled.

'Swim, Michael, kick your legs and use your arms,' I called from the safety of the canoe.

We often banked the canoe at our favourite island, where we would have a little picnic and all swim together. It was wonderful to have our freedom, lots of space and our own dugout. What more could kids want?

Even after Michael had learned to swim, we would still tow him behind; it was more fun. However, unknowingly we were setting Michael up as croc bait. Even now, the thought sends shivers through my entire body.

One weekend while we were all away on a trip to Broome, an Aboriginal man from the mission was attacked by a salt-water crocodile in the same billabong. Luckily he survived. We didn't know it, but saltwater crocodiles will occasionally go into a freshwater spring and follow a creek or freshwater seepage area to cleanse themselves of old barnacles. We never swam in that billabong again, and anytime we went near it we'd be looking over our shoulders.

On one of my father's trips to Darwin, my brothers and I got lucky. At a local auction Dad put in a successful bid on an old wartime Willy's jeep: never been driven, one out of a crate of four. Six weeks later the Willy's arrived at Melville Bay on Noondy Harritos' barge, and you would have thought it was Christmas. What a gift! A quick lesson at the bay and Bruce followed Dad home to our camp on the plateau.

From that day, when we went picnicking, fishing, or out after a buffalo for beef, the boys and I would follow behind Mum and Dad's Land Rover with our little jeep, taking turns behind the wheel and keeping a watchful eye out for buffalo. On sighting one, Dad would signal for us to stop while he silently slipped out of his Land Rover, rested his .303 rifle across the bonnet, fixed the buffalo in his sight, then pulled the trigger. The rest of the family sat elbow to elbow, hands planted firmly over our ears . . . *Bang!* Dad was a good shot; he never used more than one bullet to put a buffalo down.

Dad cut its throat to let it bleed while Mother collected kindling to boil the billy. Our job was to follow the tracks back out of the scrub and timber and head back to Yirrkala Mission to notify the Aboriginal men that we'd shot a buffalo and to come on out and get some fresh meat. It wouldn't take them long to gather their knives and steel, hop in the mission Land Rover, and take off, all laughing and talking with the thought of the feast to come. By the time we returned to the kill, Dad had boned out the cuts of meat we needed to keep our family going. On hearing our vehicles approaching, Mum would build up the fire and cook a few strips of buffalo meat for the men to sample while they were boning out. We did this a lot in Arnhem Land. The Yirrkala people are coastal, but loved to vary their diet with the odd piece of delicious buffalo meat. Towards the end of our time in Arnhem Land we discovered that the mission had done very well out of all this buffalo meat. As soon as the men arrived back at the mission, the meat was taken and sold back to them through the mission store. The day Dad found out he grabbed the red-faced reverend by the collar and gave him a darn good shaking, which left him sputtering and trembling. He promised to let the people share the meat among themselves with no money exchanging hands. To mollify Dad, the reverend pressed four packets of hard-boiled lollies on us.

There were two tribes of Aboriginal people at the mission that I can remember, both distinctive. I recall how very black they were, with shiny black curly hair down past their shoulders. Proud with their tribal markings, they carried an assortment of spears, each with a special purpose and meaning. The older women were naked to the waist with markings between their breasts, and the young girls were clothed, like the boys.

The leader of one of these tribes was a wiry old man with white hair and a long white beard. Mawwellen and his people would hunt for kangaroo, lizards and honey bees as they travelled through the bush. When on these walks they would call at our camp on the bauxite plateau, standing back the customary hundred metres. Dad would have to greet them at the edge of the clearing. Only then would they advance closer to our camp.

Gunnamullie, the elder of the other tribe, was tall and slim and much younger than Mawwellen. He always walked in a dignified fashion, a handful of spears in one hand and a .22 rifle in the other. His taut body proudly displayed his markings for all to see and his narga cloth covered his genitals.

The difference between these two men was that Mawwellen had never been outside Arnhem Land and probably never would have wanted to. He knew only Aboriginal law and custom, and was a content and happy old man. Gunnamullie, on the other hand, had flown to capital cities to dance for the Queen and Prince Philip on their visits to Australia. Gunnamullie was a wonderful tribal dancer. When he danced he captured total attention. He was also intelligent, and easily able to master the ways of the white man's world.

One lovely clear blue sunny day, with little humidity, we were preparing for a family fishing trip to Melville Bay. Bruce and Darryl went off discussing what fishing lines and nets they'd take, and I stayed in the kitchen to help Mum pack the tucker box. At Melville Bay, I'd keep her company walking along the shoreline collecting shells while the boys and Dad fished.

Suddenly a vehicle came racing towards the camp in a cloud of red dust. The mission Land Rover came roaring to a halt directly in front of Dad, showering him with bauxite gravel. Out jumped old Bob, the handyman from the mission.

'There's really big trouble at the mission! Gunnamullie just danced the stingray dance and all hell has broken loose.'

The state the old man was in said it all. Dad grabbed his .303 and off he went. It didn't take too long for Dad to confirm Bob's story. He saw a crowd: there was screaming and wailing from the women and spears were sailing through the air with one tribe trying to pay back the other, and not a missionary in sight. Dad bailed up a boy, and asked him what was up.

'Gunnamullie has been speared,' was the frightened answer.

Dad raised the .303 skywards, fired, reloaded, and fired again. As the sound of the shots echoed around the mission, there was deathly silence. The combatants lowered their spears.

Apparently Gunnamullie had been the only winner of all card games for some time, and one of Mawwellen's boys had had enough. He demanded that Gunnamullie show his hand of cards. Gunnamullie refused. Instead he went for a spear. The boy was up out of his seat, spear held high. In an instant he drove it into Gunnamullie's kidney. Not one to give in easily, Gunnamullie pulled it out and fired it back with all his strength. But at that instant his body took another shovel-nose spear, and this one killed him.

For weeks Dad seemed to be the only calm person among us all. Tension was in the air, especially among the tribal people, who were anticipating a round of payback: 'a body for a body'. Every man was carrying more razor-sharp spears than usual. I was never aware of anybody being killed in retaliation, but it took some months for the situation to get back to normal.

Two Swiss doctors of geology were boarding at the homestead while conducting a survey and taking samples from the un-developed bauxite lease that Dad was caretaking. They were well educated, quiet gentlemen, very white-skinned, with enough English to get by and not a lot of knowledge about our

Arnhem Land bush. Maybe they were a little too quiet for my brothers and me.

We took any opportunity for fun, and this looked like one. With no television, no phone and not a lot to do in the humid January evenings, Bruce, Darryl, Eric, Michael and I would often take long, leisurely walks down the track. The track was heavily lined on both sides with spear grass which rose well over our heads. Huge clumps of pandanus palms thrived in the humid atmosphere. The dragonflies were busily trying to keep their distance from Darryl's widely waving stick, which he said he was carrying to protect us from venomous snakes and the odd roving bull buffalo. The buffalo liked this track and so did we, and an old bull who had been pushed, or 'beaten', out of the herd by younger bulls could sometimes be unpredictable and dangerous.

At this time of the year – three months into the wet season – we could only walk more or less in single file, not knowing what was a foot or two behind the walls of spear grass and pandanus flanking the track. The boys and I were about half-way down the track when we heard the camp motorbike in the distance. Soon we were in fits of laughter listening to it coming along the track in unique style, starting and farting, revving high and low.

I knew it wasn't Dad taking Mum for a ride because Dad would have had it in control. It could only be our Swiss doctors of geology, trying to keep the bike going on the muddy track through the spear grass.

I had a brainwave. As the bike was lurching along the track and getting closer, I grabbed Michael.

'Lie low behind the clump of pandanus and wait for them to pass!'

Out of sight, we listened to our Swiss friends wobble past. Lying down in the mud, we gave no thought to a taipan or two that could have been up to the same trick.

Once they were past our hideaway, out we came. We couldn't possibly let them return to Switzerland without some excitement. The track was the only way in and out of the camp. It wasn't too long before we could again hear the nervous laughter, the revving high and low of the bike on its way back down the track. I outlined my plan to the boys, and then back in behind the pandanus we went. I beckoned to Bruce, Darryl and Eric to grab hold of the tallest pandanus palm with me. We waited for the bike. I then gave the boys the nod to begin shaking the palm as vigorously as they could. In between shakes we grabbed handfuls of dirt and grass and threw it into the air, all the time bellowing like a raging buffalo bull. We gave it our very best and tried to contain our laughter.

The effect must have been authentic. Dr Alexander Somm gave the motorbike an almighty rev out of sheer terror. The bike was all over the track now, revving high and low and fast and slow all at once. Screams of excitement and laughter, or maybe fear, echoed down the track as they belted towards camp pursued by an imaginary wild buffalo. We watched in fits as our Swiss visitors disappeared into the distance in complete disarray.

I was laughing so much I was crying as we wandered down the track homewards with the last light fading. From the clearing around the camp, we could see the lights and headed straight for them. I looked through the kitchen window. Both doctors were talking and waving their arms excitedly. Dad was handing them whiskys. Mum turned and spotted us, quickly came out of the kitchen and sent us off for showers.

'No need to hurry back,' she said. 'Dad is calming down our doctor friends. They have just had the most terrible experience with a raging buffalo.'

Well! It's something they can tell their kids about some day.

CHAPTER 4

Spirit Breeze

One day in the mid-1960s, my parents, brothers and I were taking a lunch break from fishing in Melville Bay. We rested on the golden beach under the canopy of a huge casuarina tree. The billy gently simmered, and the breeze carried the aroma of a seafood buffet grilling on the coals.

Fifty metres or so from our tree, stood an identical casuarina. Its branches shaded some mysterious-looking objects that had come from the sea and now circled the tree trunk. This was a sacred site. None of us dared enter it.

Some weeks earlier, a group of Aboriginal people had been hunting along the waterfront at Melville Bay. An old, thin man with unruly grey hair and a waist-length white beard stepped forward from his clan, beckoning with his spears for Dad to go forward and meet him. Dad jumped up and walked towards the old fella. I sat totally transfixed, thinking, my God, the Aboriginal man is going to spear my dad. They stood looking at each other, there was some pointing, and some discussion, and then the old man said, 'This tree belongs to my family, my people.'

He pointed to the other tree. 'But this tree we give to you and your family.'

A magnificent gift to bestow on our family, this tree gave us a lot of pleasure over the years. It shaded us; we could fish from under it as the sea water lapped the surrounding ground. Thirty metres away was Macassar's Soak, from where we drew water for our billy tea. A beautiful tree, given by an honourable old man.

I often wonder if our tree still stands at Melville Bay and how the freshwater soak is going. Or has it all been destroyed with the development of the bauxite deposit? Some months after we received the old man's gift, I was sitting waist-deep in water at Melville Bay, just below the tree, minding two little girls, Pascal and Nicky, whose mother was having a cup of tea with mine in the shade. Their father was the mining company's mechanic.

There had been a cyclone in the area just three days earlier, and the sea was stirred-up and muddy looking. I saw no harm just sitting in the shallow water with the girls.

Young Nicky moved to slightly deeper water and my immediate reaction was to reach out to her. Suddenly I felt a terrible burning sensation in my right breast. In seconds it felt as if someone had hold of my chest and was squeezing the air out of my body in the worst possible way. Soon my mother was calling my name in the distance. The pain was so severe no answer would come: sharp, rolling, terrible pains. Next thing I remember being rushed 35 kilometres over the rugged dirt track to the mission hospital. I felt as if I had left the family behind. No pain anymore, just floating. Everything seemed shapeless – no features, just a calm floating feeling, which was pretty strange considering the state of Dad's Land Rover.

The Aboriginal elders camped for three days and nights around the little mission hospital. They refused to move until they had sung me back to life. The minister at the mission,

Reverend Fall, held church services night and day, and on the third evening I woke to the sound of an old Aboriginal woman's voice singing in her language, and a sea of black faces peering through the louvres at me. Being stung by a marine stinger, the deadly Irukandji jellyfish, was the most terrible experience of my young life – it was certainly the most excruciating pain I'd ever suffered. Hard to believe the creature is half the size of a fingernail. It had got into my swimming costume as I'd adjusted the shoulder strap when I'd been reaching out for one of the children. I was lucky to have been taken to the hospital so soon; the jellyfish sting can have long-term effects on the nervous system, but I was given injections early enough to avert any lasting damage. Mum suffered so much for me she was also put into the hospital, covered in a terrible nerve rash.

Our stores were supplied to Gove by two ration ships, the *Wyburn* and the *Alanga*. The ships sailed from Brisbane, dropping supplies at Roper River, then powering on to us at Melville Bay. If we were lucky this happened every three months. It generated lots of excitement.

I remember one occasion when Dad had spent the entire day ferrying equipment from the ship to shore by barge. That evening, he was invited to dine with the ration ship's captain and crew. Since there were no women on board, my mother, brothers and I chose to remain at camp. It was a pitch-black night, with barely a star. Dad had just returned to the dock where he'd parked the Land Rover when he heard some angry Aboriginal voices directed at him.

'White bastards, you're no good, any of you.'

He pulled the crank handle out from under the seat and walked towards the group of men who had gathered around a pile of 44-gallon drums.

He had never heard such slurs before, as he had only ever treated the Aboriginal people with respect, and they him. The Yirrkala people called him 'Mr Snow' to show their respect.

'What did you say?' he challenged.

'Is that you, Mr Snow? Sorry, sorry, didn't know it was you.'

At this time, Aborigines had virtually no rights. In 1949, the year I was born, our Commonwealth Electoral Act was amended to grant indigenous people a vote, but only if they were entitled to in their particular State or if they had completed military service. In 1962 the Electoral Act was amended again, this time to grant all Aborigines their right to vote, but it was illegal to encourage them to enrol. Dad understood their rage. He learned that some of the sailors had come ashore looking for women and were supplying alcohol, then unavailable to the Aboriginal population. It was also illegal to bring alcohol into Arnhem Land.

He sympathised with them and let the matter drop. That incident was the only time I ever remember the Aborigines speaking up against white fellas, and I think they were embarrassed and wanted to put the whole episode behind them as quickly as possible.

Another time, the reverend of Yirrkala Mission upset us by publicly flogging two young Aboriginal boys for pinching watermelons. This horrifying abuse didn't sit too well with Dad. In fact, it provoked him to retaliate. He and Bruce jumped on our little motorbike and tore down the dirt track to the mission watermelon patch. They clambered under the fence, pinched two large ripe watermelons and brought them home. My father no doubt wanted to give the reverend an opportunity to flog him. That would have been a sight, the gentle man of God and the tough, hard Territory man!

I believe there were somewhere between 300 and 350 reserves, or 'ration camps' as I got to call them in later years, set up by the government around Australia. With the support of the Christian associations and churches they were later known as missions. Prior to the 1950s, when Aborigines were dragged into these places in chains, they had no basic rights, were losing custody of their own children and had no freedom of movement. In the 1960s, flogging a child for pinching a watermelon seemed a bit much to me!

If we had patronised the church at the mission, the association probably would have been better between us. With Dad caretaking the undeveloped bauxite lease at that time, in the missionaries' eyes we were probably intruders. The Aboriginal people seemed reasonably happy, healthy and content, and education was available, although the children would have preferred to run free, to fish and swim their days away.

I loved my life in Arnhem Land. We were free of most of life's restrictions. We didn't have a lot, but didn't need much. I was the only girl among four fishing-crazy brothers. Mum and I enjoyed our walks along the beach together, collecting seashells or coral that had washed up on the high-tide mark. Once Mum guided me as I painstakingly tried to sew myself a new dress; I found I needed an unaccustomed patience for this new experience. Once we left Gove, I decided that buying them was the way to go.

One day back at camp, we found a gaunt-looking Aboriginal girl of about 18 cowering in the trees surrounding our homestead. She was covered in dust and her hair was a matted mess. Her thin body was covered by a dirty cloth. She seemed unable to make much more than the odd grunting sound and certainly didn't know any English. I was happy to meet her – she was another girl, after all.

My parents guessed she had walked alone from Blue Mud Bay, in fear of her life. We never found out why, but it must have been a tribal matter – she was probably running from a spearing. Traditional law was harsh and unforgiving, but we had no right to go in and directly challenge it. I beckoned for her to follow me to the showers, where Mother had laid out a towel and some of my old clothes for her. I turned the shower on and gestured for her to step in. Then I turned my back on her and sat in the doorway.

By the time she'd finished, Mum had produced a tray with billy tea, buffalo steaks and damper. The girl was hungry – I'd never seen anyone tear at food like she did. She was also terrified; I could feel the fear vibrating from her.

She was forever looking over her shoulder, her sorrowful dark eyes wide with anxiety. Wherever I walked she shadowed me, a foot behind me day and night. My bed was a wartime camp stretcher and the girl would sleep under it on a thin mattress Mother had given her. She stuck to me like glue.

We lived like this for several weeks until my parents thought she should move on. Her fear was infectious and by now I was searching the plateau as well, looking for the man who was after her. At times I would forget she was behind me and she would bump into me, frightening us both. I was disappointed that we were unable to communicate. I may have been able to help her. She was so young and yet so fearful and sad.

My parents decided that the game must end and took her to Yirrkala Mission for her own safety. I still think of this girl and wonder about her. I hope she was safe at the mission, and looked after by the women.

The mining company Nabalco had by now taken over the bauxite leases from Gominco. Dad wasn't sure whether he wanted to be part of the new mining operation. He loved the Arnhem Land bush the way it was. Then one day he made a decision.

The spirit breeze carried the word that Mr Snow and his family were leaving Gove. We were honoured with a special visit from the elder, Mawwellen. He approached my father, his hands outstretched, and said, 'This is my land, don't you peoples go.' He continued this mantra in his broken English, searching my father's face with his milky eyes.

'I give you this land,' he added, dramatically. But it was time to leave Gove. Our beautiful peaceful camp on the plateau was slowly becoming a hive of activity as interest in the bauxite grew.

CHAPTER 5

Broome Time

I was 18 years old, skinny, with a mane of long blonde hair, blue eyes, still a virgin, and came from the bush side of the tracks. In no time at all the invitations started to roll in. Broome could come alive after sunset when the people seemed to segregate into varying groups – the pearling masters, the golf club, the abattoir workers, and the imported Malay and Japanese pearl divers. The pastoralists were just another group. They hit the town in a flurry of drinking and partying, and the new chums like us hung on the verge until the town realised we weren't aliens. We all created our own entertainment and friendships. During the day people went about their business as usual and Broome's quaint little China Town became the busy commercial centre.

After spending four years – more or less all of my teenage years – in Arnhem Land, Broome seemed all movement: people, vehicles. I was used to the idea of nothing on the road but Dad's Land Rover and our Willy's jeep. Before leaving Gove, a kind-hearted visiting policeman had just passed me on my driver's licence test after I backed into the homestead's only power pole. I wondered if I'd ever be able to drive in Broome, where there were an awful lot of power poles. I lacked confidence and found it difficult to mix. Any ambition I had for my life seemed to have gone out the window when I'd let go of my hairdressing apprenticeship, and then failed to get an air-hostess position I had applied for with MacRobertson Miller Airlines three months before leaving Arnhem Land.

'We would like to employ you, but you're still twelve months too young,' was the answer. They required that hostesses be a minimum 19 years old. I briefly considered putting my age up a year, and my life might have taken a very different course if I had.

The move from Gove to Broome suited my brothers. Not only did they always have each other and me, but being a group of boys they seemed to draw mates from everywhere. School became a challenge for Bruce, Darryl and Michael, but Eric thrived on it – he was the brain among us.

Kennedy and Son of Broome, the store with everything (it's still standing today), were looking for a shop assistant for their drapery department. I applied for the position and obtained the job, seeing a chance of becoming more independent. Old Mr Kennedy would pick up all his staff up each morning from home, take us to work, and then deliver us back home at midday for the two-hour siesta. In the afternoon, he would repeat his staff taxi service all over again.

Working helped build my self-esteem considerably. I met many wonderful people, and some were of the Broome male kind. I soon realised that it took guts for a man to come up to the drapery counter in a country store, where everyone knew everyone and everyone's business as well. I met a tough but good-looking head stockman who very nearly broke me in. He tried to convince me that 99 per cent of women 'did it' before they were married. My head was clearer than his at this point, and I explained that I was the 1 per cent who didn't.

Another man, a lovable larrikin and good-looking guy, persuaded me to go out with him. He hadn't been back in Broome long; he held a position in the local bank and had a reputation with the girls. Sadly we never made the first date together, as he was killed in a road accident the night before.

Some time later, an American from Wyoming walked up to the counter in Kennedy's Store and said, 'Lady, I'm going to take you to dinner tonight at Ma Kim's Café in China Town.' It was more of a demand than a question.

Looking back, God only knows why the hell I got tied up with Chuck. But I suppose he was rather handsome, with green laughing eyes and a head of thick blond curly hair. He was happy-go-lucky and a larrikin to boot. He and his father managed Anna Plains Station for Art Linkletter, another American. Chuck was a lot more experienced in life than I was, and a hell of a lot smoother than most men. In no time he had me under his spell.

I found it a bit odd that his father was always out to dinner with us. I would often catch his father's dark eyes boring into me. Why is he always out with us, and why is he staring at me? I wondered. He gave me the creeps. About three months later, his son proposed. 'Marry me,' he said in that same demanding way. I must have said 'Yes,' but I don't really remember. Marriage had never entered my mind, with Chuck or anyone else. But I was becoming curious about sex, and had made my mind up not to sleep around to experience it. I believed I should be married before I did.

Chuck said that if I did not marry him he would kidnap me and run off. Maybe this was his way of saying that he loved me. I arrived home from work one Friday afternoon to find Chuck having a drink with my father on the back veranda. I stopped in my stride and looked searchingly at them both. Chuck told me we were getting married in June. I didn't have the guts to say no. Everyone seemed excited by the idea, wedding plans were being made, and a beautiful bridal gown was flown from Perth for me to try on.

Both of my parents were sure that this wedding was what I wanted, that I was in love with this Yank. They were happy for me and forged ahead with the wedding plans. But I felt numb to it all. I was still a virgin. I was curious and confused, scared and anxious, but instead of getting emotional I felt distanced from what was going on around me. Chuck would visit me briefly when he came in from the station, then go off and party. Rumours were soon coming back to me of his sleeping around. Two days before I was to be married, I broke down at work and cried my eyes out to a much older lady friend. I told her that I felt Chuck was still a stranger, that I didn't really know him and I didn't wish to marry him and was frightened of the mess I was in.

I couldn't say anything to my parents. My father is a big man, whose attitude at times could be offhand and arrogant, and I was frightened of the explosion my reversal could bring. It was only in my late twenties that Dad and I began to communicate reasonably well.

Still my parents' child, not really an independent adult yet, I drifted into marriage. I didn't feel mature enough to stand up and stop the event, which had gathered its own momentum. This was also the era where the man of the house was the boss. If I'd said to Mum that I couldn't go ahead, I'd have been creating major problems for her. It was all a big misunderstanding, now that I look back on it: Mum and Dad later revealed that they had doubts of their own, but they, in their way, were as caught up in the unstoppable process as I was.

Dad arranged to open the rambling Continental Hotel to one and all. Family and friends had flown in from Darwin and Perth along with Dad's father, Grandpa Wallis, from London. My Grandpa Bond from Fresh Water Rapid Creek had died of cancer while we were in Arnhem Land, so Grandma Bond came alone. I was pleased that Grandfather Wallis had made the long trip over, as we only ever got to see him every couple of years for a week or two. He was my pen-pal and had encouraged me to keep diaries. It was a shame that I couldn't confide to him my fear of what I was about to do.

My bridal gown had cost a fortune, and was encrusted with pearls and crystals. Either Mills & Boon romance novels were full of lies – or was I expecting too much? Maybe this confused, frightened feeling of wanting to bolt back to the bush was how it always was before marriage, and maybe it would get a whole lot better afterwards?

The day arrived. I don't remember putting on the beautiful gown, but I must have, otherwise I would have been naked ... but I do remember trying to muster the courage to go to my parents and say I couldn't and didn't want to go through with this. But it had gone too far, and yet again I was afraid to upset all the plans.

I remember standing in the little white Church of Annunciation in Broome and wondering if I could announce that I had changed my mind. I glanced towards the door, and wondered if I could run away in my gown. As it turned out, I simply didn't have the courage and went ahead with the farcical event. After the marriage vows, we arrived at the Continental Hotel which overlooked beautiful Roebuck Bay in Broome, my new husband escorting me to the wedding table. I had just turned 19, and not a single drop of alcohol had ever passed my lips. I knew very little about this bloke. In fact I didn't even know how old he was! He seemed a lot older than me.

Sitting at the bridal table, half taking in what was going on around me, I was feeling I didn't belong. Seeing the guests toasting us with champagne, I toasted myself with a few glasses as well. I'm sure the champagne helped the Dutch courage to kick in, and the rebel in me came alive. I was dazed and angry and sat at the table while my new husband circulated with the guests; I refused to please anyone but myself. My dear mother and Gran tried to persuade me to change into my 'going-away outfit'. No way. It was time for the bride and groom to leave. Why should I leave? It was my party, wasn't it?

As my husband escorted me to the foyer, I glanced up to the veranda on my right and caught a glimpse of a man. He walked to the balustrade and stood looking at me. There was something special about him: his dark penetrating eyes, black hair, white creased shirt and moleskins. It was Bob McCorry, a drover and buffalo shooter from the Northern Territory, a friend of my father's and many years older than I. He was managing Oobagooma and Waterbank stations at the time. I'd first met him when he'd visited my father to discuss a walk-in freezer Dad was building for Waterbank, and he'd come to our house a few times since. I'd only caught glimpses of him, and he was reserved on his visits, not gregarious or sociable, so we hadn't spoken. But he'd certainly taken my eye.

I stopped, looked up and took in the R.M. Williams boots. A shiver went through me. I should have married him, I thought.

There was a tug on my hand. I looked up again but the dark-haired man had gone. If he had asked me to go with him right then and there, I would have. Instead, I was taken to the bridal suite by Chuck. I refused to consummate the marriage on our wedding night; I slept in a bed alone. Angry about the revelation that Chuck was a playboy, I felt nothing for him. The next night was spent at the new Walkabout Motel in Port Hedland and, after an argument because I refused to balance on a bar stool and drink with him, he spent the next two days on the booze and became aggressively drunk. I spent my time alone and crying in the motel room. I had no money of my own and felt I had nowhere to go. I'd made my bed and had to lie in it. We eventually arrived at the Raffles Hotel in Perth, where Chuck would leave me in the room all day while he went off drinking in the bar, I assume, although I never really knew where he was, except that he arrived back tanked. I realised I'd never known him at all, and soon worked myself up so much I became ill.

Dear Aunty Alvis, my mother's sister, came to my rescue, took me home to her house and tucked me up in bed with an electric blanket, assuring me everything would be all right in the morning. I now worried about being electrocuted. This was all new to me. She was thinking my problem was either the wedding or newlywed nerves. I was trying to tell Aunty that no, everything would not be all right.

I stayed with her for about three days. She seemed to understand my position, but couldn't interfere. I knew I had to go back to Chuck and make the marriage work, even though he only visited me once at Aunty's – he seemed unsure of what to do. So was I! But I was married, and had to give it a go.

Some months later, we did end up consummating our marriage and I tried to make it work. We returned to the Kimberley with two Ford F100s and a bulldozer and went contract dam sinking and fencing throughout the country, until Chuck's drinking and womanising became too much to handle. Unbeknown to Chuck, I followed him into Kununurra one weekend and conveniently walked in on an orgy that he and three others were having in a motel room. I took off my wedding band and flicked it into the air, never to be seen again. Then as I turned to walk out the door Chuck lunged and grabbed me from behind, around the throat. We fell to the ground struggling. I thought I was going to die. I couldn't scream, or breathe, froth was coming from my mouth, and I blacked out. I don't recall what happened next but he must have let go. I ended up in Wyndham Hospital with my neck in a brace, my body sore and covered in black and blue bruises. Chuck confessed to having spent time in a padded cell in his Navy days. I decided to end the marriage. There was no point going on.

I returned to Broome, neither asking for sympathy nor expecting to receive any. My father belonged to the era where people believed you should always give your marriage your best shot. Well, I had done that.

I was in my bedroom changing my clothes when my mother walked in. A look of absolute horror crossed her face when she saw the bruises and welts on my shoulders, ribs and arms. Without saying a word, she left the room immediately and spoke to Dad. They didn't push me to go back to Chuck.

Back in Broome, after moving into a flat with my brother Darryl and his wife Leonie, I landed a job with the post office and worked hard in the telephone exchange to earn enough money to hire a detective. With Mr Peter Dowding Snr, whose son would become Premier of Western Australia many years later, as my lawyer, I divorced Chuck on the grounds of adultery. It was easy to catch him out and embarrassing to see it all again.

Looking back, I wonder if it was necessary for Chuck to marry an Australian to keep himself and his father in the country to do their work, managing stations. I never discovered why that creepy old man was always looming over Chuck's shoulder. He even brought a tape recorder to one of our meetings, but I couldn't work out why. I never spoke to him. I'll never know and now I don't care, but it wasn't long after the divorce that they both left Australia. Chuck's father would later die from a brain tumour. Maybe this had had some influence on his bizarre, unnerving behaviour.

CHAPTER 6

Oobagooma Station

'*B*e at Derby airport on the fifteenth at 2 pm.'
I read the note from Bob McCorry with mounting excitement, mixed with shock – who did he think he was, giving me a directive like this? I knew Dad had asked McCorry to keep an eye on me now that he and Mum had left Broome for Shark Bay, several days' drive away. Believing Broome was growing too rapidly for them, Dad had bought a boat at Shark Bay and started fishing commercially.

I'd been quite ill the last time Dad had seen me. Perhaps it was the stress of my doomed marriage, but I hadn't been able to shake off a lingering virus. Dad had asked McCorry to check on my health, and McCorry suggested that some time in the outback might help my recovery. Maybe McCorry's intentions were good, but I resented being treated like a child. I felt I had grown up now.

On the other hand, I hadn't forgotten the man with the dark smouldering eyes at my farcical wedding, and I felt something of a thrill at the prospect of seeing him again, on his own territory. Besides, I sensed that this might present an opportunity to go mustering, something I'd never done before, and I wasn't going to miss that for the world. So I relented, and was off to Oobagooma, a station abutting the coast five hours' drive north-east of Broome.

'Buckle up and leave the seatbelt on until we land at the station. Some days she gets a little rough,' were the pilot's words after we'd flown out of Derby. Soon we were dropping altitude, seemingly to buzz a mob of wild black pigs digging in the grass. But this was the west end of Oobagooma's airstrip. My stomach lurched and there was a light thump and sound of wheels on gravel. We were safely down. McCorry managed the station for a rich city slicker, 'Monty' Montague from New South Wales. A prospering wheeler-dealer with a taste for flashy women he brought out from Kings Cross, Monty also owned several cattle properties in the southern states.

McCorry walked over to the plane from the old corrugated-iron homestead. He greeted me as warmly as if I was an old friend. I smiled and shook his hand. I stood for a moment and looked around. As far as I could see the country was harsh and rugged. The green treeline of a river and the craggy mountains marked the horizon, but there was not much around us except some broken fencing and the homestead, which was little more than a tin shed. McCorry's dusty Akubra shaded his sun-tanned face, but those steely dark eyes had a soft twinkle in them, and his colouring reminded me of a Cherokee Indian. Yes, I thought, I reckon I can handle this for a while.

As we ambled towards the homestead I could see the Aboriginal stockmen, their wives and their children moving slowly down the hill from their camp. They seemed keen to check me out. Some of the younger faces had huge smiles, giggling and talking among themselves, reading more into this friendship between McCorry and me than there was. The older men eyed me suspiciously. I had on a smart red pantsuit, makeup and painted nails. I had always promised myself that wherever I lived or worked in the outback I would try to keep myself attractive and feminine.

As my makeup melted in the exhausting heat, the mascara burning my eyes, I knew they weren't expecting me to last. I felt awkward and nervous, wondering what I'd got myself into. The quizzical look on the older stockmen's faces said they were wondering what the hell happened to old McCorry on his last trip to Broome. 'That poor bugger McCorry,' they seemed to be saying, 'he's gone off his rocker.'

That evening, I dropped my swag and a bag into a room that seemed untidily occupied. It was McCorry's bedroom, which he shared with his two dogs. While I was debating between nightie and pyjamas for bed, the staff drifted past the window and giggled at me. That made my decision for me: pyjamas! I said goodnight to McCorry and climbed onto my wartime camp stretcher, which emitted more creaks and groans than I'd ever heard coming from a bed. The mattress was paper-thin and the bed hard as hell. I felt the weave of the wire beneath me. But the sheets were spotless. I lay thinking about what might lie ahead, happy to be there with McCorry and trusting him to look after me. I had a crush on him, but wasn't sure if it was the man or his connection to the land. Either way, it didn't seem to bother me.

When I'd received the note from McCorry, I thought I was going to the station for two weeks' holiday. When he told me he was going outback to muster cattle, I jumped at the opportunity to go along. This would be my first wild cattle muster; I was excited and extremely happy, as keen as could be. His offer brought back the desire for adventure and challenge that I'd enjoyed so much as a young girl. First thing next morning, I radioed my boss asking for extended leave from the post office.

McCorry wanted to get his horses ready for the stock-camp, and get out into the Robinson River country. Word was circulating about the Kimberley that the Australian Land & Cattle Co., owned privately in America, had purchased two large properties: Kimberley Downs and Napier Downs. These two properties had about 2.25 million acres between them and probably between 38,000 and 40,000 head of cattle, a good half of them unbranded. This presented an irresistible challenge to Bob: cattle weren't considered yours to sell until they were branded, and up to that point it was a free-for-all. McCorry had been mustering cleanskin cattle, with no earmark or brand, for years. They had never been caught or handled by man and were running free for the taking. He saw an opportunity to catch and brand these cattle before the Americans got there; they would then be dollars on the hoof to him.

He wondered if these new cattlemen from America had any idea how imaginary the boundaries to their property might be, because there were no fences, no gates. By contrast, he had an unfair advantage: McCorry could read the country, line up a rocky outcrop with a schist hill in the distance and know exactly what survey features to look for. All the Americans had was lines on a map.

An old grey Land Rover pulled up at the front gate.

'Hey, come and give your cook a hand out!'

Silver had arrived. He didn't need a helping hand: he fell out onto the ground, landing like a sack of potatoes. He started scratching in the dirt to retrieve his half-smoked tailormade cigarette. McCorry had told me about the cook, and he lived up to his billing: Silver by name, silver hair and very, very drunk. I just stood staring; this was toughen-up time, Sheryl. What the hell was going to happen next? I glanced towards McCorry, but he smiled and shook his head, saying he could write a book on camp cooks.

He told Silver to get his swag, find a camp stretcher and sleep off the grog, adding: 'You start in the cook house in the morning.' While Silver was out cold I was given orders to hunt around and find all the metho, lemon essence, and anything else he could possibly mix with cordial or water and get inebriated on while we were away rounding up cattle. I hid the metho and lemon essence behind the old freezer, hoping I had outsmarted him.

The preparations were proceeding, though not without a hitch. Harry Watson, our Aboriginal head stockman, who always wore elastic-sided riding boots two sizes too big, came in from the horse yard and said, 'The camp horses are ready, but three missing, probably dead, old man, walkabout.'

This was during a wet season, a time when the crotalaria plant thrived. If the horses ate too much of it they would end up with what the stockmen called 'walkabout', walking blindly and running into trees and gullies until they died. McCorry had put some quiet cattle together to use for 'coaches'. The small mob, kept around the homestead, was mostly made up of quiet, obedient six- to eight-year-old bullocks who would step out on command from the old man. They were big rangy shorthorn cattle with speary horns that would do a good day's walk when needed. McCorry explained that it was necessary to keep coaches all the time if you are mustering wild feral cattle on horseback. When you spread the coaches out and run the wild cattle into them, they act as a buffer – coaches have the temperament of a group of fussy mothers. The idea is to get the coaches going in a circular motion and the wild cattle will stay enclosed until you can settle them down. You lose some, you retain some, but very seldom can you hold them all. The fact that the coaches might have belonged to the neighbours wasn't mentioned at the time.

The morning came for us to set off. Warm and sunny with
that outback bite in the air, the day was filled with the cattle's
calls, the ringing of the chains hobbling the horses, and the
clang of the condamine, the bell on the leading horse. Little
quails scattered in the spinifex as kite-hawks dived for them.
I was as excited as the stockmen as they mounted the lucky
horses that survived the walkabout. 'Old man', as the Aboriginal men called McCorry, took a deep draw from his
tailormade, raised his right arm and, mounted on his trusty
Arab mare, led the coaches out, closely followed by two
faithful working bull terrier crosses, Whiskey and old Jim.
Harry was in a short-wheelbase Toyota with the canopy
removed and a bull bar added – the 'bull-buggy'.

Our team included several stockmen: Malki, Churchill,
Raymond Warbi, Charlie Riley, Peter, and several other men.
They were all moving out with the coaches for the first leg of
the muster.

Yardie, an older Aboriginal stockman with white hair and
a long white beard, was the horse-tailer, minding the extra
horses and keeping them together. He'd look after the three
spare horses each stockman needed during a muster, and keep
them rotating as they grew tired. Yardie had gone on ahead
of me.

I was sitting behind the wheel of the supply vehicle, an
old-model International truck, the cab full of spiderwebs and
the tray loaded with camp swags, shoeing gear, a first-aid box,
the salted beef, drums of flour to make the dampers with, a few
onions and potatoes, a couple of jars of Rosella pickles, plenty
of niki niki (plugs of chewing tobacco) and tinned Log Cabin
rolling tobacco, tea leaf and coarse salt, but that was about it.
If I could eat tobacco I certainly wouldn't starve! McCorry was
known for travelling light and he figured that salt beef, damper
and tea leaf was all we needed. As we had packed, in the

storeroom, I'd questioned McCorry on the amount of stores we had, which didn't seem enough to me. He stopped what he was doing, looked towards me in the dark storeroom, took his hat off and ran his hand through his hair, and smiled, as if surprised by my question. He assured me that we had plenty of everything and explained gently how he ran his camp. I was to understand that this was *his* country and *his* way of life. His explanation, rather than sounding arrogant, settled me; I felt that everything was going to be all right.

As I sat in the supply truck, I listened to the radio. All the stations had Flying Doctor radios. Sessions in which station business, telegrams and medical information were exchanged took place at three set times a day. Before and after these periods, the stations could converse freely in 'galah sessions', talking, gossiping and passing on messages. So if you listened, you would have some idea of the other stations' movements, their mustering patterns and what yards they were organising road trains to and from.

Half of our team of 17 working dogs was with us, a mix of blue and red heelers and bull terriers. Glancing over my shoulder I checked on Missy, a bull terrier bitch that McCorry had given me the day before. I was touched and surprised by his gift; I'd tied her securely to the truck's centre rail where she rested peacefully on my swag. Missy was 18 months old and all white with no markings. I knew I would love this dog – she was mine. Not all the dogs would return from the musters. Some would be gored by bulls, while others would become dehydrated and disoriented and fall behind after chasing wild and feral cattle. (Having to confront this was to nearly undo me at times: I'd want to spend time searching for a missing dog, but McCorry was always set on moving the cattle along to the next camp.)

Whiskey and old Jim were McCorry's dogs, and only he handled them. The rest were purely working dogs, out on the runs to help bring in the fresh cattle to the coaches. If they failed to return to camp after a quick run with wild cattle, they were left behind and forgotten and no more would be said. I would soon realise that this was unforgiving land, and that I had better prepare for hard work and a harsh life.

The pressure was on from that first day. On our first leg out from the homestead we didn't sight many cattle; the water-hole and billabongs were further out and up the Robinson River. The stockmen did only one run and brought in eight head. McCorry was more interested in the country further out, on the boundaries. By about 2 pm we were held up, having to dig into the banks down on the Robinson so as to get the trucks over.

It was very humid among the tall spear grass, which was as thick as I'd seen. The banks of the river were muddy and slippery. In between taking turns on the shovel, we were collecting branches, bushes, rocks, anything that we could pack in the wheel ruts to make a bed for the vehicles to cross on. The bull-buggy came across first with no problems. Then it was my turn with the International. I backed it up as far as I could, then took a run at the bank, slipping into the riverbed and then gently easing it up the other side, tyres gripping the branches and rocks. Success! I had passed my first test.

While Silver sobered up back at the station, the stock-camp cook was Mary, a wonderful older Aboriginal woman. The stockman Peter was her man; he was much younger than Mary and would look after her as she grew older. Peter was from Wave Hill country in the Northern Territory, and I believe Mary took Peter under her wing to guide and protect him through country that wasn't really his. Mary and I were waiting for orders to make camp. Dusk was nearly on us as the men moved the cattle a little further ahead. Without yards to enclose the cattle, the stockmen would take turns riding around the mob, keeping them close throughout the night.

McCorry rode in later than the rest of us and gave the order to make camp. He unsaddled Little Arab, dropping his saddle to the ground. His favourite dog Whiskey moved in and settled herself down by his saddle, where she would stay until just before daylight when the camp was ready to move on again.

I unloaded all the swags, dropped all the boys' gear together, and put McCorry's and mine closer to the truck. We were only metres apart, but it gave me the privacy I needed. Mary was out collecting dry wood and I went to help her. With our arms full, we soon had the camp fire crackling.

Between the two of us we unloaded the flour drums and Mary proceeded to make damper for the next night's dinner camp. As we hadn't yet made it to the first spring on our route, I siphoned water out of a 44-gallon drum that rode on the truck. It had to do for the tea that night. Dinner was get yourself a slice of fresh damper and a slice of salt beef, boiled before we'd left the station, then eat it with your back resting against your swag. Then you'd wash it down with a pannikin of black tea.

Gazing over the top of my damper, I took a peek at the stockmen. Most of them were peeking straight back. They all seemed happy and were laughing and joking. I soon realised that the simplest of pleasures in the right company were all I needed to be happy.

During the day I'd noticed that we were following no road or track. That night in camp, I asked McCorry why.

'There's none to follow,' was his terse reply.

At first I was annoyed at his arrogance, and put it down to the hard day we'd had. It was obviously a silly question and I told myself I should trust his judgment – but I was hoping we weren't lost. I told myself to put my faith in him, and let go of my fears.

He told me that when mustering wild cattle, the idea was to 'take the yard to the cattle and not the cattle to the yard' – a good rule when working feral cattle in the Kimberley. They certainly weren't going to come to us.

I'd have liked to extend the conversation further, but McCorry was a quiet man – the brooding, silent type. I couldn't easily read his emotions in his face, and despite my best efforts he kept the conversation short. There seemed something mysteriously inaccessible about him.

The next morning was a pretty sight, the early morning shafts of golden sunlight spearing their way down through the gums, wattle and tall grass. We set off towards Tarragi River country, and occasionally a flash of gold bounced off the lead bullock's horns. We were headed towards the boundaries of Kimberley Downs and Napier Downs stations, Australian Land & Cattle Co. territory. We had no intention of crossing their boundary. We were simply going to pick up the cleanskin cattle that were lost on our side. They were only looking for an owner to take care of them! It wasn't as if we were stealing. The managers of those properties, McCorry said, spent too much time worrying about our moves and not enough thinking about how to get these cleanskin cattle for themselves. And it wasn't as if we had many advantages. Our basic mustering camp was up against a helicopter, a Cessna and three stock-camps. Trucks, bull-buggies and vehicles galore – you name it, they had it.

We made our way towards the boundaries, and suddenly we could see in the distance a roaring melee. The neighbouring stock-camps were thundering towards us, the noise of their helicopters and light aircraft echoing down the valley. It seemed like the cavalry was charging. But the noise had scared the cattle, who'd run kilometres ahead of the machines and were headed towards us. The way things were going, our neighbours would lose more cattle to us than they would yard at the end of the muster! Under grey dust clouds, from the distance, cattle were coming toward us, following the smell, the tracks and their thirst for water, and fleeing the noise behind them. Instead of going out and hunting for the cattle, all we had to do was sit back and wait.

McCorry spread the coaches into position behind a saddle in the hills. He rode to the top of the saddle and looked towards the undulating Mondooma country, and sure enough, that great cloud of dust was still travelling towards us. There looked to be 600 to 800 head of cattle. McCorry told the men to let the coaches spread out even more; the stockmen lay down flat along their horses' necks and waited. The cattle were coming through the saddle, 20 to 40 at a time.

I stayed in the vehicle and watched. For the next hour or so it was a frenzy of charging cattle, galloping horses, dust and danger. After the dust had settled, McCorry estimated that we had retained about 350 head, while hundreds of other cattle had broken out and gone on their merry way into the depths of our Oobagooma country. This was the easiest and fastest mob of cleanskins that McCorry had ever picked up.

Later, at a camp on our way back to the station, Mary and I were walking towards a spring when a huge goanna crossed our path. We often came across goannas; in fact the night before, Mary had killed and cooked one. She told me it was my turn. I had no qualms about killing it, because I knew that if I didn't, she would, and I preferred it to be dead before it went into the coals.

'Very good and fat,' Mary said, watching the goanna slide through the undergrowth.

I knew I had to do this, but felt I was being tested. I bent down and picked up a large lump of wood with a heavy end. Creeping up behind the goanna and raising my weapon, I closed my eyes and pelted it over the head again and again to make sure.

As the men came into camp that night, questions were asked about the goanna. Mary was only too pleased to fill them in on every detail. Smiles and yahoos from the stockmen showed their acceptance of me. Maybe now I could approach McCorry and Harry and see if they'd let me chase breakaway bulls with them.

The camp had been out on the run for three weeks, and we were down to the last piece of salt beef – it was green, very green. God only knows where it came from, as I'd emptied out the flour drums where we'd had the beef stacked between gum leaves. We decided we would have to eat it. We didn't really want to kill a beast now, given that we'd be back at the station in a couple of days if all went well. The meat was only green on the outside; there were no wrigglers or maggots. So I presumed it was edible. I sliced off the green bits the best I could, and cooked what remained. Surprise! It was delicious, tender and tasty. I'd had thoughts of the whole camp getting sick and having to spend all night behind a tree with diarrhoea, but luckily we were all fine.

About midday on the last day, McCorry rode ahead to alert Silver that the camp was coming in. This was to give the cook plenty of time to prepare a huge baked dinner. But when McCorry walked down the cement path towards the kitchen, he found Silver halfway to the veranda, sprawled out in his brightly-coloured jocks, amid a pile of empty cordial bottles. The water bottles from the fridge were empty too. Silver had discovered a full bottle of metho that had been hidden in the store many, many musters ago. Raising his head slightly, with bleary, bloodshot eyes, he slurred, 'If you're looking for McCorry, he's mustering.' Then he dropped back to the cement, out cold in a drunken sleep.

The cattle were yarded well before sundown. The yard – built between two huge boab trees – was old, the post and rails held together with wire twitches (pieces of twisted wire used as fasteners), but it was still sturdy enough to hold about 400 head. The stockmen nose-bagged the horses and gave them a little extra chaff and nuts as a reward for a good job, before letting them go in the horse paddock for a spell. We had a week to draft the different lines of cattle out – divide them into bulls, cows to keep, weaners, mickeys (young bulls) that needed castrating – then brand the cleanskins, and truck the 'meatworkers' to the abattoir in Derby, 130 kilometres away.

With Silver out of action that night, I willingly took on the cook's job, preparing potatoes, pumpkin and onions, throwing them into the largest baking dish I could find, with a generous sprinkle of salt and some rendered fat that still looked healthy.

I hauled from the fridge a very large rump, cutting it into half-inch-thick slices for grilling. The full baked dinner we were all looking forward to would have to wait another night. Better still, we might catch a huge barramundi from the Robinson River just below the homestead.

Oobagooma did not have the most elegant of station homesteads. Constructed mostly of corrugated iron, it had no ceilings or doors but plenty of window space. The cement floors were as corrugated as the roof and the toilet was 4 metres from the dining table. Sounds and efforts were advertised for all to hear. Sometimes the noises from the bathroom were enough to start the dogs on a barking frenzy. I timed my visits very carefully.

The next day, after a good breakfast of steak and onions, the stockmen and all the Aboriginal kids headed towards the old wooden cattle yards to give McCorry a hand with the drafting. I had already organised a road train, via the Flying Doctor radio, so that at first light on the following morning the cattle would be trucked to the Derby meatworks.

While cleaning out the yard we had a visit from McCorry's old hatter friend, Cec Rodericks. (A 'hatter' was the name given to people like Cec who lived lonely and eccentric lives in the bush or outback.) Cec was an odd sort of character, but likeable. His wiry frame was draped with well-tanned skin, more like a hide, exposed to the elements of the Kimberley for many years. His face, which looked like a well-cooked johnnycake, was framed with unruly grey hair and a long white beard that hung to his navel. Old Cec would nearly always be dressed in a narga or loincloth when McCorry saw him, but if I was present he would put on an old worn pair of shorts, tied on one side with a number 8 wire twitch.

When Cec was near the station, he would camp under the pandanus near the billabong, a stone's throw from the wooden yards where we were drafting the cattle. His camp was basic; one old wartime wire camp stretcher covered in tattered canvas and supported by some Dingo Flour drums.

Cec would wander over from the billabong to have a chat and give a hand in the yards while the drafting was on, although at the end of the day on our way back to the homestead, we would often wonder if he would ever let the cattle loose – he never liked seeing them trucked off the property to the meatworks, and we suspected he would prefer to set them free, to roam like him.

I always worried about him: we never knew where he was, or where he would pop up on this million-acre cattle run.

I always hoped he was alive and happy, as he was only sighted for about three days every 12 months.

On the other hand, three days was definitely the limit. I saved any newspapers we'd scored from passers-by and store runs, which Cec would study solidly for two days, then give us a burst in the evenings on the state of the nation.

On this visit, Cec was sharing his camp by the billabong with about eight very large feral pigs and their piglets. Each pig was named after a politician and Cec would refer to them as if they were old friends. I was terrified of these bloody politician friends of his, who'd roam into the homestead at will. One snort from Whitlam, who had a broken tusk and seemed to be the daddy of them all, and I ended up in among the flour drums on the old wire bed. Once when McCorry and I visited, Cec was upset, as Malcolm Fraser had spent most of the morning rooting up his camp, and Whitlam hadn't shown up at all after a night out.

My biggest worry was that if Cec was ever unwell, or fell down and hurt himself and was unable to get up, the pigs might just eat him alive.

At day's end, McCorry and I would relax together in two 'Queenslander' deck chairs, talking over the day's events and plans for future moves with the musters. I was pleased he chose to talk about work with me, and I was eager to listen and learn all I could.

A worry had been working towards the front of my mind: I had to tell McCorry that after six weeks at Oobagooma I still held my job at the telephone exchange in Broome and must return soon or lose it.

When I did tell him, he said he would 'fix that in the morning'. I thought he meant he'd organise a charter flight out for me. I couldn't believe it, and was saddened by the thought that the next day I'd be gone from this man who had made me feel safe and secure as we mustered cattle together.

Only that day he'd held my hand as we strolled along the banks of the crocodile-infested Robinson River. We'd had a beautiful drive along the riverbanks, missing gullies and deep holes formed in the wet season. Every now and then, crocodiles would take fright from sunning themselves on rocky ledges and splash into the water. Away from the river, I spotted a billabong surrounded by blue waterlilies. A mob of wild pigs hurried their piglets away from us. I was walking through waist-deep grass towards the billabong when I came face to face with a huge goanna standing straight up on its tail. Spinning in my tracks, crying out, I ran smack into McCorry's arms. While I was madly fighting him to flee the predator, his grip tightened.

'Slow down, slow down,' he said, holding me firmly. 'It's just an old goanna, too old to get out of your way.'

I relaxed against McCorry and rested my head on his shoulder. He held onto me for a while longer. It felt so right.

That was the first time we'd touched. At the homestead, we slept in the same bedroom – there was no other – in single camp stretcher beds. We had completed a couple of musters together and he had not attempted to touch, let alone grope, me. All he'd done was lovingly hold my hand in his hard callused one, or offer me a welcome, strong arm around my waist. In the mornings he would bring me tea and toast, and kiss me on the forehead. He was of the old school, of 'getting to know you', and I appreciated this.

I knew deep down that I was falling in love with him. There was a mysterious magnetism around McCorry that both inspired and fascinated me.

Morning arrived before I was ready; I'd had a restless night churning over what lay ahead. McCorry woke me at what seemed an earlier than usual hour with tea and toast, plus pen and paper. Not properly awake, I asked him what he wanted me to do with this. He said to write my resignation to my boss, Mr Gauld, the Postmaster in Broome. McCorry said he would send the telegram immediately on the Flying Doctor session that morning.

At first I was shocked and confused. I'd had thoughts of visiting my parents in Shark Bay. But then, while having my tea and toast, thinking about the telegram I was to write, I couldn't help but smile, thinking this was a funny way of asking me to stay with him.

I could have refused and demanded a charter flight, but I wanted to remain, to work with him and be with him, and I did. He said nothing, as if he'd expected me to do so all along.

A week later, we were up before the break of day. McCorry and I had a pannikin of tea and a couple of slices of toasted damper before heading for Derby to replenish the station store. The next day we would head out for another sweep in the back country.

The road into Derby, about 130 kilometres, was very narrow and terribly sandy in places. McCorry's rather new black-and-white Valiant was in the middle of the track, its wheels in the deep ruts. Every now and then there would be an almighty whack from a rock or branch hitting the floor. I prayed all the way.

Our first stop was at the post office to collect the mailbag, then the bank, and on to Elders (a rural trader selling anything and everything) to collect the stores and the bits and pieces needed for repairs to the saddles. We loaded the Valiant with as much flour, sugar, Sunshine powdered milk, tea leaf, niki niki, and Log Cabin rolling tobacco as we could fit. Then the perishables went on top. There was no alcohol on board as McCorry ran a dry station, a rule for one and all.

With the boot and back seat loaded to the roof, the Valiant's nose was now in the air and I joked that we looked like a DC3. The last stop was for McCorry to have a few cold beers with his old mate Jock Pontant, a mechanic in Derby, before heading back to the station.

I couldn't believe my new life! Here I was, perspiration trickling down my forehead and between my breasts, having my very first cold beer with a couple of old-timers from the Kimberley! Sitting up between them, listening to their yarns about the bush, I was happy, knowing McCorry would get us home to the station safely. Back in the Valiant, he pointed the nose in the general direction of Oobagooma and took off, both of us sharing a mood of great contentment, this time the vehicle cutting slightly deeper into the road.

Sorting through the mailbag the following day, I was surprised to find a letter from an old boyfriend, a well-to-do businessman in the Broome and Kununurra district, trying to convince me that I would be lost and totally bored to tears in the outback. 'Please think about coming back,' he wrote. I carefully tore it into tiny pieces and went into the loo to dispose of it.

I was having a hell of a job repeatedly flushing the toilet and trying to bash the sodden paper down with a mottled old toilet brush, and could hear McCorry's spurs tapping on the cement kitchen floor. He hollered out, 'Having problems, love?'

I was having bloody problems all right – the bits of paper wanted to float. McCorry knew what I was doing, I'm sure. When I returned inside, the smile on his face told me. But the assurance in his dark eyes said it was okay, and not to worry. We were together now and this was the life we would build upon.

McCorry was in the homestead drafting out, or separating, the rations of flour, tea leaf and sugar that would be needed on the next muster. I was at the round yard to give the men a hand drafting out the horses. I was inquisitive to see if our resident frill-necked lizard would be there to watch us. Each time horses were brought into the yard, the 'keeper of the yard' would run up on his post, perch himself on top, raise his frill, and drop it down again. The Aboriginal stockmen would say that the 'keeper' was drafting for us. He would never leave his yard post until all the horses had been drafted out and let go. As soon as the yard was empty, the 'keeper' would disappear, not to be seen again until we needed fresh horses.

During that muster, I asked McCorry and Harry if I could go bull-running with whoever was chasing the rogue bulls. Both men went silent. McCorry started scratching at the ground with a twig, while Harry started kicking at the dirt with the toe of his over-sized R.M. Williams boot. The toe of the other boot was cut away, and Harry's big toe was protruding. I could see some serious thought was going into this and I wasn't really impressed about the amount of time they needed to give me an answer.

McCorry pulled his Log Cabin from his top pocket, took the right amount of tobacco out of his tin, slowly rubbed it around the palm of his hand, pulled out the cigarette paper, set his paper in place along it and then applied exactly the correct amount of lick along the edge of the paper. Harry found an excuse to walk away and I decided I might as well walk away too. It looked as if I wasn't going to get an answer – not that day, anyway.

I was cross with him. I thought I was getting to know McCorry, but his refusal to answer left me stunned. I had walked 100 metres away, to where the stock-camp was set up, when McCorry sang out.

'You can ride with Harry.'

I knew this wasn't to be a pleasure ride and that once Harry had knocked the bulls down with the buggy, I was to tie their hind legs for him. This made my day! The next morning, I sprinted to the buggy filled with both excitement and fear. This was what I really wanted to do. I jumped in, ready to offside Harry. Looking back, I don't think I was really supposed to make it past the first run. Since I had no instruction or preparation, they probably thought they would frighten the living daylights out of me straight up, and that would be the end of it.

No sooner had my backside hit the front seat than Harry cranked the starter and we were off with such force that he nearly launched me into space. The boys had done a run already, and fresh cattle were running into the mob from several directions, splitting and breaking off. I was on my first 'bull run', charging at breakneck speed with Harry behind the wheel, trying to muster these untamed cattle into the mob or knock down the ferocious ones and strap them.

Hanging on white-knuckled to the Jesus bar, a handrail running across the top of the glovebox, I was terrified that the sweat gushing from my palms would loosen my grip and the next bump would throw me out. I wedged both feet at an angle to counteract the swaying of the bull-buggy, and held on for dear life. We were winding in and out of low-hanging branches, just missing the rim of the breakaway gully, which looked more like the Grand Canyon. With inches to spare and dust flying, Harry would swing the buggy in another direction to keep the wild beast, 'the scrubber', heading for the clay-pan flat where we would take the animal down. We made the claypan flat safely; I was well and truly shaken, but still in the buggy. I was scared, but determined not to give in. Harry lapped the scrubber around and around.

Every chance the bull got, he would charge and hook the buggy with his horns. At just the right moment Harry came in and put the edge of the front bull bar in behind the old scrubber's ribs. As he turned to hook the buggy, down he went, nice and gentle.

My job was to strap the scrubber's hind legs together. I flew over the side of the buggy with limbs like jelly, and a metre of strong leather bull strap in hand. How the hell was I to get his massive hind legs together?

Casually Harry climbed out from behind the wheel and up onto the bonnet of the buggy. Resting his chin comfortably on his skinny black knee, he proceeded to give me instructions.

'Grab that strap below the buckle,' he called, demonstrating the action in mid-air. 'Put it over one leg, wrap the rest of the strap around the other, and pull up, thread it through that buckle and pull the hind legs together.'

'Right, got it!' I yelled. There was no way I was going to miss; it was a case of get it right first time, or my life in this Kimberley stock-camp was over. I felt there was no place for me in the camp if I couldn't pull my weight. I wanted to show McCorry I could be useful, that I wasn't just a pretty face.

The next challenge was to get the coaches over to this rogue bull and remove the strap without injury. Up the scrubber jumped, every muscle in his powerful body rippling, still full of fight, his eyes wildly looking for an opening in the mob to make a break for freedom. Up close he was enormous, seemingly as big as an African rhino. But we settled him all right – success!

The stockmen were all alert, watching and waiting. We held up the mob for an hour or so and had smoko. Once the fresh cattle and the scrubber had settled, we moved on again. I had achieved my first bull run. I was relieved and proud of myself and, more than ever, ready for the chase again.

We spent the rest of the day picking up small mobs of cattle. Late in the day, Malki, one of the stockmen, and I were given orders to kill and butcher a beast – a 'killer' – for the camp to eat. Circling the cattle slowly, we had to select a well-conditioned, medium-weight, barren or 'dry' cow and nudge her gently out of the mob. As soon as we had her out and the distance was right, Malki pulled out the camp .303 and shot her dead, right between the eyes. I flew over the side of the buggy with butcher's knife in hand, intending to cut her throat and bleed her.

'Missus!' Malki called, his hand out for the knife. This time he would do it. I didn't have the heart to tell him that as a kid in Arnhem Land I'd seen my dad cut the throat of buffalo to bleed them for meat for our family. I knew I was capable of this.

As the killer was being bled, Malki took the rest of the butcher's knives out of the buggy's glove compartment and unwrapped them from the old rag they were tied up in. Running the knives down from tail to hock, Malki and I started skinning out the killer, taking the cuts of meat as we worked our way up. The first side completed, we rolled the beast over and started again, taking everything we wanted, including the sweetbreads, curly gut and rib bones. Having fresh meat in camp would only happen every three or four weeks, so dinner would be really something.

Sundown was on us and it was back to camp. Before we drove off, we collected gum leaves to protect the meat from picking up dirt and dust in the back of the buggy. At the camp, Mary had the fire going and a flour drum of water close to the boil. Some of the stockmen were already in. Charlie and Raymond helped us unload the meat and lay it out on an old stretcher bed.

Sweetbreads and rib bones were the firm favourites on killer night, although I also liked the fine strips of belly flap and the meat around the kai bone, just off the hip. There was nothing better than warm fresh damper and chewing on a rib bone cooked gently over simmering coals, with a slight touch of salt and a pannikin of fine black tea.

The parts that we didn't eat straight away would stay on the stretcher bed and cool through the night. The next morning, Mary and I salted it down and packed it with the gum leaves into the flour drums.

Sitting beside Harry in the buggy, the next day, with the mob poking along at their own steady pace, soaking up the wonderful warmth of our Kimberley sunshine, I thought: *I love my life on the land, and I'm happy, and free to roam.*

Life was never dull; it was peppered with exciting and fresh challenges. One day, I dreamed, I would manage and own my own cattle station. While this aspiration seemed far off, I never let it go; I had a powerful determination to follow it through. Women just didn't run stock-camps or stations in the Kimberley back then. But I knew with McCorry's knowledge and my determination to learn all I could from him, my vision could come true. In fact, I dreamed that McCorry and I would achieve it together.

I was jolted out of my daydream as Harry's foot hit the accelerator. We were heading out to back up the stockmen who were running a fresh mob of cattle to the coaches. We raced up behind three wiry-looking cows and in they went to the coaches without any trouble. Now it was a young mickey's turn. A 'mickey' is a young scrubber bull that hasn't had his balls removed. Around and around him we went, dust flying, dodging anthills and overhanging branches, until we had the young bull on Harry's side of the buggy, running neck and neck. The temptation was too much for Harry and he decided to bulldog the beast. Bulldogging is usually performed from a stockhorse, where the rider leaves his horse at just the right moment, takes the beast by the horns and throws it to the ground. A good bulldogger can make it look neat and easy. My stomach took a sudden lurch into my throat as Missy, my bullterrier, and I became the sole occupants of the racing bull-buggy.

Thank God there were no large trees or anthills directly in front. Flinging myself behind the steering wheel, my vision blurred with dust, I swung the buggy in the general direction of Harry and the mickey. I noticed that several of the stockmen had left the mob of cattle and were galloping towards me, waving and pointing. Lifting my foot from the accelerator, I was damned if I could see what was wrong until one of the men rode up close.

'Missus,' he pointed. Poor Missy was flying in mid-air out the side of the buggy, connected by her chain around her neck, but luckily unhurt. I made a mental note to shorten her chain right up. McCorry rode over and said something to the effect of, 'So you'd rather lose the mob of cattle than lose the dog.' He was blaming the men for caring more about the dog than the cattle, if only for a moment.

'It was my fault,' I tried to explain. 'I should have shortened her lead.'

This was the first time I saw any sign of annoyance from McCorry. He swung his horse around and rode back to the mob of cattle. Through my inexperience, we could have lost the cattle and blown weeks of hard work.

Meanwhile, Harry had bulldogged the mickey and tied him firmly with a bull strap. Sheepishly the men turned their horses around and rode back to the mob. By sundown, McCorry had forgiven us all and we were laughing again.

The following afternoon, as we were slowly moving the mob of cattle down a creek to a wire yard we'd built on the side of a schist hill, we heard an aircraft flying low. We stopped the cattle in the shadows of the overhanging trees. It was the same 180 Cessna from the neighbouring property, Alpha Charlie Charlie, that we'd seen yesterday and the day before. Henceforth the spotter would be known, due to the regularity of his swoops, as 'Five O'Clock Charlie'. On arrival at the homestead we were greeted with a Flying Doctor radio message from the manager of Napier Downs Station: 'Stay out of my country or you will be in serious trouble.'

With all the stations tuned in for the galah session, this would at least give them something to talk about. As far as McCorry was concerned, it was water off a duck's back – he hadn't been on Napier Downs in the first place. In reply he drafted a message to Department of Civil Aviation in Derby, stating that a 180 Cessna, marking Alpha Charlie Charlie, had been flying over his country, Oobagooma, at treetop level and was this legal? He already knew that no aircraft was allowed to fly below 500 feet. The same afternoon McCorry drafted another message to Jack Fletcher, the Managing Director of the Australian Land & Cattle Company: 'Your aircraft Alpha Charlie Charlie has been flying over my country in a dangerous manner for some time now. Please cease.' Five O'Clock Charlie never worried us again.

Some weeks later at another draft, we had in hand about 400 head of cattle, of which about half were branded from, or owned by, Napier and Kimberley Downs. Before we left for home, McCorry and Malki would cut out these foreigners and let them go. We were holding the cattle up around a waterhole and letting them feed and have a drink before yarding for the night. The camp was nearly out of meat so McCorry drafted out an older steer, a bullock, moved him away from the mob and shot and bled him. He then asked old Yardie, our Aboriginal horse-tailer, and me to bone out the kill. As we were working on the carcass, Yardie looked up and said: 'Horses coming, old man.'

I turned and looked in the direction his nose was pointing – the Aboriginal people never pointed a finger in the direction they wanted you to look. Sure enough, coming over the rise, still some distance away, were two riders, two packhorses and four spare horses. I was told to cut the brand and earmark out and to shove them up the beast's arse with a stick. It was the one place police patrols failed to look!

McCorry rode out to meet the party on Lychee, a big brown gelding. One of the riders was an Aboriginal fellow we knew worked for Napier Downs. He was good with his fists and a smart horseman too. The other person was a beefy, strong-looking bloke wearing the biggest black hat I'd ever seen. McCorry asked him where the hell he thought he was going. Black hat was American. He said his boss had sent them to help muster along the boundary, to 'tender muster', and that they would be assisted by 'Five O'Clock Charlie'.

Back then, with no fences, if you tender mustered with your neighbour on a boundary you would usually split the cleanskins. But these men were well inside McCorry's country; he knew where his boundary was. Several years earlier he had accompanied Lands Department personnel into the depths of Oobagooma with their maps. They showed him what land-marks to look for. Joining them with an imaginary line, he could easily define his boundary. He did this for his own good, because as far back as the 1960s and 1970s there were 'range wars' on cattle properties throughout the Kimberley. The cattlemen would stop just short of taking pot shots at each other. I know McCorry enjoyed these challenges on the boundary; he had a touch of larrikinism and a good dose of scepticism about authority. On this occasion, though, he knew he was on his own land.

The stockmen from Napier Downs pulled their horses up and sat looking at McCorry.

'Turn your horses around or I'll gut-shoot them,' he said. 'Tell your boss to stay out of my affairs.'

It was a savage threat, because McCorry loved horses too much to ever shoot any in the guts. We watched the men turn their horses around and ride back over the ridge out of sight.

'I guess they were only carrying out orders,' McCorry reflected later. 'If they hadn't been so far off course, we might have asked them to dinner.'

Back at the station, McCorry and I took every opportunity to be alone together. He would pack the tucker box and the swag into the buggy, and we would drive down past the homestead to the river and spend time in each other's arms. This was our 'getting to know you' time. Away from the hard work he would relax. He was a kind and gentle man. Sometimes he would patiently drive me from billabong to billabong so I could cut waterlilies for the homestead. He would sit on a log, roll a smoke, and watch me from under the brim of his Akubra with those dark laughing eyes. McCorry knew I liked the old homestead, but it was very plain and a bunch of flowers brought life into the home for me. He was beginning to understand that I would live anywhere with him.

Time at the station was precious for us, because once we were out on the run and working, we seemed to have an unspoken agreement of not touching or showing affection to each other in the presence or sight of the stockmen. It wasn't that we didn't want to. It just seemed the right thing to do.

Mary and I had the supply truck loaded with the swags and what we thought were sufficient rations, ready to leave on another muster. The fresh coaches were stepping out well in the lead, heads held high taking in the crisp morning breeze, while the buggy was sitting patiently on the tail of the mob. I was in charge of the Inter, bringing up the rear. I had been watching old Yardie, a natural in the saddle like most Aboriginal stockmen. Yardie had the stockhorses in hand and sat patiently behind while they moseyed along, chomping on any juicy morsel of grass in their path. Again we were following the course of least resistance – no roads, no maps, but this time heading towards Pardaboora country, an area on Oobagooma north-east of the homestead.

As we came closer to Pardaboora, some of the young stockmen rode ahead with me and Mary to erect a temporary yard to handle some of the flightier horses. In no time the young stockmen had started on the yard, selecting a group of trees which they could 'Cobb & Co.' using number 8 fencing wire. To 'Cobb & Co.' is a bushman's way of securing posts together to build a yard when there are no tools, only wire. Rails were made from young trees, which were 'Cobb & Co.'d together to make a round yard. We had it in place and working in no time flat.

Large shade trees were few and far between on this part of the river. Mary and I decided to make our camp in the bed of the river where some young river gums were growing. As the cool Kimberley breeze began to blow, we dragged an old wire stretcher bed down to the creek and set it up with the pannikins and tin plates. Mary soon had the fire going and the dampers were just about ready to go into the coals. We filled flour drums with water and set them by the side of the fire. I decided I would drag my swag further up the riverbed for a little privacy, as any movement from McCorry's or my swag during the night would draw attention.

I had no sooner pulled the strap from my swag when I heard Mary yell out: 'Missus, come – bullock!'

Mary was walking towards the tall young river gums. In the riverbed was a big old-man bullock, eight or nine years old, decidedly lean and unhealthy looking, with a very large set of speary horns.

Mary picked up a billy can, swung it around her head a few times and let fly at the bullock, hoping to frighten him off. It only enraged him. He charged her, but after a few steps began to stagger. The bullock then focused on Missy, my white bull terrier, and came through the camp, hooking billy cans, flour drums and camp ovens with his sharp horns. Mary, Missy and I ran for our lives up the riverbed. I could see about half a dozen young gum saplings ahead, no thicker than my arm. Up we went – it was like trying to claw your way up a 3-inch water pipe, but it's amazing what strength you can find when you need it. Although she was close to 60, Mary's screams and yells were as strong as a young woman's. The mad creature kept charging and staggering, determined to get us. Missy continued barking at him from the rear, heroically trying to draw the old fella's attention away from us. Then, suddenly, the bullock fell in a heap.

'Him proper mad bugger, Missus,' said Mary as she climbed down from the tree. With feeling, I agreed.

The bullock was still sleeping there while Mary and I put the camp into some order again, collecting wood for a fire, refilling the billies with water and retrieving the plates and pannikins that the old bullock had sent flying all over the riverbed. McCorry and the stockmen arrived on sundown and Mary told them about the afternoon's events. I suggested to McCorry that we might move. I could not see myself sleeping too well with this beast in the middle of the camp, and it wasn't as if we had the inconvenience of a houseful of furniture to move. But McCorry couldn't or wouldn't understand why I was upset. He seemed tired that night, and his 'horseman's walk' seemed more obvious than usual. I suspected he had back pain.

'He's got red water, he's nearly dead,' rapped McCorry. I was trying to say that he might have red water, or tick fever, but he wasn't dead yet and he was in the middle of the camp.

'Please, can we move the bullock or move the camp?' I asked again. He tried to calm me, saying the beast wouldn't be going anywhere. So McCorry had the last word – we had to camp with the bullock. Uneasy, I gave the bullock a wide berth and headed off in the direction of the camp fire for my ration of beef and damper and a pannikin of black tea.

It took some time for me to fall asleep that night, and when I did I slept with one eye open. About two o'clock in the cool of the morning, the bullock hit his feet, sized up the situation, then charged towards the glowing camp fire. I flew out of my swag with a blood-curdling scream before realising it wasn't me he was after. All hell broke loose in the camp. The stockmen were trying to claw their way out of their swags in the moonlight and the bullock was charging into the fire. There were stockmen, swags, flour drums, the old wire stretcher bed with our cooking gear on, plates and pannikins flying in every direction. Then, as quick as the old warrior had had risen from the night air, he dropped in his tracks, dead, right in the middle of the camp.

As usual we were all up before sunrise. The billy was boiling and I was helping Mary with the flapjacks for breakfast. I couldn't help overhearing the Aboriginal stockmen talking among themselves about the night's events. They were very quiet and whispering that something bad might happen today, because the bullock had died in our camp.

'No', I whispered, 'no, we haven't done anything wrong.'

I noticed we were all talking very quietly. The men were going about their breakfast much slower and quieter than usual; they seemed to have lost their happy selves. A little frightened, maybe? I was starting to feel their uncanny fear myself.

It was nearly an hour later when it happened. Malki and the boys were drafting out their horses for the day's work when one colt, the biggest of all, hit the gum sapling rail in the round yard, catapulting it out of the wire ties and straight into Malki's temple with the force of a spear. With an almighty crack Malki went down in a heap. McCorry tuned in the Flying Doctor radio and alerted Derby Hospital. While he was on the radio, Monty, our station owner who had just flown in from Sydney, picked up our medical call on his Cessna's radio.

There were no roads or airstrips nearby and the closest the Flying Doctor plane could get would have been the station airstrip, close to 80 kilometres from where we were. McCorry packed the side of Malki's head with a clean towel as he took instructions from the doctor over the radio. Monty called in and said he was on his way in the Cessna. We selected a good claypan flat for Monty to land on. With axes, shovels and tools improvised from the bush, the men put everything they had into clearing away anthills, tufts of grass or anything they thought might endanger the landing. McCorry said that if anyone could land under these conditions in this country, it would be Monty.

I had never felt so relieved as I was to hear the droning of the Cessna. For the first time since the accident, the men started to talk to each other again. Monty dipped his wings to signal he had spotted us. He did one circuit to check out the strip length and condition, and came in without hesitation. By this time I had made Malki as comfortable as I could on the old wire camp stretcher that was used to hold the cook house utensils. He was a very heavy man and we had to lift him from the accident site and carry him about 100 metres to the Cessna. Malki was out cold and losing a lot of blood. Amid a cloud of dust, Monty was slowing the aircraft to a halt at our end of the strip. There was no time wasted on pleasantries. Out came the back seats of the aircraft. Harry, Monty and McCorry helped lift Malki's stretcher onto the aircraft floor and strapped him down. McCorry sat on the floor beside this good man and held his hand until they arrived at Derby airport where an ambulance and doctor were waiting. McCorry told me on his return that every so often he would squeeze Malki's hand and he would get a faint squeeze in return.

That night as I lay in my swag, gazing at what stars were about and reflecting on the day's events, McCorry came and lay with me. He told me he was proud of the way I'd handled myself in the crisis. He was scared of losing Malki.

After six months in Perth hospital, Malki returned to Derby. We were later informed by his doctor that Malki was a very lucky man to have survived the accident at all. If he hadn't been as strong as an ox, we would never have had him back. He came back to the station, but couldn't do the work he'd done before; he was never the same man. He moved into Derby town and several years later passed away.

Immediately after we'd evacuated Malki, McCorry ordered us to pack up the camp gear – we were moving back towards the homestead. He estimated we had 350 to 380 head of cattle in hand, including 60 feral bulls.

This was the last big muster for the cattle season. The wet season was charging in, its early storms having already washed clean the grass and leaves. The country was turning green as it shot to life. Most afternoons we'd watch the mountain-ous thunderheads building up until they exploded. Then the thunder would rumble and the lightning would dance as the monsoonal influences hit the area, torrential rains spreading across our once-scorched earth. The cool helped salvage our sanity from the effects of a long season of gross heat and then humidity.

Once the 'wet' set in on Oobagooma, there was no point in being there. The May River would 'run a banker', or overflow its banks, and the Robinson would be up at our back door. The road to Derby and the homestead airstrip would turn into quagmires, leaving the station completely isolated for months on end. The wet season's rainfall would exceed 600 millimetres, starting any time from October and running through to April. The bush would come to life, and the biggest green bullfrogs would dominate the landscape.

Before the rivers ran and the country flooded, the men would race to hit the towns, to renew old acquaintances or just spin yarns and prop up the bars. McCorry and I also took this time to get away from the station. That first wet weason, I met his mother in Beaudesert, Queensland. A devout Catholic, she was somewhat surprised to see Bob with a woman, let alone such a young one, at this late date. She and I became friendly and later exchanged letters – once she wrote a poem about Bob. Introducing me to his mother, Bob showed no nerves. I wish I could say the same for myself! But no matter where he was, Bob was Bob.

When we went back to the station after the wet season, Mary and the stockmen's wives started watching me closely. I knew they were curious about McCorry and me: Mary was forever hinting that I was pregnant and carrying a boy child. She was watching over me closer than ever and would growl at me if I went into a billabong for a swim alone. I asked her why she worried about me so much. Mary's answer was, 'We want you safe, Missus, for Boss.' I certainly wasn't pregnant, although McCorry stepped in and told Mary he was going to take me away one day and get married. Then we were going to have a boy child, a girl child, then another boy child.

This confession ended all their curiosity and made them all very happy – and me too. I'd come to love Bob's indirect ways. He might not have been able to make such confessions directly to me, but he arranged things in such a manner that I was sure to know how he felt.

One night after our return I was tired, checking my swag for any unwanted visitors of the eight-legged kind. All I wanted was to sleep. McCorry and I were now sleeping in a double swag, much to the stockmen's amusement. About 11 pm I was partially woken with a nudge to my back. Grabbing hold of the blanket, I moved over on my pillow. Several hours later I was nudged again. I kept my hold on the blanket as I moved onto the edge of my pillow, this time asking, 'Is that you, McCorry?'

No answer. I was too tired to check. Near daybreak I turned over and was confronted with the ugliest face ever. Old Jim, McCorry's bull terrier dog, his breath rank and coated in dried blood from a day's work, was my night-time visitor. He'd been successfully stealing my swag from me, little by little, throughout the night. Jumping up and grabbing my pillow, I proceeded to belt him out of my swag. I loved this old working dog, but not enough to share my pillow with him. McCorry thought it was hilarious.

We'd had a good wet season with 600 millimetres of rain falling around the homestead. Now the terrain was covered in billowing spear grass, their golden heads near bloom and their sharp spears ready to spread havoc through the property. Not even the donkeys would eat it.

McCorry suggested we go for a drive around the country to find where the cattle were hanging. The sweet grass areas always attracted them first. Without fences, we had a million-acre paddock to deal with. If we could spot stock in sufficient numbers, there might be a chance of an easy muster and an early shipment to the meatworks.

With grass towering above us, we travelled by bull-buggy: McCorry, Charlie and me, with Jim and Whiskey, McCorry's favourite bull terriers. Charlie sat on the bull bar guiding us through the thickets, dodging antbeds and pointing out dangerous breakaway gullies.

'Little bit this way,' he called. 'Little bit that way, Old Man.'

We were steadily weaving our way towards a billabong when we came upon a mob of coarse-haired feral pigs with piglets. Jim was the first dog out of the buggy, diving into the mob in full flight, setting off the squeals and screams of protective sows and aggressive boars. Within seconds we'd lost Whiskey as well.

McCorry powered the buggy ahead, without thought for me or his head man. The old bastard was driving like a madman, caring only for his dogs and to hell with the rest of us. This sudden change of attitude frightened me, if only for a moment. Sometimes I think McCorry loved his dogs more than me.

We tracked the squealing mob to a watercourse fringed with young saplings. There, old Jim had a death grip on the ear of a mean-looking black boar. The two of them were locked in a dance of death, flying around in circles and sending the grass spraying about them.

McCorry drove the buggy towards the boar, yelling for the dog to let go. But Jim wasn't about to give it up. In an instant both McCorry and Charlie jumped out of the buggy waving tyre levers, but it was too late. The tough old boar had slit the dog from groin to throat, literally spilling his guts on the ground. As Jim released the boar, it bolted.

I emptied the butcher's knives from a hessian bag in the buggy, slit the bag lengthwise and wrapped the wounded dog in it. Whiskey turned up a minute later, unhurt.

McCorry turned the buggy around and we began the slow, sad journey home.

I was sure Jim would die. How could any creature survive being gored like that? At the station, McCorry carried Jim, guts spilling and saturated in blood, to the radio room, where we kept the medical kit. He laid down his beloved dog and we went to work on him. McCorry washed the dog's intestines with antiseptic and gently pushed them back into his body. After covering the wound with antiseptic powder, he stitched him up.

For three days there were few signs of life from the old dog, and everyone was miserable. He was so well loved as a working dog and companion, he had many visitors, including most of the stockmen. On the evening of the third day, McCorry came in from a horse muster, tethered his horse and headed straight for the radio room. The tap-tapping of McCorry's spurs on the bare floors of the homestead blended with another sound, which seemed to get stronger the closer the spurs came to the sick room. It was the whimpers of the embattled dog, trying desperately to lift his head in greeting.

It took many weeks but Jim miraculously survived the accident and returned to working with the scrubber bulls in the stock-camp. What they say about dogs was definitely true in this case. He was man's best friend, in particular McCorry's.

At the end of another busy day at the station, McCorry and I were lounging in our favourite Queenslander chairs on the front veranda with a pannikin of tea each, watching the sunset and letting our bodies soak up the cool of the evening. Monty's Cessna buzzed the airstrip, panicking the two retired pack-horses who scattered to one side. Then he came in to land.

Monty was always arriving with a new scheme for his station. This time he brought David, a young pilot from New South Wales, who was to stay and fly for us when Monty returned south.

The scheme this time was to muster donkeys for pet meat. The other bright idea, said with tongue in cheek and to shock me, was to sell the donkeys' pizzles to the sex shops. I thought Monty was rather sick-minded, but on the donkey muster I decided to take a bit of notice. Believe me, those jack donkeys were well hung! But donkey mustering was of no interest to me or McCorry. During the exercise we slipped off quietly to the banks of the Robinson River, where we spent a couple of wonderful hours together making love on a saddle blanket under a pandanus tree. It was strangely erotic to hear the rustle of the pandanus leaves as we lay on the blanket, our eyes open for snakes. Then we were rudely interrupted by the diving and circling of Monty's Cessna, which we nicknamed 'Death on Arrival' after his radio callsign, DOA. Our life was always thrown into disarray when he turned up. I quickly pulled on my jeans and shirt and laughed at McCorry doing the same dance on his side of the blanket. We stuffed the saddle blanket back into the buggy and returned to the big donkey muster, feeling much better about everything and determined to take charge of our own destiny. I thought, fancy asking a cattleman to muster bloody donkeys!

As soon as Monty headed back to the southern country, McCorry asked David to fly to Derby to collect the necessary papers for us to be married. In between the musters throughout the year, we had been receiving messages from the Managing Director of Australian Land & Cattle Co., offering McCorry better money and conditions. McCorry had been such a powerful adversary, they would rather us work for them than against them. At the same time we had a visit from the company's Kimberley Downs manager, Gordon Bryce, assuring us that things were good on the other side of the boundary. At my urging, McCorry accepted the manager's position on Napier Downs, but on one condition: that they send over a road train so McCorry could load his faithful coaches and return them to their rightful home on Kimberley Downs, from which we'd 'borrowed' them.

Even though the Australian Land & Cattle Co. had been after him for some time, McCorry didn't really want to go – he'd have been happy spending his whole life in his swag. We'd been paid about 180 dollars a week at Oobagooma, and they were offering to double it at least. I was the one to push Bob along, and Monty accepted our departure regretfully but readily. Later, he sold Oobagooma to the federal government as an army training reserve.

CHAPTER 7

My Kimberley
Man

*B*ob McCorry and I were married by the Clerk of Courts in Derby on 7 December 1973. It was a balmy, humid evening. At 44, my Kimberley man was 20 years my senior. Some people may have considered it was me who was barmy!

We planned the marriage with military-style precision, with help from the clerk, who was kind enough to open the courthouse at seven o'clock on the evening of 7 December. McCorry had as many wild friends as he had quieter ones, who would have loved to celebrate our happy event. The wild ones, after a dry spell on the stations working, would probably have wrecked the town. But neither McCorry nor I wanted to make a spectacle of getting married, because in our eyes we were already married anyway. This was only the paperwork!

As much as McCorry loved his mother (his father was deceased), and as much as I loved my parents and brothers, neither one of us told a single person. Isolated at Oobagooma, I hadn't seen my parents for about a year and wasn't sure what their reaction, or their shock, would be to find their daughter marrying for the second time by age 24 and this time to a man 20 years older. I feared that my father wouldn't take too kindly to it. It was simpler to just get married than explain it to everyone. Three weeks after the wedding I posted a letter to Mum and Dad telling them the good news and asking for their blessings. They wrote back, accepting my marriage without question, realising I was a maturing woman who would make her own decisions and follow her dreams. Their acceptance took a huge weight off my shoulders. I was confident in McCorry's and my love for each other and knew I was marrying the man of my dreams. My Kimberley man!

The three-minute ceremony was witnessed by Cynthia and Les Smith, two very good friends of McCorry's. After a few drinks at home with the Smiths, we retired to the Boab Inn, one of Derby's two motels. Next morning our black-and-white Valiant had 'Just Married' plastered all over the front and back windows and the inside strewn with rice – just in case we'd forgotten what we'd come to Derby to do.

McCorry threw in our one and only bag. We looked at each other and agreed it was time to leave town. But there was one more obstacle. As McCorry reversed, we heard terrible metal crunching and screeching noises. An inspection underneath the car revealed bundles of old cans tied up, an old bushie trick. I grabbed the pliers. We cut them loose and threw the cans in the boot, and away we went, heading out to Napier Downs. I think we both had red faces.

Because of our age difference, the word was it would never work. McCorry was known as a confirmed bachelor and nobody knew much more about me than what they could see on the surface: makeup and well-manicured, painted nails. But the rumours and gossip didn't worry me a bit. To me, McCorry was a good, hardworking man with a kind and gentle heart. I knew who I was as well: a girl who had grown up to love the outback life. My plan was to learn all I could from this rugged cattleman of mine. I believed he would be a good father for my children and could think of nothing better than the prospect of working side by side with him and building a future. I loved him.

McCorry hadn't been sure about marriage all these years, although he certainly hadn't ruled it out. He was from a family of 11 children and was brought up during the Great Depression and its aftermath. He often spoke of seeing more dinner times than he had dinners. He could remember the anguish and heartache his mother and father went through when they couldn't feed and clothe their children. This was the reason he had stayed single. If things got tough then there was only himself to feed.

This was not to say McCorry couldn't be romantic. His version went like this: 'Then fate stepped in, a blonde-haired girl 20 years younger came on the scene. If I had gone to a horse sale and there were 100 horses there, she would have been my pick.' At least he tried!

Apart from all these feelings, romantic and otherwise, fate had opened up the perfect opportunity for the beginning of our married life: Napier Downs. I had some regrets about leaving Oobagooma but also excitement for this new adventure. In this outfit we were only a small cog in a big machine. The company we were now working for, Australian Land & Cattle Co., had something like 8 million acres of land. The Napier homestead was actually a nice house – with windows and doors! It was an old transportable nestled back against the limestone range and looking north over a horse paddock towards the picturesque King Leopold Ranges. It wasn't as isolated as Oobagooma, being only a kilometre or so off the Gibb River Road, a well-maintained gravel road that runs from Derby to Wyndham. The siting of the homestead wasn't accidental. Two earlier homesteads, the first on a freshwater spring in the Napier Range, the second on the banks of the Barker

River, had both been inundated during big wet seasons, when the Barker, Womberalla and Lennard rivers all flooded. Such events were disastrous for the Aborigines and there were stories of people found dead in the forks of river gums after the flood had receded.

The homestead's huge walk-in freezer coolroom was full of rotting vegetables, cakes, fruit and bread. Things must be good here, I thought to myself. I made a mental note to put an end to this over-ordering. In the saddle room, most of the saddles and bridles were in need of repair. On Oobagooma, we had absolutely nothing but we were always able to keep the saddles in top condition. Looking around at the other buildings I found we had a good-sized storeroom with four cartons of tinned sauerkraut and not much else, a large workshop and windmill shed and a cottage for a windmill mechanic. Each station in the group had a Flying Doctor radio plus a company radio, which was on all day, crackling with messages and instructions. It sounded like an all-day galah session.

We read back through the monthly report sheets. Napier cattle figures showed about 24,000 head. We didn't believe it. The company had been offering an incentive to managers, a trip to America, for the highest numbers of cattle branded during a muster. We reckoned the previous managers must have been counting the cattle with a forked stick – two lines in the ground instead of one – to double their numbers.

Still, whatever the actual numbers, it was a large operation. The stations had to pre-book killing dates at the meatworks, and if these cattle did not show up it would throw a spanner in the works. We already knew that however many head were on the station, a big percentage were wild and feral cattle. No, let me keep telling the truth; the *whole bloody lot* were wild and feral cattle. What little fencing there was was in disrepair, so it would be a huge challenge to meet these meatwork dates.

Word was out and in no time we had a good team of Aboriginal stockmen. The only whites were McCorry and me. We found the Aboriginal stockmen to be smart ringers, good on their horses, good on their feet and happy in their family unit. McCorry and myself were knocked many times for our hiring policies, because we hired only Aboriginal men, and were often called blackfella lovers. But I remember out of the company's eight cattle stations we were the only one that never had a shortage of stockmen. We made sure our men were paid a healthy living wage, better than the going rate, well before it was made compulsory by award.

One would think that with the mustering we had done and other experience picked up along the way, we would not have had much trouble meeting the kill dates at the meatworks, but this was not always the case. When mustering with horses, we were able to hold about 50 per cent of the cattle we came across during the day. The other half were galloping away from us, mostly strong, valuable 'meatworkers' we'd want to send to Derby. If management had given us a quota of, say, 300 to 400 head for the meatworks and 10 days to get them, we would have to ride the arse out of our trousers. It was hard on the men, hard on the horses and hard on us. These work conditions ratcheted up the pressure and tension.

The buzz around the Kimberley was that a Yank, an ex-wartime fighter pilot, owned an old Bell 47 chopper and could do just about anything with it. He sounded like the man who could solve our problem. With a ton of guts, and his helicopter, we hoped he would muster cattle into the yard for us – a first for the Kimberley.

Stuart Skoglund was tall, lean and bow-legged, with a white Stetson pushed back slightly on his head to reveal a weathered, craggy face. With his wonderful smile, he struck me as a man with guts and charm. We agreed to supply the portable yard panels, the race to run cattle into the loading ramp, the men and the bull-buggies. 'Skogy' also wanted us to supply the aviation gas and oil for the chopper.

We set up the portable yard at Billyarra, on the banks of the Lennard River, extending the wings out from the yard by erecting two fences to look like a funnel feeding the yard. We covered these with hessian to stop the cattle taking fright, or spooking, as they ran down the laneway into the yard. We dropped two drums of Avgas on a claypan flat about halfway between the starting point and the yard. The muster was now in Skogy's hands. McCorry said it was like preparing a racehorse: once you legged up the jockey it was out of your hands. At piccaninny daylight, the faint light just before dawn, with barely enough light to see, the old Bell 47 fired up. It sounded like a scene out of *Apocalypse Now*. We watched with pride and terror as the Yank lifted off the airstrip in front of the homestead. He could fly a chopper, all right. Since he was the first helicopter cattle musterer in the Kimberley, we had nobody to compare him with, but it was doubtful that we could have found anyone in the world so fitted to the work.

Of course, no-one's perfect. After several musters we worked out Skogy had a bad habit of trying to cover too much country in a day and was yarding cattle in the dark nine days out of 10. He was determined to clock up 10-hour days. Since he was paid by the hour, I suppose you couldn't blame him.

McCorry and I were in the buggy following the tail of the cattle at the end of another long day. It was pitch black and the dust thrown up by 600 head of cattle wasn't helping our visibility much. Right at the yard a cunning old scrubber bull broke from the tail at full gallop with one thought on his mind:

his home back in the hills. I gripped the Jesus bar tightly as McCorry stamped his foot flat on the accelerator. Whack! Straight into a bloody stump, which drove the front diff housing and everything connected with it halfway back along the chassis. Nothing but the whites of our eyes showed through the dark and the bulldust.

We were now on foot and hoping there were no more wild surprises in the dark. Somewhere just ahead, I could hear Skogy landing outside the gate of the yard. I ran like hell and gave the boys a hand to pull the panels across and close it up. We'd done it! The stock boys jumped into the front of the Toyota with McCorry and set out for the homestead. I'd ride with Skogy in his chopper. That way I could shower and get the evening meal well on the way before the men arrived home.

As I buckled in, the Bell 47 was burning and leaking a hell of a lot of oil. During the day Skogy had poured between three and four gallons into the old chopper and there was none left.

'I had an electrical failure,' said Skogy. 'We don't have any instrument lights.'

'Or any bloody lights at all,' I said, looking at the instrument panel.

He asked me to light a match and check the oil pressure. He also had one control gear playing up and had tied it into position with his seatbelt. We were low on fuel, about 10 minutes short of reserve time. Hell, I thought to myself, I've had better days.

We took off okay and steered in a direct line for the Napier Range, which stood out even on the darkest night. I could see the faint glow of the homestead lights. With one match left and very little oil, we put down on the home strip just in front of the house. This would be a full bottle of whisky night for Skogy, a few cans of beer for McCorry and a decent-sized pannikin of tea for me, the non-drinker. The stock-camps and the Aboriginal camp were dry, but the station wasn't. This was a change from Oobagooma, and Bob needed and enjoyed a beer after a hard day in the cattle yards – but only after the sun went down. Skogy wouldn't have worked for us if he couldn't have a whisky or two.

There was more pressure and action working for the big company than working for Monty at Oobagooma. Some nights I'd return to the homestead so tired I would flop down and just fall asleep. When this happened, McCorry would suggest I stay behind and rest the next day. It showed he cared about my health, but resting was hard for me – I preferred to be where the action was. I was becoming more confident with each muster, and it never once occurred to me that I was unable to do the job. With McCorry by my side, I felt we could achieve anything.

Following the tail of the mob all day, we noticed that the big rogue bulls would travel all right from daylight till about 10 am, and then pull up under a shady tree. Skogy could turn the chopper inside out trying to move them, but they would just stand their ground and shake their heads as if to say, 'This is as far as we're going.' Some people used shotguns to scare them out, but we didn't want to pepper our stock with lead pellets. What we needed was a decent bull-buggy.

There was a bloke I knew called Jamesey, from around Halls Creek, a tough ex-Queenslander, a hard worker and hard player. Jamesey had caught quite a few bulls in the East Kimberley. There were a few men around the Kimberley that were calling themselves bull catchers, but they were really more like bull killers, breaking legs and badly bruising the animal. Jamesey was the real deal.

I contacted Jamesey and put our idea to him. He was at the homestead three days later. McCorry rode as strapper with him all morning to check him out. Back home, McCorry pulled me aside.

'This bastard knows what he's doing,' he said. 'You go with him and strap.'

That evening I could reflect on Jamesey's skills. He gave me one of the most hair-raising rides in a bull-buggy in my entire life, as he fiercely charged and spun the buggy about the bush. Either he wanted to put the wind up me, trying to impress the little woman, or he was so centred on catching the bull that nothing could distract him. The chase was exciting, but the bulls went down gently, the way we wanted.

Head office, after some persuasion, eventually gave us the go-ahead to bring Jamesey over. He rolled up with two trucks, a dog trailer and two bull-buggies, and set up camp by Warragee, a waterhole on the banks of the Lennard. He employed two Aboriginal men, one as an offsider to cart the bulls to the yard, the other to cart the bulls to the Derby meatworks each night.

One morning about three weeks later, Jamesey pulled into the homestead at daylight and said he had to go to Derby to see a doctor, as his penis was all swollen. I knew he had spent a night in Derby town a week earlier, and thought perhaps he'd picked up the pox. It seemed like a good idea to go and check this out with a doctor, as his oldfella (reportedly) looked like it might be ready to explode. The same afternoon he arrived back at the station with a huge grin all over his face. The doctor had found the culprit; a spear grass seed had gone in through the eye of the oldfella and kept travelling. Jamesey was another of that Kimberley breed who saved the underpants for special occasions. Whether he changed his ways after this, I never discovered.

Every station has one mechanic-cum-windmill man; ours was hardworking, hard drinking, bad tempered, red haired, covered in freckles and skin cancers and at times hard to keep up with and hard to keep track of. Bluey was on rations of four cans of beer per day. We were no longer a 'dry' camp, and this allowance was just enough to stop his hide from cracking. This morning Bluey was making the odd joke or two as he loaded his two blue heelers into the back of his new red ute and his wife of many years, Rita, into the passenger seat. They were headed for Derby for some rest and recreation. Rita was a lovely person, a Broome girl of Aboriginal descent, who had inherited a strong Catholic background from her white father. Bluey knew just how lucky he was to have Rita as his wife.

Three days later we had a radio call from Meeda Station to say Bluey and Rita were crashed out in the ute by a boab tree, rather drunk and abusive. The nose of the ute was facing towards Derby. Apparently on waking from a drunken sleep, Bluey had started the ute up and driven off in the direction the nose was pointing. Driving down the road he must have sobered up enough, or spotted another landmark, to realise he was heading for Derby again, so he wheeled the ute around and headed for Napier Downs Station once more. On this attempt he made it to a boab tree on Kimberley Downs, and again woke with the nose facing Derby. He set off again in the wrong direction until they realised. Bluey, Rita and the two blue heelers were slowly getting closer to home at Napier.

On his way up the Gibb River Road, one of the local Department of Agriculture men spotted old Bluey and Rita out cold. He pulled over, woke them and asked if they were okay. Bluey woke, shivering and shaking, and told him to fuck off. Apparently he woke enough to start the ute and take off in the direction of the nose and, would you believe it, towards Derby again! Rita realised they were heading in the wrong direction; old Bluey swung the ute around and headed in the direction of Napier Downs once more. Late afternoon, as the sun was gently sliding down behind the Napier Range, Bluey turned onto the Napier track. Sitting up and concentrating behind the wheel with a tailormade hanging out the side of his mouth as usual, he was cruising very steadily up the dirt track towards the homestead. Then, God only knows how, he clipped the side of the loading ramp at the cattle yards and wrote off the driver's side of his ute. Shaking his fist in the air, staggering but winning the battle to stay standing, his freckles pale against the red glow his drunken and untidy appearance presented, he abused us all for putting the loading ramp in his way. The cattle yard and loading ramp, needless to say, had been in the same place for 20 years.

We'd been on Napier Downs for three years when, in July 1975, there was some great news for McCorry and myself – I was pregnant! We'd been married three years and after many, many trips to Derby balancing a urine sample on the dashboard of the car, we were over the moon. God could not have given either of us a greater gift. The outback, which gave me total peace and contentment along with sheer hard work, would be the best place in the world to bring up healthy and happy children. I have to say I enjoyed the effort that we put into becoming parents, although making love under a chuck wagon when the temperature was about a hundred in the waterbag and a few native bees were biting me on the bum wasn't one of the better times.

Our old hatter friend Cec walked into the Napier homestead, after living off the land for the previous 12 months, to a loud welcome from the camp dogs and Aboriginal children. I had just been listening to warnings of Cyclone Wilma, which were being broadcast hourly.

Cec was dressed in his visiting clothes – worn-out khaki shorts kept up by a twitch of wire. His long grey hair and white beard were clean and combed. Cec had made the most of the Barker River before coming on up to the homestead. I was so pleased to see him and to see that he was healthy and had survived another year out in the Hawkstone Hills alone, with nothing to sustain him except game and what he could beg, borrow or steal. The usual handout was a sugar bag of salt beef and some niki niki tobacco. He told me it was tough out in the hills that last season. He'd had one .303 bullet but found not one beast – donkey or kangaroo – that he could have shot for meat. Instead the grasshoppers were out in their hopper stage by the thousands, so he would bound along with them and pounce and grab what he could, pull their hind legs off and eat them. Cec said they were quite good and tasted like salted peanuts.

I bundled up the six months' supply of newspapers and magazines I'd saved to help him catch up with the world. He was hopping from one foot to the other, a man in a hurry to return to the safety of his beloved hills.

'What's the big hurry?' I asked.

It seemed he wanted to cross the Barker River before it flooded and get back to the country he called his own. After loading the drygoods into the bull-buggy I picked four large pawpaws, his favourite fruit. I waited for him to farewell the camp people, then delivered him to a cave he had on the Hawkstone side of the Barker River. I imagine he sat out Cyclone Wilma there, keeping up to date on the news, waiting for the flood to recede.

We were lucky to receive only moderate winds from the cyclone, which turned into a deep rain depression, dumping heavy falls across the station, causing flooding and running the rivers a banker. Only weeks later the whole station seemed rejuvenated, the paddocks flushed with green grass.

CHAPTER 8

A Hundred in the Waterbag

*I*n April 1976, my doctor in Derby advised me not to return to McCorry and the station. 'You'll have your baby any time now.'

Good! I expected this would happen in the next couple of hours. By 10 am on 23 April, the labour pains had started. They continued all afternoon and through the night. On waking the next morning, I decided to start raking some leaves at the house where I was staying, with McCorry's friends Cynthia and Les Smith. The raking and the pains went on all day until I decided to have a shower at 4 pm and head up to Derby Hospital.

On arrival I was put into the good hands of a Catholic nun, the midwife. I spent another two hours without much luck in the delivery room. I vaguely remember a rush to theatre on the evening of the twenty-fourth . . . and nothing more. My baby had become terribly distressed and my blood pressure had gone sky high. I remember sometime the following morning opening my eyes to see my husband sitting in a chair at the foot of my bed with tears streaming silently down his face, nursing our baby boy. It was overwhelming. At long last, this old Kimberley cattleman had the son he'd always wanted, this beautiful baby, our baby boy, Kelly McCorry, named after an Irish uncle, a name that we had chosen well before I was pregnant. Kelly was delivered by caesarean section at 7.30 pm on the twenty-fourth. I was told that we'd both had a rough time of it, and it was three days before I could actually hold my dear boy. During this time the old nun was expressing my milk to feed Kelly and she asked me if I'd mind them using my excess milk to feed a premature little Aboriginal baby girl. Years later I found that the mother and her little girl were in our camp at Louisa Downs. The mother never forgot.

Once back at the station, although slightly sore from the caesarean, I settled into a routine with Kelly of bath, feed time, cuddles with Daddy, and sleep. I always timed the evening feeds so McCorry could sit and nurse his son. Some nights, while having a beer after a hard day in the cattle yards, he would sit for hours just looking at him, informing me of every sigh or burp as I moved around the house. The company's head office in Perth had given me the okay for a nanny, and we found Nanny Kate in outback Queensland. Kate was a wonderful person. I knew that when Kelly was left with her he was in good hands, which gave me the confidence to keep pulling my weight. Life could not be better. God had given McCorry and me many gifts: our boy, a good nanny, good Aboriginal stockmen and, it seemed to me, a significant life in outback Kimberley.

Tommy, one of the stockmen, brought me in a dingo pup, a good-looking, dark-red male. I called him Dingy. I gave him no special treatment; he was just another one of the dogs, if a big one, well fed and content.

I had just turned the lawnmower off when I heard a mob of horses galloping in the distance. I knew it had to be in the horse paddock and now I could see that the dogs, including Dingy and our blue and red heelers, had mustered the horses together and were chasing them down the fence close to where I was standing.

McCorry had a very staunch rule – no dog was ever to chase horses. I ran towards them, yelling and waving my arms, trying to stop them without getting run over myself. McCorry pulled up in the Land Rover and my stomach dropped. He had the old station .303 rifle. With my heart pounding, I screamed at him, 'No, no, please don't shoot, don't shoot the dogs!'

Because McCorry had worked with horse plants (teams of working horses) most of his life while mustering cattle outback, horses were his most valuable possession. He lifted the .303 and fired. A blue heeler went down instantly. Dingy, who was in the dogs' lead group, somehow dodged the first bullet. As soon as he heard the shot he dropped back from being the leader of the pack to about a hundred metres behind and crouched behind the spinifex. My screaming and pleading with McCorry was to no avail. As I turned away, the second shot thundered out. Lifting my head I saw Red stagger, then drop. Dingy could not be seen, though I knew he was still hiding behind the spinifex clump. Picking Kelly up from his cot, I walked into the homestead feeling broken, deflated and in need of a very good cry. Dingy lay low for several days, but he survived.

I stewed silently, unable to believe that Bob would shoot our dogs and let the dingo get away with it. But Bob was obsessively old-fashioned about horses. He'd never even wanted to change to bull-buggy and helicopter mustering. Horses were the thing. But the incident rocked me to the core, showing me an unforgiving, even cruel, side to Bob. The silences were thick around the homestead in the next few days.

Some months later, I arrived home from Derby loaded with stores and noticed a presence of someone, or something, in my bedroom. It wasn't the first time. My bedroom door was always closed, just as I'd left it, but the flywire screens had been pushed open about 40 centimetres. It was becoming a bit of a mystery. With Kelly on my hip, I headed for the bedroom. He was feeling tired and I always liked to put him down for a sleep as soon as possible. Throwing the bedroom door open, I caught Dingy totally relaxed, stretched out on the bed with his head on my pillow. The fly screen was wide open. I yelled at him, chasing him out the door with a broom in my hand. He propped and stood his ground, baring a fine set of fangs. It was enough to call my bluff. I should have known better than to have reared this dingo. He belonged in the wild, and the sooner he went back to it the better. One of the older camp women warned me to 'watch that dog, might be milk smell, Missus'. I kept a watchful eye on Dingy and told Nanny Kate under no circumstances to let that dog near Kelly. We stopped looking after Dingy, keeping him out, and some months later we heard he was showing his face at a Department of Main Roads camp on the Gibb River Road. We never saw him again.

Nineteen seventy-six turned out to be one of the driest years I can remember in the Kimberley. A very late wet season was made more difficult for us with the company very short on funds. Just before the adverse weather, the company had accrued a lot of debt, and was now stricken with a cash shortage.

Working for this company could never be boring or dull. There were times when there were more pay days than actual pay packets. There were times when we personally had to pay the whole station's living expenses and registration of the motor vehicles to keep the station together. We had to borrow and steal fuel from the mining companies and sweet-talk local businesspeople into extending credit. At times we had to sign and make ourselves personably responsible for debts the company had incurred. We always guaranteed the fuel account. We never thought for a moment that the Australian Land & Cattle Co. would pull the rug out from under our feet. We knew that the dollars were on the hoof, as did the management. Our capital was right before our eyes, grazing all around us on the fertile black soil plains.

McCorry and I took over managing Kimberley Downs Station as well as Napier, a total of 2.25 million acres. They had trouble finding good station managers who would work for them without capital in the bank for repairs or improvements, or willing to wait a month or six for their pay packets. There were times when I was convinced that management never really understood the dire straits we were in. But I do know they thought we were capable. There was no point falling in a heap – we could only do what we could, with what we had.

Kimberley Downs's bores had been badly neglected, partly due to a lack of funds and partly to mismanagement. Cattle numbers were still too high, a problem we'd inherited. Napier Downs's water could support about 16,000 cattle, but we estimated that we had closer to 20,000.

By October all dams, creeks and springs were drying up and with both properties overstocked we were flat-out, day and night, trying to keep the water up to them by dragging a jack pump (a portable pump) from bore to bore and filling up each tank. It was so dry that the last camel on the property was found dead in what was left of the Congra waterhole. In a good year Congra was full all year around, one of our most reliable waterholes; this year it had all but dried up.

We were lucky that Bluey and Rita had stuck by us. Between his benders Bluey could be a reliable mechanic, repairman or manufacturer of spare parts from the rubbish dump. He made up two portable jack pumps that we could tow behind a vehicle. With no rain, a dry wind and the temperature ready to blow the thermostat, we had those jack pumps going day and night. We'd tow a pump to a bore, pull the stays off the windmill tower, back the portable pump into place, clamp it onto the column, disconnect the windmill rod, start the pump and hey presto, instant water. With the surface water dried up, we were watering a thousand head or more on each of these bores.

One evening over the nightly ration of beers we had a talk with Bluey. We all agreed that we should split the bore run in half. Bluey would look after the bores on the south and west sides while McCorry and I would take the north and east sides.

This meant that we had to hook up the jack pump for 12 to 14 hours on each bore. When the circle of bores was completed, we'd start again. You didn't think about it too much: there wasn't time. We just kept going day and night. There was nothing more we could do about the situation: there was no money!

Barnes Bore, on Kimberley Downs, was one of the bores that Bluey had to keep the water up to. At the time there was a mining company prospecting in the area with a basic camp consisting of five men with five little pup tents and a cook tent. In the cook tent they had a freezer and fridges powered by a portable generator. Two days and nights after Bluey had gone out there, I was starting to get worried, as we hadn't sighted him. In the morning we asked Rita if he'd been in yet, and she said no, but she wasn't concerned, and was making the most of a few beers while Bluey was away. At 3.30 pm we checked at the station, but still no Blue. At daybreak the next morning we left the station to track him down. Many possibilities were running through my mind.

At Barnes Bore, we were checking to see if Bluey had pumped the tank full when one of the prospectors arrived. We were disturbed but not really surprised to hear that Bluey had hooked up the jack pump and then decided to visit their cook tent while the miners were out on the job. There he'd decided to have a drink and reflect on how good life could be at times, especially when you had unlimited quantities of someone else's wine to drink.

He'd managed to get back to the station – we followed his Land Rover's tracks weaving from side to side and sometimes off the dirt road, another mark showing the jack pump still attached and bumping along behind it. For a while afterwards Blue kept out of our way. You couldn't help but feel sorry for the old bugger – he suffered shocking remorse when coming off a binge.

Face to face, we couldn't resist teasing him.

'Hell, Blue, it was bad enough you drinking their beer, but you could have left their plonk alone!' He denied it, as he always did.

'Well,' I said. 'There was something wrong with you when you came back from Barnes Bore. You spent more time crossing the road than you did on it! After that, you nearly tipped the jack pump head over heels several times. There are five of those prospectors and they're rather tough-looking men, so next time you pump Barnes Bore don't hang around too long.'

McCorry wanted to muster closer to the boundaries of our neighbours. Since the properties were well overstocked, we could do with a culling of 'cracker cows' – cows that were too old to breed or send to the meatworks – rangy old bulls, and bullocks that had escaped previous musters.

We set up the portable yards in the usual position, hessian-covered wings leaving an obstacle-free run for the cattle. Again, Skogy flew his helicopter for us. His orders were not to cross the broken-down old fence which marked the boundary, and to muster no more than 600 to 700 head of cattle. Any more made it too difficult to process them through the yard.

By 10 am, watching the broad cloud of dust rising in the distance, we could see Skoglund had far too many cattle. Waving our arms frantically, we signalled him to cut the tail, usually the weaker and younger cattle, off from the rest of the herd. Oblivious, he kept on coming. It was too much for McCorry. Giving in to his natural hot-headedness, he slammed the buggy into gear and wove in and out of the bulldust and moving cattle, cutting off the last hundred head himself. We closed the yard immediately. As soon as Skogy landed, there were heated words. By now the scene was chaotic. The yard was jammed with bellowing cattle and road trains were pulling up to the loading ramp. McCorry drafted them directly into the trucks, to be dispatched immediately to Demco Meatworks in Broome. Our neighbour, Merv Norton, the manager of Meeda Station, had got wind of the muster and arrived on the scene. Since Kimberley Downs and Meeda were on a party-line phone system, it wasn't hard to pick up the news and Merv arrived at our yard, all puffed up with managerial importance.

'Why wasn't I informed?' he demanded.

'Seeing we were mustering Kimberley Downs and not both sides of the fence, why would you be informed?' was McCorry's angry reply.

The puff slowly left the man's stout little body. McCorry, usually taciturn, could only take so much before exploding. He suggested the manager send a truck over to collect any branded Meeda cattle that might come through the yard and any cow with a bag of milk that he could 'mother up' with a weaner.

Merv left the yard, since there was nothing he could do. But he went home and called the Stock Squad, or cattle police, and had them sit out on the Gibb River Road to pull over our road trains and run checks on brands. God only knows what absurd stories he told them. Possibly he thought we were stupid enough to send unbranded cattle to the meatworks. No – we trucked them to another yard on the property and held them for three days, waiting until our nosy neighbour had given up his surveillance, branded them and then sent them off. All legal, of course!

Between October and December 1976 we were hit with anxious times. We had been working flat-out trying to keep the tanks full of water and now that the rains were coming, the dams were becoming deathtraps for thirsty animals. The Wombrella, Barker and Congra waterholes turned into bogs. Wading knee-deep in a moving, black, muddy sea of maggots, stretching to put a noose over the horns of a cow that could still be dragged out . . . it was enough to test a saint. One cow's dark eyes told me she still had plenty of life even as I brushed away the maggots. With the noose around the horns, I slowly moved one leg after another, trying to keep my boots on and not fall over. I clambered onto another dead animal to get out. I untied the rope from my waist and fixed it to the shackle on the Land Rover. Putting the vehicle into reverse, I pulled the cow over the other carcasses and onto the bank. I pulled the noose off her horns and tried to help her up. She had enough strength, after several attempts, to get up. I was lucky that time: at other times they were so weak and poorly that I left them to try by themselves. Some made it, some didn't.

We became very frustrated. It was hard to believe that the company fully understood the desperate position the stations were in. They weren't sending money or coming out to see how bad things were.

CHAPTER 9

Hide the Cattle Truck

*W*hile away visiting central Queensland in February 1977, we had some wonderful news: I was pregnant again! I had always wanted to have my children close together so they could grow up not only as brother and sister, but as happy country kids who could be mates and learn to love the outback as I had with my brothers. Overjoyed, we couldn't believe our luck. McCorry, not one normally to shop for children's toys, went straight out and bought a pink teddy bear. A bit on the superstitious side – and not one to count my chickens – I hid the teddy until the birth.

Head office was short of funds again. The company's other property, Camballin Farm, a couple of hours' drive away, was growing sorghum. The parent company, while building huge dams and developing the Camballin farming operation, had accumulated massive debts against the cattle stations. Their feed lots were draining the stations of resources and the push was on for more cattle. Then, during a big wet season, the raging Fitzroy River stormed down through Camballin, wiping out the sorghum operation and dam. This left the company's dreams in limbo and the debt collectors on the fence. Word was circulating that we might have to hide the cattle truck, grader and even the old station furniture from the spectre of repossession.

It was one of the years when you still got rain in April, May and a couple of showers in June. The country was far too wet for mustering, but with the company in dire straits we had no choice. We had a reasonably good paddock at Billyarra, about 43 kilometres from the homestead. We gathered the stockmen around us, squatting in a circle, and explained our plan and the difficulties we expected. Our plan was to get Skoglund in to muster the cattle into Billyarra paddock. We would set up the portable yard partly in the paddock and partly on Gibb River Road with the loading ramp on the road itself. The stockmen, on horseback, would walk the cattle about the paddock for several days, enough to quieten them, push them up into the portable yard, then load them into the road train from the road's firm surface.

At the station we loaded swags, tucker and fencing gear onto the Land Rover. We'd need the fencing gear, as a lot of the paddock would be covered in debris from the floodwaters. Five men would sit on top of the swags, on top of the Land Rover; not one of them volunteered to stay behind at the station.

The station had a tractor and we towed a 7-metre trailer behind it. We loaded it with the camp gear and some extra passengers: three Aboriginal women and their four children. They never liked to miss out on a muster and would often get bored if they were left sitting around the station camp.

Billyarra was a big billabong, with good shade trees and plenty of bush tucker. On the way out we had the Wombrella Flat to cross, 6.5 kilometres across and under water. The tops of anthills rose above the murky floodwaters. I was on tenterhooks as we left the gravelled Gibb River Road. The first time we made it across all right, but on the second run we broke through the surface beneath the brown floodwaters and fell into a deep pit. The boys jumped off the vehicle and more or less carried it through.

On Skogy's first run we ended up with close on 600 head in the Billyarra paddock. It was a battle, but the plan more or less worked. We reached the billabong by sundown and set up camp.

The evening was darker than usual, with a large cloud build-up coming from the south and a cool, gentle breeze. The wet had more or less finished, but the country was still covered in water, a sign that there was more rain coming that winter. We would only get winter rains every six or seven years, and it wasn't looking good for us that night, I thought, lying in my swag. Three hours later the heavens opened up. It continued to pour all through the night and most of the next day. By the following evening we'd had a good 150 millimetres. Everything was completely soaked and covered in mud and we were all wringing wet, but the Aboriginal men and their families never complained. They knew that in a day or two the sun would shine and dry everything out.

We hadn't noticed that Mary, Robert's wife, was very pregnant. I asked her how long to go, and she said, 'Could be long time, Missus.' Fair enough, I thought, but we knew they never kept a counting stick. On the fourth morning, just as we were pulling the saddles from the back of the Land Rover to ride the paddock, Robert walked over to me and said, 'That girl got pain, Missus.' I asked him to lie Mary in her swag on the trailer towed by the tractor, and we would return to the station. I knew I'd worry too much otherwise.

I checked and timed Mary's pains. 'Robert, you ride with Mary,' I told him. 'If she has any trouble, you wave and I'll pull up.'

McCorry warned me to keep the revs up going back across the Wombrella Flat, because if I didn't, that's where we would sit until the country dried out. I jumped behind the wheel and told Mary and Robert to hang on real tight. I pointed the nose of the tractor at Wombrella Flat and we slowly moved off. I kept the revs right up and a tight grip on the wheel as we ploughed, slipping and sliding across the flat. The moment I hit a bit of hard country I slowed enough to check that I hadn't thrown Mary or Robert off. They were hanging on still, covered in the mud and spinifex that the wheels had thrown up, soaking wet but with huge smiles on their faces, their beautiful white teeth gleaming through.

Once we made the gravel road I pulled up and checked Mary again. So far, so good. I kept going at a steady pace. As soon as we were home and all cleaned up, I put Mary, who was suffering her contractions in stoic silence, into the Land Rover and headed straight for Derby Hospital. We made it by 10 minutes! Mary safely delivered a very large baby boy, who they called Robert after his father. I promised Mary we'd pick her up from Derby on the next store run, and Robert and I headed back to the station. At daylight the next morning, we met the camp as the cattle were being pushed along a sandy ridge into the yard. The truck driver had to unhook his 13-metre trailers from the prime mover, hook them up to the tractor and turn them around on the gravel road without going over the side.

Robert and I put together a small fire on the road once the cattle were loaded and the stockmen branded them on board. Whoopee – the dollars were on the truck! We could hear Bucko, the driver, blowing the horn as he slowly manoeuvred down the wet, gravelly road towards Broome.

My life seemed to be travelling along a beautiful, winding, dusty outback road. There would be some little hiccups on the bends, often due to the company's cash shortages, but I would pick myself up on the straights. We were a family now, and it felt good. I was pregnant and all was going well. The only cloud in our family life was that McCorry seemed to be drinking more in the evenings. Never during the day. But sometimes the pressure of chasing cattle all day and battling with scant resources seemed to be getting to him. He would sit alone, brooding silently.

Looking back, I think he must have been showing the first signs of depression; but at the time it just seemed to be the way he was. He didn't need people. He thought he could figure everything out on his own.

Parenthood also brought its anxieties. I had to fly to Perth with Kelly, who needed a minor hernia operation. 'A small incision, and all over in five minutes,' my paediatrician informed me from Princess Margaret Hospital. Those five minutes turned into the most traumatic time of my life to that point. As I watched my baby wheeled away, down what seemed an awfully long corridor, my heart pulsed heavily and I burst into tears, reliving a silent fear I'd carried on the station: that if anything ever happened to our son we mightn't be able to get help quickly. But I was comforted by a kind nurse and Kelly was soon returned to me. It took me longer to recover than he did. He sat up in his cot laughing and clapping and very soon we returned home, my faith in our medical profession renewed.

My parents and younger brother Michael arrived in early 1977 to spend some time with us on the station. Mum and Dad set themselves up comfortably in their caravan and Michael moved into the homestead. Dad always found something to do in the workshop: if it wasn't a broken-down vehicle or machine, he'd overhaul the water pumps. In the meantime, Mum and I, between drinking bucketloads of tea, would fill each other in on the gaps in our lives since we'd last seen each other. Michael would race out and join McCorry with whatever he was doing on the 'run'. It was a holiday of sorts, and we found a lot to do together. McCorry and I were pleased to see them, but more than anything proud to show off our little man Kelly, who was ten months old.

One day while my parents and Michael were there, we were out on a muster. I jumped into the Bell 47 chopper with Skogy, buckled up and waited while he secured his thermos full of black coffee (although I sometimes wondered if that was all he had in it). The peace and tranquillity of the early morning was rudely broken as the old chopper roared into life. I was to show him the area we wanted mustered while the others, including McCorry, stayed to manage things on the ground. Skogy would then drop me off, downwind of where the cattle would come through to enter the yard.

As we did a gentle lap around, moving the herd in the general direction of the yard, I pointed out the schist hills that were the boundary for this muster. Skogy winked and I took that as an okay. I was in no hurry to return to earth, enjoying the beautiful feeling of flying. We dived and prodded at a rogue bull who was being a bit too territorial. After several more runs, I signalled to Skogy that I was ready to get out. I knew he was better off without the extra weight. Heading straight for the highest granite hill in the area, he landed the old Bell on top of a precarious, slippery boulder – just to be a smart-arse. Then he dropped me back at the yard. A little while later, I looked up to see the chopper heading towards the yard, making a hell of a racket. As Skogy came closer to the ground, I could see the chopper was way out of control. It landed heavily, bounced high and, the main rotor roaring, rocked wildly, the blades nearly collecting the ground.

As the dust settled, we came out from behind the granite boulders like rabbits from a warren, keeping an eye on the slowing blades. As we rushed forward, a deathly-white Skogy waved us away. He wasn't joking. As the rotor came to a standstill, Skogy stepped out, shaking his head. 'It was close this time,' he said. Too right. We were all shaken up.

Skogy, McCorry and Dad did a full study of the chopper's rotary section, finding a couple of bolts snapped off. They were talking about Cobb & Co.-ing the base of the rotary section with fencing wire. I thought, God, no! and walked away. They were forever jimmying up machinery and this time too much was at risk. Skogy said, 'If you can secure it, I can fly it!' – so the challenge was on.

First they doubled no. 10 wire and gave that a go. Skogy kicked the engine over and the blades started to rotate, but the chopper started to rock and he shut it down again in a hell of a hurry. After much discussion, the bush mechanics proceeded to Cobb & Co. the rotary section again, this time with some no. 8 plain wire.

Skogy told everyone to clear the deck, as he had seen a blade fly off a chopper before and go through three sheds. He kicked the engine over. The chopper held – there was no rocking this time. He brought the revs up to full throttle and it was starting to look real good, no rocking at all. Skogy gently lifted her up from the black soil plain and I peeped out from behind the boulder as he manoeuvred a full circle and landed her.

He jumped out and ran over to us, all smiles, giving a thumbs-up. 'She's great, better than ever, I'll finish the muster!' And away he went to bring in the cattle. It turned into a long day as we sat and worried and waited, but I knew Skoglund was no fool; he wouldn't tempt fate for the sheer hell of it.

Later, with the chopper back on the ground, we drove the tail of the herd up into the yard, closed the gates and headed for home. Thank God the day's over, I thought. It would be another full bottle of whisky night for Skogy.

One beautiful sunny day at the station, some of the women from the camp were having smoko on the back lawn under a giant frangipani tree. Old Yardie, who had appointed himself my minder at the homestead now that his horse-tailering days were over, was also having his smoko; only he sat three to four metres out on his own. From the kitchen window I watched him jump up and head to the front gate to question some strangers who had arrived. Yardie never let anyone in the house yard; they were all made to wait at the fence while he came to collect me.

For months newspaper headlines, radio and television and the outback radio galah session had concentrated on the unrest among the Aboriginal people on Noonkanbah Station, 145 kilometres south-east of Napier. A mining company wanted to drill for ore samples in one of the sacred sites on this property, supported by Western Australia's very conservative Premier, Sir Charles Court. The Aboriginal people were coming from far and wide and grouping together to protect this sacred site. The Kimberley, and particularly the cattle station personnel, were in turmoil.

We'd never seen a disturbance like this. We believed they had every right to make a stand – surely the mining company could drill somewhere else close by. But we also wondered if the Aborigines' resistance would set a precedent. The Shell Oil Company had been involved in exploration work on Napier Downs for years without complaint, but McCorry began predicting that that might change. He was proven right when Steve Hawke, the son of the future Prime Minister, and his colleague Sarah arrived at our Napier Downs front gate. They were white activists who had become involved with the Aboriginal people who opposed the exploration work on Noonkanbah.

'Missus,' was all Yardie would say. I followed him to the gate and shook hands with the young man, whose name had become publicly connected with the conflict.

'What do you want?' I asked Steve Hawke.

He explained that they had received a complaint from an Aboriginal man working on Napier Downs that Shell was interfering with sacred land and sites. It was just as well McCorry wasn't home; the one thing he detested most was what he saw as outside interference.

'I don't believe that either one of you knows or understands the Aboriginal people well enough to speak to me on their behalf,' I said. 'How long have one of you lived, worked and sweated side by side with these people? Not bloody long enough to come here stirring up trouble. I can guarantee that Napier will not become another Noonkanbah.'

I asked them to name the person behind this complaint. I had to smile; the man, in the camp on the Barker River, was a sacred-site robber himself, I told them, a grave robber!

'I have about 15 stockmen to back up what I'm going to tell you,' I said as I told them the story. We had just set up camp at the original Napier site and Yardie had come in from hobbling the workhorses. The stockmen were grabbing a slice of damper, a pannikin of strong black tea and were settling down in their swags for the evening. It was to be an early rise for the muster. Then the cards came out, and the first hand was dealt. This boy scratched around in his shirt pocket and pulled out a tooth – an eye tooth from a nearby burial site. The bodies in that particular cave had been laid in rows, one behind the other, over the years. My brother Michael had found the cave on a visit to Napier several years earlier. We respected it, and therefore no-one went there. But this boy had no respect for the dead. He was questioned loudly and extensively by the stockmen. Two of the older ones walked over to the camp fire, and sat down beside me.

The head stockman said, 'The boys don't want to camp here – the spirits, Missus.' They were frightened because this person had robbed a tooth from a skull in a burial cave.

'Load up,' McCorry said, 'Move camp back to the Barker River Junction.' Two hours later, the stockmen were dropping their swags on the ground again and settling down for the night. I went up to the boy who had stolen the tooth.

'Maybe the spirits will collect that tooth tonight,' I said, hoping like hell the damn thing would disappear by morning.

Now, having told my story, looking straight at Steve, I suggested he and Sarah jump back in their vehicle and drive out of Napier Downs a darn sight faster than they came in.

There never was a problem with the mining company. Some years later at Louisa Downs Station, Steve Hawke returned. Here we go again, I thought. McCorry and Steve went out behind the homestead, sat down on the hill in the midday sun and had a good two-hour discussion. We have been friends ever since, and I would encounter him many more times over the years as he worked hard representing the Aboriginal people.

The Main Roads department from Derby were camped at the one hundred mile jump-up, the rise in the road as it passed through the King Leopold Ranges. They were filling and grading the Gibb River Road. One of the bosses, Ivan Watson, was a friend of ours who would often pick up and drop off mail on his way past the front gate. They would collect mail or machine parts for us, and we'd give them some meat. One day outside of the mustering season, their camp cook called by radio asking if we had any spare beef, as they were cleaned out. As it happened, we too were in need of a killer.

Had it been mustering season, the job would have been easy: we'd drop one in the mob. Now it would be tougher. It was hard to get in for a close shot at wild cattle. To aim behind the ear or go for the lung shot was not so easy when the target was galloping at 60 kilometres an hour. Making sure we had the waterbottle and butchering knives in the back of the old Land Rover, McCorry and I headed out in the direction of Mungawheeler, a billabong along the river heading south.

I was eight months pregnant now and it was a rare pleasure for the two of us to be out alone, and we were laughing together and enjoying each other's company. Crossing a gravel road into the Mungawheeler track, I slowed down and took it steady. Thunderheads were building up and the sun was setting. The wild buggers would be coming in for water. We needed to get a killer before we ran out of daylight. McCorry had the .243 in hand as I nosed the Land Rover up out of the scrub and onto the plain, where we could see cattle watering. We spotted a bullock who, judging by his size, had escaped many musters. Very carefully I manoeuvred the Land Rover closer, making sure to keep downwind of the cattle. McCorry thought a standing shot would be easiest, a head shot behind the ear.

Stepping out of the vehicle, using the open door to steady the rifle, he fired. The bullet went in halfway down the bullock's neck. He took off across the buggar buggar – black soil plain – at a flat gallop. I had a sinking feeling in my stomach. We had to get this bullock. Calmly but quickly, McCorry took aim again behind the bullock's shoulder, hoping for a lung shot. Getting desperate, he frantically fired off another four rounds, and on the last shot the bullock hit the ground.

Thank God, I thought as I drove over to him, but when we were within 10 metres of the bullock he jumped up.

'Knock him down!' yelled McCorry.

I'd had enough and wanted it all over with; I knew we both did. Slamming my foot flat to the floor, I pushed the bullock over. Within a split second McCorry jumped out and cut his throat.

We'd never experienced such misfortune in getting a killer for meat. The day had all but gone; it was getting dark. Because he was worked up, McCorry mistakenly grabbed a long, thin boning knife from the pouch instead of a wider siding knife, which would have been safer and more effective. He bent over and was running the blade from the butt of the tail down to the hock in a hurry. He had quite a lot of pressure behind the knife and halfway down the hind quarter the blade slipped out of the hide and into the inside of McCorry's left arm, above the wrist. The point of the knife came out the other side, just below the elbow.

'My God,' was all I could say. I very nearly fainted He had 20 centimetres of cold steel lodged in his arm, his hand locked up in a tight fist. I stood in shock, staring. 'Shit,' said McCorry, and pulled the knife straight out. A cold shiver ran through me – it was a stark reminder of how easily you could lose someone you loved out here.

Grabbing an old towel from behind the seat of the Land Rover, I cut it into strips and put pressure on the wound. We left the bullock and headed for home.

It was now that the Land Rover chose to play up. We must have dislodged some dirt in the carburettor, and a couple of spark plug leads had bounced off. We were getting along like a sore-footed duck on a stony road. I pulled up and we replaced the spark plug leads, but there was nothing we could really do about the carburettor out there in the dark. The sooner I could get McCorry to the hospital, the better.

At the homestead I ran in and grabbed the keys for the Kingswood. McCorry grabbed a few cans for the road and we headed for Derby. Two and a half hours later, we arrived. The doctor refused to touch the arm that night, due to the six cans of beer Bob had consumed on the trip.

The following day, we were informed that the median nerve in Bob's arm had been severed. After four hours on the surgeon's table he ended up with a crazy, mixed-up hand with no feeling.

Years later, I believed the power of the mind and Bob's determination to keep on using his hand – even without it retaining any feeling at all – had stopped it from curling up into a hard, lifeless claw. Not long after the accident, while I was servicing the power plant, a job I rather enjoyed, McCorry dropped by to see if I needed help. I was in the process of tightening the fuel filter when I smelled a strange odour coming off the engine. Bob had rested his numb hand on the hot exhaust and it was cooking! He never felt a thing.

Hardly a breath of air, no leaves moving: it was October, and I was due to have my baby. The grass was crying out for rain and so were we. I looked out towards the Leopold Ranges at the massive wet season thunderheads coming our way.

'Send it down, Hughie!' I called to the Almighty. My parents were up visiting from Kilto Station, a small property in the Kimberley 50 km north-east of Broome and about three hours from us. They had moved there from Shark Bay in 1976 to manage the station. Having been connected with the bush all their lives, they'd had the urge to return to the outback.

Dad, ever mechanical-minded, was working on the grader. My mother, who kept herself busy around the homestead, had tolerated my cravings for raw onions throughout this pregnancy, and was setting up for smoko in our favourite spot on the front veranda overlooking the horse paddock. Kelly was in the bedroom having his afternoon nap.

Out of the blue, a huge bolt of lightning struck the middle of the horse paddock. Horses were squealing and galloping in all directions and the paddock was on fire. With my heart pounding from the closeness of the strike, I stood transfixed. Then a water glass exploded on the table, shattering into tiny fragments.

'Mum, come on!' I grabbed her arm, wondering where the next strike would be. We ran into the dining room and within seconds the next strike was directly behind the homestead, hitting the Napier Range. We stood, staring through the windows, then moved further into the house to get away from the glass. This time we could hear the thunder grumbling in the distance. Sinking down into the sofa I thought, thank God. My big baby was kicking away inside me.

Then the pains started.

I timed the labour pains, and then they eased off. False alarm, I thought, and slept well through the night. In the morning I packed my hospital bag and headed for Derby. I was admitted to hospital and by 1.30 am, after another rush to theatre, beautiful Leisha Marie was born, weighing nine and a half pounds (4.3 kilograms). How lucky we were. McCorry and I were over the moon – we had two precious children.

I felt very confident looking after Leisha. Whereas Kelly was my first-born and had arrived under more traumatic circumstances, and was also a smaller baby, Leisha was bigger and I'd well and truly mastered the breastfeeding. Though slightly sore from another caesarean, I was allowed home early.

Father Lawrence of the Catholic Church in Derby would often do station rounds to check on the followers, have a cup of tea or whisky, a smoke, crack a joke and move on to the next station on his round. He had always been there in my time of need and yet he knew I was a bush Baptist. After helping Father to load his trusty ute, I always had a parcel of beef for him.

'Next door's beef?' he asked.

'No, Father, ours,' I replied, and winked. 'You should know, Father, that to eat one's own beef, we must eat the neighbour's.' This was a common joke in the Kimberley, referring to the unbranded cattle that roamed freely between stations.

He blessed me and said, 'Goodbye, Mother', and headed off to Derby town.

Bob was constantly unwell during 1978, vomiting blood and getting so sick he could hardly move. With this he drank more in the evenings and grew moody with his pain. He would pass out while working, and I'd drag him under a tree to recover. I first feared Bob was having health problems the year before Kelly was born, but whenever I mentioned seeing a doctor, he would explode. As Bob grew harder to live with, my brother Michael left Kilto, where he'd been helping Mum and Dad and came to work for us permanently.

One day after Bob passed out near the toilet, vomiting blood, I erupted for the first time. I'd had enough. I dragged him from the bathroom to the radio room, laid him on the camp stretcher by the window where a cool breeze was gently moving the curtains, and returned to clean up the bathroom. When I went back to him, McCorry was coming to, a terrible deathly grey colour. I was frightened he might die, but upset and angry too.

'I'm calling the Flying Doctor,' I said as I picked up the radio handpiece. 'I'm taking you to hospital right now. Do you understand? You must see a doctor!'

I had the microphone in my hand, the cord stretched to its limit.

'I'm not going anywhere, I'm not going,' he said, angry with me, refusing point-blank.

My voice raised, I thumped the radio desk hard. 'Go on, McCorry, go on and die, take the easy way out!' I screamed. It was the maddest he'd ever seen me. The bed was creaking as he battled to sit up. He looked so sick, so terrible, but his eyes never wavered from mine. They were black and watery. He had nothing to say.

'When you're dead and gone, you'll be happy – no pain, no worries,' I said. 'Is that what you want?'

He never answered.

'The easy way out,' I repeated, the tears flowing freely now. 'Don't worry about the hurt it'll cause me and the children.'

He tried to speak.

'No!' I shouted. 'You don't care! The children won't have a father and I won't have a husband because you're too pig-headed to let me take you to the hospital, for God's sake!'

McCorry raised his hand, a weak smile on his face: it was a peace offering. It seemed I'd got through to him. He agreed to go to Derby Hospital, where he was diagnosed with a massive bleeding ulcer the size of his fist.

Through 1978 and 1979 my frustration was mounting with the company we worked for. I could accept the long and hard days of work, but no longer the many months of waiting for the pay cheque. This bothered me more than it did McCorry. As long as he had beef, bread, beer and tobacco, he would ride along forever. But now we had two beautiful children and I had begun to think about their future. I really couldn't see one for us remaining where we were.

Unbeknown to McCorry, I had applied to the Lands Department in Perth and successfully obtained two 10-acre blocks on the outskirts of Broome. He wasn't particularly pleased with me at first, but came around in the end. The blocks were leasehold at 45 dollars each a year. Once we'd planted some mango trees and laid down the slab for a house, we could apply to buy them outright. I wanted to freehold them as soon as possible.

After many months of agonising, I saw another way of getting out of our rut. Without telling McCorry, I applied for the position of General Manager of Mount Hart, Silent Grove, Ellendale and Blina stations, a group of stations owned by Sir Leslie and Cecil Thiess, who also owned the Demco Meatworks in Broome. In October 1979 we received a message over the Flying Doctor radio from Doug Halleen, the chief of Thiess Bros Pastoral, to say the General Manager's position was ours if we wanted it.

Bob took the radio message and ran to me with a thundercloud over his head.

'What's this about Blina – Thiess Brothers?' he bellowed.

I stood my ground and said calmly: 'I've applied for the General Manager's position.'

'You've done what?'

I ignored his anger and asked: 'Did they say we've got the job?'

'Yes. And what are you going to do about it?' he asked, as if I was going to turn the offer down.

'I'm going to start packing right now.'

All hell broke loose. McCorry hated change. He and I had never really argued before, but this time I laid it on the line; I'd had enough of wondering if the staff, or ourselves, were going to be paid, even though the dollars were on the hoof. I'd had enough of being told to hide the station trucks. I didn't need to make excuses for what I'd done. I needed change, and if McCorry wouldn't take the first step, I would.

I accepted the General Manager's position on our behalf, and told McCorry, 'We do it together, or I go alone.' I can't say for certain what I'd have done if he'd resisted, but I think my determination shocked him into compliance. Once he saw I wasn't going to back down, he fell into line. The next thing I knew, he was helping the boys load the truck. He never said much, never put his arms around me and said what a great move it would be. But he came.

CHAPTER 10

Blina and Beyond

*T*he Blina landscape differed considerably from Napier Downs, even though we were more or less neighbours. Blina country was flat and scrubby, with part of the southern end circled by the Erskine Range.

An elder from the Wungundin and Dutchie Aboriginal groups asked if they could move with us from Napier to Blina Station. McCorry and I were extremely happy to have these devoted and faithful stockmen and their families follow us. Bluey and Rita also joined the crew. There were currently no staff on Blina or Ellendale stations, but as it turned out we always had more ready and willing people than we could possibly hire.

The Blina homestead was an older-style transportable, very large and airy. There was a little windmill man's cottage and kitchen, white men's quarters, corrugated-iron individual huts for the Aboriginal stockmen and their families, and a huge workshop for Bluey. A good-sized saddle and tack room and station storeroom completed the list.

We'd been on Blina three months when Sir Leslie Thiess arrived from Queensland in the company jet. We found him a delightful and charming gentleman. Kelly and Leisha had their first flight with Sir Leslie on a trip to Broome, where they stayed at their cousins' place while Sir Leslie and I watched a load of the station's cattle killed at Demco Meatworks.

Two and a half months later, we had a visit from his brother Cecil. Cecil was more of a rough diamond and we had many laughs with him while doing the rounds of the company's four stations. His only worry was whether the ice cubes would set during the day and be ready for his whisky at night.

One of the first jobs that needed attention was cleaning up the station store. I don't think I'd ever come across so many cartons of outdated tinned fruit, some of it two years past its use-by date. The walls were covered in cobwebs and heavily coated in dust. I had one of the stock boys pull up the big camp trailer a metre or so from the door. Three of the stockmen's wives who had followed us from Napier – Betty, Janey and Maisie – came up from the camp to give me a hand and we started going through box after box, discarding anything rusty or out of date. Many of the cans were ready to explode. While dusting the bottom shelf I found a wooden box of what I thought were antique bottles, containing a pinky mauve powder. Proud of my find, I was holding the bottles up and showing everyone. After I took them up to the house and washed the powder out, I sat the little bottles on the kitchen ledge to look at. Some days later we had a visit from an older couple, Len and Sylvia Connell, our caretakers from Mount Hart Station. While preparing lunch with me, Sylvia spotted the bottles, walked over to them and demanded to know where I had found them and what I had done with the contents.

'What's the problem?' I asked.

'Strychnine powder,' she said. It was used in the early days for baiting wild dogs. My heart started working overtime. I'd heard stories from doggers about terrible deaths from strychnine. I threw the bottles straight into the bin.

During muster we'd noticed that there weren't as many calves as we'd expected. McCorry and I thought from day one that there may have been a problem with the bulls. Previous management had had the bright idea that Santa Gertrudis bulls were the way to go. Normally, tough shorthorn and Brahman were the dominant breeds in the Kimberley. Santa Gertrudis bulls, shorter in the leg and a softer breed, had never before been seen in the area to my knowledge. They were brought onto the station – big, fat and lazy, dragging their pizzles along the ground like giant vacuum cleaners and picking up spear grass seeds, which of course rendered them useless for anything more than decoration. We ordered a single-deck road train, loaded them on and sent the whole lot to Demco Meatworks.

It was the middle of the wet season and Blina was awash. One afternoon in February Maisie came up to the homestead. 'Missus, Missus, that Margaret she having a piccaninny.'

'Are you sure?' I asked. 'Margaret has said nothing and she doesn't even look pregnant.'

Maisie, who'd had several of her own, was sure. I followed her back to camp to check on the girl, who at 16 might have concealed her pregnancy because she was frightened. Who could blame her? When I got to the camp the older women were pulling her out of a hut and seemed to be growling at her in their language.

'Come on, Margaret, we must go to Derby Hospital,' I coaxed. I radioed the Flying Doctor who organised for an ambulance with a doctor, named Gaudier, on board. They would meet us on the road. I explained that we were having a very wet season, the lake in front of the homestead was overflowing in several places, and I would have a battle getting through to the highway. Most importantly, I didn't know how long this girl had been in labour.

I put her on a mattress in the back of the F100 truck and told her to knock on the cab if she thought the baby was coming. The dirt track out to the main road was covered with water and very boggy and soon we were slipping and sliding from one side to the other with mud and grass flying all around us. I was hanging onto the steering wheel with all my power; there would be no hope if we slipped over the embankment.

I stopped where the creek crossed the road. The water was deep and moving fast. In the cab I had a large canvas mailbag, always handy in an emergency. I climbed into the back of the F100 and checked Margaret and her pulse. It was rapid. Why the hell hadn't she admitted to being pregnant? I was feeling really sorry for her. I hung the mailbag over the radiator and slammed the bonnet closed. The idea was to stop the pressure of incoming water from pushing the fan back through the radiator.

'We're going into deep water. Hang on, Margaret!' I yelled over the sound of the engine.

No answer. Entering the water, we gently made our way across the creek and up the other side, sounding like a sick submarine. As we had another dip to cross within a hundred metres or so, I left the bag hanging. I was starting to wonder what the hell I was doing when the next lot of deep water came up. I sang out to Margaret again: 'Hang on, deep water!'

Again there was no answer. I glanced back and thought that as soon as I hit the main road I would stop and check her and try to comfort her – she was only a young girl.

Hitting the Great Northern Highway was a great relief. I immediately pulled over, removed the mailbag from the radiator, then climbed over the tailgate to do another check on Margaret. Her only sound was a deep moan. She hadn't spoken a word since we'd left the station. I thought the sooner we got going and met up with the doctor, the better. It was 154 kilometres to Derby from the homestead and we had about 90 to go.

There was not another vehicle on the road and I was travelling as fast as I could. At the 80-kilometre peg I saw a distant flash of light. Dr Gareth Gaudier – what a relief. Margaret was transferred to the ambulance to continue to hospital, and I turned the vehicle around and headed back for the station. Later that same afternoon I received a call on the Flying Doctor radio, telling me that Margaret had given birth 10 minutes after arriving, but that her baby boy was dead.

I was left with a lot of mixed emotions, thoughts and unanswered questions. What value does life have? Did she really want the child? I didn't know, but I felt angry that we had lost the little boy.

The following weekend the Aboriginal families asked me to be godmother to 18 of their kids whom Father Lawrence was arriving to baptise. The camp women and I decided to put on a smoko for all, with cakes and little party pies and homemade sausage rolls, lemonade for the kids, tea for us adults and a whisky for Father Lawrence. It did something to relieve the anger I was still feeling about Margaret's baby.

My disquiet was only a shadow, however, of Bob's. He just couldn't settle at Blina. The challenge of mustering was nowhere near as great, the country not as rugged, as Napier and Kimberley Downs. And the pay cheques were coming in every fortnight! To top it all off, the owners were happy with the profit. But McCorry wanted out of the station. The harder the mustering was, the better for him, even if his body was racked with pain. With this easier job he seemed to be moody, suffering pain of some sort, and was drinking more.

I never wanted to leave Blina. McCorry just needed more time to accept the change. But in the end I was prepared to move rather than see him so unhappy. This was part of the give-and-take in the marriage, but I wondered where it would lead us next.

Sir Leslie Thiess flew over to visit and wanted to hand over Mount Hart Station as a gift. Yes – literally give it to us. Sadly, we couldn't accept it, even with the offer from the Aboriginal stockmen to work without wages. We never had the finance to back a cattle station and because of McCorry's age he'd always refused to take out a bank loan. I was keen to take up the offer. I knew we could survive and keep our heads above water there and maybe add a small tourist venture to it at a later date. But McCorry had the last word, and his answer was a firm 'No'. We offered the management position to Errol Appleton, a young, smart cattleman from Clermont, Queensland. The Thiess brothers were happy with our choice, if regretful that we'd decided to move.

The day before we pulled out from Blina, I spent some time gazing out over the beautiful lake that had appeared after the wet season's rain. I watched the birds feeding, the swans gliding against the evening sunset, and wished for many good wet seasons to come and for the swans, ducks and hundreds of other water birds to be left in peace.

We didn't leave without having made plans. The Managing Director of Australian Land & Cattle Co., Jack Fletcher, made the kind offer for us to manage Kilto Station. By moving there we would still have a hand in the cattle game, but also be only 50 kilometres from one of our 10-acre blocks north of Broome where we wanted to build a log cabin. My parents, who'd been caretaking Kilto, had moved back to Broome, so they would be nearby too.

The move to Kilto Station was on. At 86,000 acres, you could almost spit from one side to the other. It was the size of a real good horse paddock, made up of sandy ridges and mostly wattle scrub with several nice flats and the odd cabbage gum.

It would just be my younger brother Michael, Kelly, Leisha, Bob and myself – the smallest camp ever. Kilto was more or less a poddy-dodging block – because it was so small, you couldn't run enough cattle there to make a living, so the only viable way would have been to set up traps for wandering cleanskins from the neighbouring properties and hope to capture and brand them. There was no money to spend on the place and at the time the company didn't have a cent to bless itself with. But Bob was happier with the tougher challenge. He and I knew that a darn good cleanup, replacing post and rails, cost nothing, so with the help of Michael we got into it.

It was a pleasure to have Michael working with us now, as our jack-of-all-trades. We all got along extremely well and the kids just loved him. We cleaned up around the old homestead, removing the odd king brown snake that was in the way, and cut bougainvillea from outside the loo. At night it was hard to tell the difference between a bougainvillea runner and a snake.

In the cool of the afternoons we gave Kelly and Leisha their first riding lessons on Sirocco, a lovely Welsh Arab stallion. They took turns bouncing around the homestead bareback. Kelly was a natural in the saddle and Leisha developed a little later. This was really an idyllic time in our lives: a beautiful and precious period for our family. McCorry and I had more time with each other and the children, and Michael was our added bonus. I'd often sit on the front steps of the Kilto homestead and watch the children playing with their toys in the red pindan sand that was the colour of dark oxblood.

They played well together; Kelly was always helping Leisha push her truck along their sandy little track. He would then have to catch her pet green frog when it escaped and jam it back into the cabin of her truck. The frog was the driver! They were good children and we loved them dearly. I never needed to be told how lucky I was to be a mother.

The wet season had started to settle in. Bob had ploughed the cleared ground again and now the seed was going in: luccrne, buffel and sorghum. We were amateur farmers just having a go.

One day Missy, my bull terrier, charged into the old homestead and Sally, the blue heeler, followed as backup. Kelly and Leisha were playing games on my bed. Michael and I were over at the yard working on cattle spears, for setting up traps for cleanskins. With the dogs going berserk and sounding aggressive and agitated, we were alerted to the danger. Yelling, 'Snake!' we sprinted across to the homestead. Michael grabbed a post-hole shovel and I grabbed the station killer rifle. We burst into the room. The kids looked up from their game, wondering what the heck was going on. Guided by the dogs' incessant barking at one point in the wall, Michael launched the shovel and made a hole about twice the size of a dinner plate, poked in the handle of the shovel, and felt something soft. I handed him my bedside torch.

'Come here and have a look at this,' Michael said. It was the biggest and fattest king brown snake I had ever seen. He had been living well on the oversized rats. I had to walk past the snake to get out the door, with Kelly on one hip and Leisha on the other. Michael kept an eye on the thing. A snake this size would have enough venom to kill a horse in 20 minutes, so he wasn't spending another night with me. I put the children safely down and got a gun. I shone the torch down on the king brown to get some idea of where his head might be, then stood back and fired, blowing another hole in the wall. There was blood and fibro everywhere. The brown really came to life, but seemed too big to get out. Mick broke more of the wall down and pulled the big bugger outside to finish him off.

Early in April 1981, after only 18 months at Kilto, we were offered the manager's position on both Louisa and Bohemia Downs stations, adding up to 2.5 million acres owned by the Australian Land & Cattle Co. Bob and I sat up that night and gave it some thought. We had achieved what we wanted on this break, planted more mango trees on our block and started the log cabin. We were champing at the bit for more of a challenge and some excitement in our working lives, and this sounded good.

There were several things that bothered me, though. For the 2.5 million acres of these stations, there had only ever been 600 to 800 head of cattle trucked per year. That was reasonably small numbers for large acres. Also, managers in the past had spent an average of two years on the stations and moved on. On the upside, there was a large permanent Aboriginal camp on the property and they were keen to work.

I suggested to Bob that we go and look it over first. His reply was for us to take the position and if for some reason we were not happy, we could always leave. Bob had his way.

Moving day, Friday 17 April 1981, came and the easterly breeze was gently carrying the banging and rattling sounds of a vehicle along the corrugated sandy track into Kilto.

'Here they come,' yelled Kelly, his blue eyes lighting up.

He and Leisha stuffed his metal toy Cat dozer, a gift from Mrs Higgins of Water Bank Station, into the front of the Ford. This was a very precious gift; therefore the tucker box would have to travel in the back. After a quick cuppa with Nan and Grandpa, who were moving back to Kilto to take over its management from us, we were chugging down the track towards the main road.

Occasionally glancing into the rear-vision mirror, I felt happy to see our convoy steadily moving along together. It was a great new adventure, since neither Bob, Michael nor I had ever been to Louisa or Bohemia stations.

My little man Kelly was my 'spotter', sitting up high to keep a lookout for straying cattle that would occasionally drift across the main road. It was also an opportunity to draw his sister's attention to any birds or animals that he thought might interest her. Before leaving the station we had all agreed to pull over under the first shady tree beyond the Fitzroy and have a corned beef sandwich and a pannikin of well-earned tea. It was also a good opportunity for the kids to stretch their legs. All fed and watered, Michael checked the horses, Bob checked the load of stores and fuel, and we were off on the last leg of our adventure.

The two stations were semi-desert, slightly undulating spinifex country. The Mary River ran the full length of Louisa Downs and a big watercourse called Christmas Creek ran through Bohemia Downs. As we travelled through its vastness we couldn't help but gaze in wonder at the rich ochre- and cream-coloured plateaux away in the distance on what must have been Bohemia. We were travelling through undulating country with many deep but narrow creeks on the Louisa side. My body tingled with excitement. I was wanting to look about and take in as much of this new country as I could, while struggling with the wheel of the F100 to stop it from jumping all over the road like a disturbed kangaroo.

The road was deeply corrugated and I very nearly missed the Twin Sisters, two hills that rise like perfect breasts out of the spinifex and mark the way to the Louisa turn-off. I carefully turned in and followed the two-wheel track. I could see no sign of gates, fences or yards until I spotted the horse paddock and then the homestead. Kelly jumped out at the gate, gave Leisha a helping hand down, and they unhooked the chain together. As the gates swung open, huge smiles lit up their beautiful faces as they looked back at me. Yes, we were there at last.

The children walked the hundred metres as I crept along, seeing for the first time our low-slung homestead atop the red gravel rise. The homestead was fronted by the airstrip, with a huge jacaranda tree and low scrub and spinifex at the sides. The only other trees of any height were the river gums bordering the Mary River, which flowed around the foot of the hill just below the homestead. The lawn seemed to be more brown and brittle than green. The house itself was old, made of fibro and corrugated iron but in reasonably good order. The back veranda with its cracked cement floor and fly screens and huge old dining table looked like it would become a very happy place for smokos and evening meals. The enclosed front veranda was equally welcoming. I knew that I could make this a good home.

It was time to visit the camp to meet and greet the Aboriginal people. I found it silent and eerie, about 30 old humpies and bow sheds – shelters made from spinifex and chicken wire – billy cans still hanging from meathooks, flour drums that were used for water containers or chairs, old wartime camp stretcher beds and about three dozen hairless, blue-eyed inbred dogs cowering in the shadows. There wasn't one person in sight.

These people were so proud of their humpies that they'd swept the full expanse of their camps so often as to create little gullies around the perimeter. I could tell from the sweepings that the people had only been gone one to three days. We deduced that they must have moved to the neighbouring towns and were homeless, thinking the white managers had abandoned them. Whenever there were changes of management, the Aboriginal people tended to take fright, fearing that new managers might evict them – even though the camps were, in reality, their home.

On Easter Monday, a young fellow with a wife and baby drove in from the main road looking for work. He confessed that he had no money or food and was desperate. But Danny said he had some mechanical knowledge, so we put him on the payroll to offside Michael. Later that same day we had a visit from an old Aboriginal fellow called Alex Gordon. Alex had a sad tale to tell.

'Louisa my home country, Missus, we been told to leave, new manager come. Please, the peoples are hungry; they have no meat or money.'

'We don't know this country, old man,' I said. 'We need stockmen, good stockmen, who belong to this country, who know this country well. In fact we need them by Monday; otherwise I will bring Aboriginal people from the Napier area.'

Alex said he would pass on the message, so I fuelled his old bomb car with super petrol and gave him some beef to carry the message to the other stockmen.

Two weeks later we had more Aboriginal stockmen than we could possibly afford to hire. Alex, being the elder in the camp, with a good knowledge of this Louisa and Bohemia area and a good horseman as well, became our head stockman. We left the drafting of the stock camp to three older men: Alex, Ringer and Frank. We knew they would select well.

There were more visitors. Bull Pup and Sally, our two faithful dogs – Missy had died when we were at Napier – drew my attention to the front gate, where, in front of her white dust-covered Toyota, stood a blonde girl in her mid-twenties.

'I'm Julie,' she said. 'I'm the travelling kindy teacher.'

Her arms were loaded with educational toys and story-books. I welcomed Julie with a quick cuppa while the house staff mustered all the kindy-aged kids, including Kelly and Leisha, onto the back homestead lawn under the shade of a beautiful mature jacaranda. The back lawn soon became a hive of excitement. Leisha and her little friends were willing partici-pants, happily drawing and painting. Kelly and Jeffrey, his Aboriginal mate, were forever escaping school and climbing onto the laundry roof.

Later the same afternoon, I was feeling a little tired and weary after a trip to Halls Creek hospital with a sick child from the camp; then I'd had to wait an hour at the station turn-off for the Greyhound bus to drop off Sharon, the station cook. Katie, my tall, slim house help, came running into the kitchen.

'Missus, Missus, that Kelly boy, Jeffrey and that baby girl Leisha, they gunna jump, Missus!'

She grabbed me by the arm and hauled me outside to the laundry shed. Sure enough, on the corrugated-iron laundry roof I counted three children. There was Jeffrey with his thin black legs dangling over the edge and Leisha and Kelly standing with what looked to be homemade parachutes tied loosely around their waists. A cold shiver ran through my body, knowing one of them could break an arm or leg, or at worst break their neck.

'Sit down, sit down carefully,' I told them gently so as not to frighten them. Jack, who worked around the house yard, grabbed a ladder from the nearby shed and I coaxed them down. Kelly was five and Leisha three at the time.

In the weeks following our arrival on Louisa we covered as much of our 2 million acres as we could, assessing the work that needed doing and the potential of the place. The horse paddock

turned out to be the only decent paddock between both properties, and there were many sorry sights of burnt, rusted, twisted
barbed wire lying around from years gone by. I couldn't blame
past managers for this neglect, as there were never enough
funds. All of us had battled along without wages for months on
end. Some were strong enough to hang in; others simply retired
or pulled the pin. Who could blame them? This was hard
country which ran more or less on a 350-millimetre annual
rainfall. A tough country for the white man to survive in and
make a profit from. Many hard men had tried and many of them
had walked off with nothing but their swag.

There was a lot of excitement at the station as the stockmen
got their new gear and swags ready to move out on the muster.
We had more men than we needed, but the extras just wanted
to work for their keep. Some of the stockmen's wives joined up
as cooks and about half a dozen kids from the camp decided to
come for the ride.

We set out to find a reason for the previous years' low
cattle turnoff numbers – the cattle sent to the meatworks.
Maybe past management had been covering and mustering the
same country, the same old pattern year in and year out. We
explained to old Alex that we wanted to muster new country,
extend our work to the boundary of our properties first, and
then, with subsequent musters, come back in stages towards
the homestead. The reason? The cattle in this country were
wild, cunning and mostly rogue. As soon as they picked up
strange movement and sounds, they scattered among the desert
sandhills, spinifex ridges and rugged ranges. They favoured a
peaceful existence, and who could blame them? By mustering
boundaries first we reasoned that cleanskin cattle not picked
up in our first sweep would flee inwards, and eventually be
mustered anyway.

'Lead us to places that no other managers have mustered,' McCorry said to Alex. He lit up his tailormade, tapped Little Arab on the flank, and men and horses moved out.

Alma, the yard man's wife, and I would hole up in camp each morning baking fresh damper in the coals and boiling salt beef in flour drums for the day's dinner camp. We would then follow the cattle tracks until the mob was in sight. With Jack and the help of several stockmen, we would erect the portable yard panels. Once the cattle were yarded, the horses could be hobbled out for the night. A week after leaving the station, the first cattle were picked up on the open watershed country out from Christmas Creek. By this time we were travelling through some rough areas new to both Bob and me. Prior to leaving the station we had studied the old maps. It soon became apparent that we were close to the invisible boundary of a million-acre neighbouring station, Go Go. I had suggested carrying the maps, but Bob's answer was always that the old Aboriginal stockmen knew their country. I suppose I wasn't really worried that we would get totally lost, but I was concerned that we stay on the right side of this invisible frontier.

I rode over to Bob and mentioned my fears. Feeling the same, he beckoned old Alex over.

'Where are we, old man?' he asked.

'A little bit Go Go,' was his reply. He said no more and rode away. We were on Go Go Station, it seemed. I was worried about trespassing, but Bob was happy to turn a blind eye, as Alex was the elder and guide. In any case, there were no cattle there.

Several days later we crossed over a rough rock ridge. Looking east I could see the outline of a huge square abutment. Both Bob and I had flown past this landmark several times on our way to Halls Creek. We also knew that at the foot of this landmark was a big spring known as Morgan's Grave. At last we had some idea of our position. Bob reasoned that we could be travelling along the edge of Fossil Downs country – another neighbour with whom we shared a boundary. He again beckoned Alex to ride over to him and asked the same question as he had before. In other words, *Wherethehellarewe?*

'A little bit Fossil,' was the reply. Bob had asked Alex to lead us into country where no other manager had gone before. He had done that and more!

As we did all our life mustering vast areas in the Kimberley, we followed this rule: let go all the branded cattle that did not belong to us, but hold onto all the cleanskins. So Bob decided to work back towards Morgan's Grave, which was on Louisa country, and then head home.

Kelly and Leisha were always with me in the stock-camp, and on the days I mustered with the boys Alma our cook would watch the children closely for me. But this was the second day Leisha had been showing signs of being unwell. She was tired, miserable and now running a high temperature, and Panadol, cool wet flannels and an abundance of water were not easing it. I was concerned. Bob's old Trager two-way radio had seen better days, and I was angry he would not carry the newer Codan. He seemed intractable lately and kept moving along as if we didn't seem to exist. He had a goal and was heading for it, alone if he had to. He had no fear. Whenever I demurred or raised a question about our whereabouts, he ignored me. He had a cold, tough edge, even with his own daughter sick. Instead of talking to me, he'd ride along with the mob while we followed in the vehicles. I was beginning to think he belonged, spiritually, to the long-gone era of the bushrangers.

With the Trager too hemmed-in among the ranges, crackling and static dominated when we tried to communicate with the Flying Doctor. I decided to take the Toyota on the rocky two-hour drive to the homestead, with nothing to follow but our own earlier tracks. With some trepidation, alone with Kelly and Leisha, I was able to follow our tracks back to the gravel road before sundown. Finding renewed confidence, I steadily progressed towards the homestead. Tuning in the Codan back there, I was able to make contact with the doctor, who prescribed some antibiotics that we already had in the Flying Doctor medical kit. I gave both children a warm flannel wash before settling them in bed.

Mid-afternoon the following day, I received a telephone call from John Hendwood, the manager of Fossil Downs Station. He was most irate and wanted to speak to Bob, who was not home, of course. Hendwood as good as accused him of cattle stealing. Thinking about it now, it was understandable. As a Kimberley cattleman, Bob's reputation as a formidable musterer, able to find cattle where nobody else would go, was enough to put the fear of God into all his competitors, most of all the neighbours.

For four days the phone calls continued. I tried to assure Hendwood that I understood his apprehension, but said that Bob did not set out knowingly to muster Fossil. Hendwood said that he would put the matter in the hands of the Stock Squad.

'Tell Bob to call me as soon as he returns to the homestead.'

I assured him that I would. Later, Bob told me the story. Following my departure from the stock camp, the men had caught and saddled their horses, and ridden over to the yard to let the cattle out. One of them pulled his horse up, turned to Bob and said, 'Aeroplane coming, old man.' Sure enough, a plane came into sight, and circled the yard and the boys at a height of 50 metres. Under this intruder's continuous surveillance, Bob and the boys were unable to let the cattle out of the yard. Mustered only the previous day, the fresh cattle could be stirred up by the aircraft. Bob decided to hold up and wait for this intruder to 'piss off', as he put it.

One of the little camp kids who followed the stockmen towards the yard said, 'Something come down, old man.' It was a piece of white paper, a note. There was a light breeze around that morning. Bob said to the boy, 'You chase that paper.' It took some time for him to get hold of it – it would float gently down just within his reach, then the wind would pick it up and carry it further, as if a mischievous spirit breeze was having an early morning game with our little friend. The message from the heavens read, 'You have been mustering my country, you will hear more about it.' These words were not exceptionally worrying to McCorry – he had mustered no branded cattle belonging to the neighbours, and the yard and cattle were now well and truly on Louisa country.

A week later, Kelly and Leisha picked up the distinctive sound of Bob's Wave Hill spurs tapping the path.

'Daddy's home, Mum!'

I was anxious to relay the messages and hear what he said. Bob, showing no concern or distress, showered, got a cold can and made the phone call. I was worried, and his nonchalance annoyed me. Naturally, by now, Hendwood had worked himself up and was quite upset. When he stopped talking to take a breath, Bob chipped in.

'Well, John, it's like this. I can't read maps and the country is all new to me and if I had strayed over the border line it was by mistake.'

This infuriated Hendwood.

'You old bastard, you can't read maps but you seem to get to exactly where you want to go any time you choose. I've put it in the hands of the Stock Squad, so you can deal with them.'

'Holy hell,' I said, listening to the crackling on the other end of the phone. 'What shit are we in this time?'

The Stock Squad did contact Bob. He was open and honest and laid it on the line. The detective said he wanted nothing to do with it, and for us to work things out among ourselves. Hendwood called again, and Bob passed on what the detective had said. Hendwood suggested he bring his brand and earmarking pliers over to Louisa and mark half the cleanskins for himself. Bob pointed out it was illegal to use a brand on any station other than the one it was registered for. Hendwood slammed down the phone in Bob's ear and that was the end of the matter. When a cow calves and the weaner grows up and leaves its mother, it's impossible to tell which cow owns what. When you are mustering 2 million acres plus, with no boundary fences or any fences at all, it has to be first in, best dressed! My dear husband, a man of few words and quiet strength, never let accusations bother him. He loved his family and worked and treated every day as if it was his last. But there were times when it bothered me and I envied his placidity in the face of threats and accusations. Sometimes I thought he was pushing me, his boundaries and his luck too far.

My brother Michael was flat-out on the grader putting in a road to the Larawa mustering site. The camp had been out for six days and had a reasonably good mob of cattle in hand, mostly cleanskins and not many branded ones. A few rogue bulls had got away, but we would pick them up another day with just the buggy and bull truck.

The sun was on its way down and the boys were holding the cattle on the water. In that country, there was no such thing as a permanent yard; we took it in turns to ride through the night to keep them in. Kelly and Leisha gave me a hand to collect firewood for the camp fires. The nights were still quite crisp and cool, and the cattle dust was hanging in so close I could smell it and taste it in my mouth.

On such a typical Kimberley desert night, a two-blanket night or a 'two-dog night', the men were busy haggling over who should take first watch riding the mob. They hobbled their horses and nose-bagged them for the evening feed. Dreamer, our horse-tailer, would see that all was done well. As each man settled his horse he would move steadily towards the glow of the evening camp fire, his spurs tinkling through the black night. Sitting on the edge of the coals waiting for these weary ringers was a flour drum full of black tea, a good thick slice of fresh damper and some cooked beef.

It had been a long day. Both Leisha and Kelly had snuggled down into their swags and I could hear Kelly telling 'Bub' about the big bulls he saw today. I'd managed to relieve him of the bull strap he'd worn across his shoulder. He always liked to dress just like the stock boys.

With the children close to sleep in the tray of the Toyota, I unrolled Bob's swag next to mine on the ground nearby. As I settled down to sleep, Bull Pup, my faithful bull terrier, moved over and settled himself comfortably on my feet. It was cold and I rather welcomed the foot warmer. I lay awake for a while, listening to the distant bellow of a rogue bull, and then a clash of strong horns. This was followed by the sound of stockhorses and gentle voices. Knowing the boys had everything under control, I drifted off to sleep. I always felt secure out in the bush and sleep came easily.

But during the night I was woken several times by the bellow of another bull. He obviously wasn't too happy with us camping the cattle on his dunghill. Before drifting back to sleep I watched the boys moving quietly about, stoking the fires. On and off throughout the night I could hear the constant bellowing of the rogue as he moved closer to our mob of cattle. I hoped and prayed he might join our mob peacefully, or better still stay out far enough for us to put him down with the bull-buggy in the morning, away from our hard-won beef. The morning just wasn't coming fast enough. As that thought crossed my mind, the deep bass note of the rogue sounded again, this time too close for comfort. The camp fires were putting out a golden glow, but it was still very dark.

Next I heard the heavy clash of horns, a raised voice, a horse whinny, more voices and the frightening sound of tonnes of beef on the move, the thundering sound of cattle rushing. The dust was thick from the moving mob. Cattle, horses and stockmen seemed to be travelling in all directions. Some baulked at what was left of the fires, others charged through or tried to jump. A thousand tiny shining embers rose high into the night sky as our secure world unravelled.

'Let them go!' I yelled to no-one in particular. Of course no-one would have heard a word over the thunder of the cattle as they galloped their way to freedom on the edge of the desert.

Kelly was sitting up, all wide-eyed. Leisha had slept through the lot.

'The cattle have got away, my darling boy,' I said. I tried to settle him for another two hours' sleep and then took a look around to take stock. No-one had been hurt in the rush. The stockmen stoked the fires up and I filled the flour drum with water again for tea. Dreamer had taken the buggy to bring the panicked horses in. Sitting down on my swag, trying to find some warmth in my mug of hot tea, I whispered to Bob:

'Bloody hell! Eight days of hard riding for a good mob of cattle and this happens. What about the boys' wages? And we haven't been paid for months! There's never any money in this bloody company.'

He turned and looked at me with his piercing dark eyes, put his pannikin on the ground beside the swag, got hold of my arms just below the shoulders and lifted me straight to my feet. Holding onto me firmly, his dark eyes staring into my blue ones, as he did when I was in need of reassurance, his voice was soft but firm.

'Girl', he said. 'Get it together, you're stronger than that.'

I calmed down immediately, drawing on his strength. This was the thing about Bob – his self-sufficiency could be annoying, frightening and alienating, shutting me out and leading him to take big risks as if I wasn't there, but on the other hand, there were moments when that very same self-sufficiency was a deep source of reassurance for me. At a time when he had every right to be angry and frustrated, he was calm and solid and trusted me to look after myself.

He dropped my arms abruptly and moved off in the direction of the horses.

It was piccaninny daylight and the sky was filling with the beautiful soft pastels of first light. As I swung up into my saddle the breeze sent a cold shiver running through my body. I pulled my coat collar up firmly around my ears and decided to let the loss of the cattle go now so I could pull my weight, just like Bob said. We'd scout around for a couple of hours and maybe pick up the odd few head of cattle that had split from the mob.

The stockmen's spirits were down over the loss of the cattle. I told them not to worry, this sometimes happens, and we should remain strong. We were lucky and picked up between 30 and 40 head. I jumped back into the truck and told the men to head for the homestead. We would leave the Larawa area for now and give it a spell. We'd muster the island in the Mary River and make up for the loss. The boys knew the cattle were there and so did we: sweet country always draws them in. We would still get the dollars. This brought smiles to all our faces.

Sure enough, three days later we had a good muster and yarded about 300 head in the old wooden yards below the homestead. At daylight the following morning, we drafted and branded 69 cleanskin heifers and 61 cleanskin mickeys – young bulls. We let go bush 163 cows and calves and were left with 71 good bullocks for sale. It was by no means a disaster.

It was a beautiful June morning on Louisa Downs, three months after our arrival on the station, the clear blue skies reaching down to embrace the sunburnt earth. The desert wind was cool and at this time of the year it carried a glorious crispness. We were now well into the dry and as I watched the gentle breeze ruffle the spinifex heads around the storeroom, I was filled with the joy of life. Since our move to Louisa we had enjoyed a season of contentment, not without challenges but positively good for each of us.

Walking back to the homestead after distributing the morning's bread and beef rations to the camp, I heard Bob's cheery call.

'Sheryl, come for a drive with me and Kelly.'

Light-headed with my optimistic mood, I ran towards the back gate to join them. There I found Bob with his head down rolling his tobacco in the palm of his hand and Kelly sitting up on the bull-buggy beside him, pleased as Punch. I felt over-whelmed at the sight of father and son, one as dark as the other was blond. Then Kelly's childish laughter, as he gazed up at his father – he loved his dad – they were probably telling jokes. No, I thought, it wasn't hard to imagine my son's future. He'd be a Kimberley cattleman.

As I clambered into the buggy, Kelly climbed out and tried to get up on the bull bar. I grabbed him back immediately and tried, as gently as I could, to explain how dangerous that was.

Bob lit up his cigarette, pulled his Akubra down firmly on his head and off we went across the cracking claypan towards the windmill that supplied our water to the homestead. Because of the wind drought, the tank was low, which meant the jack pump had to be hooked up and cranked over. Kelly played around the tank while I helped Bob. Soon the old pump was blowing black rings of smoke as it spluttered into life. Satisfied it would continue, we got ready to return home.

Again, Kelly climbed straight up onto the bull bar and again I grabbed him.

'He'll be all right,' said Bob. 'I'll drive slowly.'

'No!' I said very firmly. 'He must not ride on the bar. Can't you see we'll lose him like this?'

I wrapped my arms protectively around my son and we rode home in deep silence. My body was trembling with the fear of that awful thought. How could any mother bear to lose her son?

At the beginning of June the wages cheques arrived on the mail plane. It was time to do a store run. By 1 am I was out of bed and was soon ready to carry my sleeping little darlings to the Ford. I had packed a thermos and corned beef sandwiches the evening before, so by 2 am I was carefully manoeuvring my way to Derby.

It was a five-hour trip: gravel and corrugated to Fitzroy Crossing, then bitumen from the Crossing to Derby town. It was slow and I would have to be alert at all times, particularly in the early hours of the morning as the cattle started to roam for new grounds to feed on.

At around seven we had breakfast at the Colac Service Station. I crossed the road to Elders, where Brian Moore always had the station stores packed and ready. Next came the post office to collect mail, then the ANZ Bank, then the chemist. Whoopee! It was worth checking the mailbag before leaving town, to make sure the company had been able to pay us our May wages as well. Before leaving Derby, I dropped by Lee Leiver's station outfitters. Kelly needed new desert boots and Leisha had an order in for ladies' shoes. Kelly's desert boots didn't fit – they seemed half a size too large – but he said he liked them and insisted on wearing them, as kids do. By 7 pm I was back at the station, more than a little weary, and the kids were sound asleep.

The following day – 13 June 1981 – was my thirty-second birthday, really just another day on the station. Bob seemed to be in some sort of pain, his horseman's walk more pronounced and his left arm – the one he put the siding knife through – was giving him hell. Pins and needles were going off in all directions, he complained. To kill the pain he drank too many gold cans and fell asleep at the dining table. At 2 am I woke to find Bob's side of the bed hadn't been slept in. This was unusual for him. We had a few unpleasant words as I tried to help him back to bed. It was rare for us to argue, but I was determined that the children not see Daddy, dirty and covered in cattle dust, still at the dining table where they had said goodnight to him the evening before.

CHAPTER 11

The Blackest Day
of My Life

*T*he morning after our disagreement, Bob was up, showered and busy as always. Men like Bob have very good work habits and the occasional night on the grog or a blue with the wife makes no difference. The stockmen were holding a small mob of cattle out on the river. Bob would pick up the rogue bulls that were upsetting the herd. My plan was to stay at the homestead for a change.

I noticed that Kelly was hanging very close to his dad and wanted desperately to go out on the muster with the men. I had never let the children go out to a muster without me.

'Kelly wants to go,' Bob said, looking straight at me.

'You know I don't agree and I don't want him to go,' I replied. I was still upset over our argument, even if Bob was in an apologetic mood this morning. But Kelly had recently turned five, and I could see how much this meant to him. I gave in and let him go. I put my arms out, gave my boy a big hug and kiss, told him to be very careful and let him go. Kelly put on his bull strap, his Akubra hat and his new desert boots. He raised his beautiful blue eyes towards me, put his hand out and touched me.

'Thank you, Mum!' he shouted as he ran towards the truck.

I turned to Bob and made him promise not to let Kelly ride in the buggy while he ran bulls – he must stay in the truck with one of the young stockmen. Bob agreed. I waved goodbye, with Leisha by my side. We watched their dust as they roared through the homestead gate in the direction of the river camp.

At sundown, Katie, who worked in the house, sang out to me from the laundry shed.

'Boss and Kelly boy coming, Missus.'

We ran to the front garden where we watched Bob pull up at the homestead gate. They were still some 250 metres from the house. I saw Kelly jump out to help his dad open the wire gate, and then help him drag it back against the fence. This told me the boys were following with the truck. From where I stood with Katie, it was almost like watching a long shot in a movie. The actors were performing on cue and everything was looking good. Had the scene been in close-up, I would have picked up the fatal flaw. Kelly had climbed up on the bull bar. The buggy drove through the gate but now I could see something was awfully wrong. I saw Bob get out of the buggy again. What was he doing? I stood there and watched as Bob picked Kelly up from the ground, lifted him into the buggy and raced to the house. Bob was in shock as he carried Kelly, unconscious, into the bed in the radio room. I couldn't make sense of what was happening, but I checked his pulse: it was terribly slow. He was not breathing. I screamed for someone to try the phone. It was out of sched time – the hours we had access to an operating line, which were limited to three set times per day.

'Just keep ringing!' I yelled.

Bob kept pushing the emergency button on the Flying Doctor radio, but it wasn't functioning. I grabbed the company radio's microphone and begged that if anyone could hear me, please answer, we had an emergency. Unbeknown to me, my mother picked up the faint call at Kilto and then phoned Kimberley Downs, who in turn contacted the Flying Doctor service. At long last Derby base answered. I gave my location and said I needed an aircraft in a hurry.

'Is the patient dead or alive?' asked the operator. I wanted to scream at him that this was my beautiful boy he was talking about. How could he possibly be dead?

Shawn Murphy, a friend from Halls Creek, picked up on my desperate call. He chipped in and said he was leaving immediately; he would fly into the station in 30 minutes.

'Good, please come quickly, Shawn,' I answered with my heart bursting. 'The strip will be lit with fires, you can land.'

Michael, with the help of those at the stock-camp, lit the fires down each side of the airstrip. It was completely dark now. I knew Shawn would come and I knew he would land safely.

I began to give Kelly mouth-to-mouth, holding his little suntanned arm and feeling for his pulse. Bob was hovering in the background, seeming lost, with nothing to do. Every second seemed like an endless, terrifying hour. I remember seeing Shawn through blurred vision, and everything else was in slow motion.

Then I felt the last three beats of Kelly's pulse. Tears were rolling down my face. I felt cold, I was shivering and shaking. Everything was out of focus.

'I can't find a pulse anymore,' I whispered to the others. 'Please, someone check, I can't find Kelly's pulse!'

I heard a gentle voice beside me.

'He's gone, Sheryl.'

Everything turned black. I remember nothing more. Sometime during the night I woke with every cell in my body aching. I got up and found Bob sitting at the dining room table with his head in his hands. I went looking for Kelly; I found Leisha curled up asleep and safe, but no Kelly.

No, nooooooo! It can't be true!

Suddenly I was screaming and out of control. Everything seemed like a nightmare. Someone gently led me back to bed. Bob's suffering was as great as mine, probably more, because his tortured mind would be blaming himself.

Somehow, without Bob being aware, Kelly had climbed up on the bull bar and sat there as his father drove slowly through the gate. In those fatal few moments, his foot slipped out of his too-large desert boot and he went under the buggy. There were no marks on him. He hadn't been run over; just a little scratch on his chin. Bob didn't know it then, but our boy's spinal cord had snapped high in the neck. Kelly's father was already a broken man.

The next day Martin Pearson Jones, owner of the Kimberley Hotel, Halls Creek, picked us up from the station and flew Bob and me to Halls Creek to identify Kelly at the small hospital there. My parents had arrived during the night to take care of Leisha, and took her on to Broome, where we joined them later that day. Father McMahon from Broome and Father Lawrence from Derby gave Kelly the most beautiful service and burial in Broome, the town where it had all started for Bob and me. I remember very little; I was caught up in my own private world of grief and pain.

Somehow in the weeks and months following, I struggled through the foggy cloud of emptiness and continual heartache. In the mornings I awoke with my body so tired from suffering, it was a battle to lift myself from the bed. There were black days when I so badly wanted to be with my son I would beg God to let me die so we could be together again. When the darkness lifted a little, I would remember I also had a beautiful three-year-old daughter – Leisha, who seemed lost and confused. Just by being there, and needing us, she gave Bob and me comfort. I could never accept my mother's view that my son was only on loan from heaven. If Kelly was God's child, why did He give him to me, only to take him away barely five years later? In my grey, cloud-filled and isolated world, I tried in vain to find a reason for his death. I started to read the Bible, which I'd never done before, in the effort to believe his death had some reason and to discover where he might have gone. But none of it made any sense to me.

My doctor prescribed medication, which sent me into a numb and unfeeling world of total blackness, but it was the only way I could get through the nights. As awareness returned each morning, so did the terrible realisation that Kelly was no longer with me.

During this time I dressed only in black. Like a cocoon, the traditional mourning colour covered my feelings and shielded my hurt. Whatever I picked up, I seemed to drop and break. I was frightened my life was spiralling permanently out of control. If Kelly wasn't coming back, how could I ever get better? Deep inside, I felt guilty: I knew Kelly had reason to be disappointed in me. I had always been so strong and in control, and I'd failed him.

As if things could get any worse, my Grandma Bond, from Fresh Water Rapid Creek, died from cancer three weeks after Kelly's tragic death. My mother took it stoically as ever, absorbing her own grief while shielding me at the same time. So deeply buried in my pain, I was barely aware of Grandma's death.

After another hysterical call from me, my parents decided to come over from Kilto and stay. Observing how badly Bob was affected, my mother was worried that he might do away with himself unless I pulled myself together. Her wisdom – not to mention the reassurance of Mum and Dad's very presence – allowed me to move out of my terrible black trance. I had to realise that I wasn't the only one suffering. I threw away the medication and discarded my cloak of black clothes. I also regained the ability to hold onto objects.

Soon enough I was back on the job; with the caring and loving support of the Aboriginal women around me, with their understanding and kindness, I got through it somehow. We would be working alongside each other when I would burst into uncontrollable sobs. I'd feel a supportive arm around me and would hear them whisper their own comforting mantra: 'Poor Missus, poor Yumun.' Jeannie had that natural empathy which many women, especially older women, have. Alma and Katie made sure I was never left alone; they looked after me as if I were one of their own. Looking back, I realise that there was much in their own lives that made grief, and death, no stranger to them.

One day I called out to Kelly and Leisha that dinner was ready, then was shocked to realise I'd overlooked his absence. Then I burst into tears. The women around me understood the pain my heart was suffering. I clung desperately to the support of my dear Aboriginal friends, these people with big caring hearts who helped keep me on track in some of the darkest days of my life. With their help, I was able to find the strength to survive and face the future.

When I look back on this time, I can see the beginning of a change in my life with Bob. His grief knew no bounds, but rather than express it he banished it to some dark recess of his soul, from whence it would surface in ever stranger ways. Bob was a changed man. Distancing himself from me, he kept repeating, 'It should have been me.' He knew he wasn't meant to outlive his son. I would try to find comfort with him but he would push me away. The silences grew longer, and longer, so that I found it difficult to communicate with him. Then he began drinking himself to sleep at night to take the pain away. Even though I never brought up the fact that I had warned him, he must have remembered. He seemed to hold it against me, that I'd had a premonition. But whatever was going on inside Bob was a mystery to me. He wouldn't let me in. He was a stranger to me. I could never bring myself to talk about the accident, and nor could he. In my heart I had blamed him, for a while, anyway. It was altogether too painful for words.

CHAPTER 12

Finding
a Future

Katie and Alma came to see me on the back lawn.
'We go picnic to Palm Springs, Missus, take Leisha.'
'Can we swim, fish? Are there shady trees?' I asked.
'Yes, yes!' They both nodded and their eyes lit up.

I quickly put together a tucker box of bread, beef, two
large packets of sweet biscuits and some fruit. Then I washed
out and put wire handles on two large Sunshine milk cans –
they make good billies and the water boils faster in the light
metal. I stopped by the camp on our way out, where Judy and
Biddy, two of the oldest ladies in the camp, climbed aboard to
join us.

As there was no such thing as a road into this secret place,
the girls guided me from landmark to landmark. The entrance
to Palm Springs was a gap between two high hills, wide enough
for only one vehicle. As I steadily wove my way in and out of
the rocky outcrop, I was stunned by the sight of beautiful
crystal-clear pools of water. I parked the Toyota and looked on
in amazement. The hills had closed in on us and formed a
gorge. Here was nature resplendent, from the brilliant colours
of the walls to the clear pools of water surrounded by evergreen

water plants and lilies. There were hundreds of tropical Livingstonia palms, their forked fingers pointing in all directions, and several majestic fig trees pumping the sweet aroma of their fruit through the gorge. Everything about the place was beautiful, so peaceful and cool with just the gentle sound of the spring water moving gracefully from one pool to the next. In the background I could hear the happy chattering of colourful birds going about their daily business. Occasionally the demanding squawk of a black cockatoo would break the spell.

The springs started high up in the rugged range, where waterfalls cascaded from one perfectly round granite pool to the next. Soon our trips to the springs became a regular treat. Every couple of weeks I would take the old people, mothers and children, for a picnic, sometimes to Palm Springs, other times to a waterhole called Me-No-Savvy, or to any one of the numerous lovely places on the station. These were rare moments of quiet amid a turmoil of grief. The moment I'd calm down enough to seek some happy memories, I'd break down crying again: those memories would remind me of what I'd lost.

Michael was bulldozing the track from the valley to Goat Paddock at this time, one blade wide. The fog was starting to lift from the valley as the first light of day appeared between the peaks of the rugged O'Donnell Ranges, spreading its golden glow around the valley floor below.

Bob and I were due to run the bulls that day. I followed him out with the bull truck. Soon we sighted a beauty, between 600 and 800 kilograms, all rippling muscle, in top condition with a set of horns that could punch a hole through the buggy as if it were cardboard. We stopped. I left the truck and jumped into the passenger side with the bull straps all hanging from the Jesus bar, which I was gripping fiercely with both hands, legs wedged firmly to left and right.

Bob's determination to down this huge beast was evident in the set look on his face, his old bloodstained hat pounded firmly down on his head. We swung in and out of the back-breaking gullies, around the edge of the buggar buggar country, pushing the bull back towards the flat, nearly wiping ourselves out with a low-hanging branch.

I found it hard to glance sideways to register the speed we were travelling, but knew it was fast. I remember wondering *Is he mad, or does my husband have a death wish?* I was absolutely terrified, for the first time ever. He was driving like a madman, carelessly, fearlessly. He seemed full of aggression and anger, prepared to do us both in. This was the first time he had driven this bull-buggy since Kelly died. Was Bob losing control? Fine, mustard-coloured dust was billowing up behind us. My pulse was racing, my palms sweaty. I tried to tighten my grip on the bar, and my legs held firm as we came up on the near side of this racing tonne of beef, every muscle in his well-formed body stretching out for freedom. As we lapped him around the claypan, his pace started to drop. Bob turned the wheel and gently nudged the rogue, who took offence and hooked the buggy. In response Bob accelerated harder, and brought him down with the bull bar over the near-side horn.

Over the side of the buggy I leaped, strap in hand. I wrapped the strap firmly around the bull's hind legs and buckled it before the brute had time to start fighting and hooking his way up and out.

Bob drove me back to the truck. I took the truck to the bull and dropped the slide down near his head. With Bob still in the buggy, I looped the head rope over the bull's massive horns and signalled Bob, who slowly pulled the huge weight up the slide and into the truck. In this time not a word was exchanged between us.

When the bull's head first touched the truck, I was on the top rail of the cattle crate on the truck's rear, pulling off the long rope and throwing on a short head rope. The rogue came alive. Now he was snorting, muscles rippling, head down, hooking and charging the truck every time it moved.

By now I had worked my way along the top rail to shorten up his rope. He saw my movement and charged toward me. Good! I tightened his head rope up short, took a deep breath and jumped from the crate to the dusty ground, sending up a small cloud of claypan around me.

I was to follow Bob, who had charged off in the buggy to hunt for more; we needed another nine to fill the truck. I was trying to understand the way he was, but he had unnerved me with his ferocious driving and his silence. So instead of following him, I turned the truck around and went home.

Bob arrived back an hour after me. From the kitchen window I watched him walk towards the homestead. He leaned against the kitchen door jamb and rolled a cigarette. I spun around, my fists clenched.

'Why? Why did you drive like a madman? You could have killed us both!'

He took an awfully long time to roll his cigarette.

'Is that what you wanted to do?' I screamed, in tears. 'Do you think Kelly would want us dead?' Answering my own question, I went on: 'No! He wouldn't want that! We have a beautiful daughter, remember? We have to get it together!'

I put my arms around him, but he wouldn't be comforted. After a pannikin of tea, he returned to chase bulls with the men.

Having finished our next stores trip to Derby, Leisha and I left the town later than usual, loaded to the hilt with the station stores, including cartons of bread and many cases of beer. The night air was humid, with some cloud about and hardly a star in the sky.

The road was slow, as a construction gang had been working to build it up ready for the blacktop. As I slowed to change gears and manoeuvre the Ford steadily down into the dry bed of Gap Creek, I felt my driver's side back tyre blow out.

'God, no,' I said aloud as I pulled the Ford out of the deep creekbed onto the rough verge of the road.

Leisha woke with a start. I explained our predicament as best I could. I comforted her; she was with me all the time now, but I worried because she hadn't asked about Kelly.

'Mum will fix it,' I assured her. 'If we're late, Daddy will come looking for us.' With my torch in one hand and Leisha on the opposite hip, I took one look at the vehicle and my heart sank. We were right down on the rim. Since leaving Fitzroy Crossing I hadn't sighted another vehicle, not unusual for this part of the Kimberley at this time of night. Our main road was rough, rugged and corrugated with lots of short deep creeks between Fitzroy Crossing and Halls Creek. Pulling a small tarp out from under the seat, I settled Leisha on the ground beside me.

'Stay there, while Mummy finds the jack and spare tyre.'

This wasn't nearly as easy as it sounded. I knew I would have to unload boxes and boxes of shopping to reach what I wanted. The night was pitch-black and my heart jumped when I heard a rustle in the high grass close by. Next came a *thump-thump* from further out. Leisha was on her feet, clinging to me for comfort. I reminded her of something Bob had often told us: if you can name the noise, then you don't have to worry. The first noise was probably a little snake or lizard that I had frightened when I placed the boxes on the ground.

'The thump-thump was a kangaroo checking to see that we were okay.' I probably sounded more confident than I felt.

There was no way I could get the jack under the Ford, with the vehicle so heavily loaded and the ground rock-hard. I gazed into the distance, searching for the glow of headlights and listening for the sounds of the station's Toyota, but no such luck.

I began unloading Bob's beer supply – carton after carton of Gold – until the Ford was half empty. I desperately needed to dampen the ground to help make it easier to hammer and chisel my way through the surface and get a block of wood and the jack under the vehicle. Using one carton of Gold as a seat, I dragged another carton up beside me and started popping tops. As the warm beer flowed over the side of the cans I took a swig.

Uuugggh! No wonder I don't drink beer, I thought.

Can after can I poured into the area, digging with a screwdriver to try to loosen the ground. About three-quarters of a carton later, and still stone cold sober, I had the block of wood and jack in position under the Ford. I always carried a water-bottle for times of need, but saved this for emergency rations for my girl. Fixing the wheel spanner in place, I climbed onto the handle with a grip on the canopy to steady myself and rock-and-rolled the first nut off. Then I repeated the procedure until I had them all loose.

Once the wheel with the flat was off, I wedged a tyre lever under the spare to lift it up and into place. Then I found I was able to push the tyre back onto the studs with my legs. It was an unladylike position, but a girl has to do what a girl has to do. After tightening the nuts in reverse fashion, I reloaded the station stores and the remaining golden ale. As I gently lifted Leisha from the tarp on the ground, she woke, rubbing her eyes.

'It's all right, my girl, Mummy has fixed the tyre,' I whispered. I settled her back in the front seat and manoeuvred the vehicle back onto the road. With both windows down hoping for a cool breeze, I heard the lonely sound of the curlew calling from the dark of the night. I remembered a story an old Aborigine had told me when I was little: that the call of the curlew was a sign a child had died in camp. A shiver ran through my weary body. The curlew seemed to express exactly how I was feeling.

All the lights were blazing as I pulled in by the freezer at the station homestead at 2.45 am. I carried Leisha into the homestead asleep in my arms and was hurt and dismayed by what I saw. The dining room was littered with empty beer cans and empty rum bottles. Maybe it was a hard day – who knows? Two of the contract bull runners were out cold, and Bob was asleep over the dining room table. This was becoming an increasingly regular event and I was just too numb to address it. It was another of those things I couldn't talk to him about. I closed the door, and fell asleep with Leisha in our bedroom. I planned to let fly on my 'rescuers' tomorrow, or today, or whenever I woke.

But the next morning, everyone was up and working at dawn. Over breakfast I had a crack at Bob and the stockmen, but they were looking so sheepish, with their weak and apologetic excuses, that I gave up. There was no use holding a grudge: there was too much to do.

The evening was cool for a wet season night and a good soaking had gone some way to quenching the thirst of the red earth and spinifex plains. There was little movement in the camp, just the old bomb vehicle that farted its way through the homestead gates around 10 pm. With Bob away at the Mango Farm near Broome, Leisha and I were sharing the double bed. I lay listening to the broken chatter as the Aboriginal men laughed their way through the homestead to their camp at the foot of the hill. Bull Pup ran out to the fence and gave a bark or two, then settled himself back on the toilet floor of the back veranda.

Kissing my girl goodnight, I thought that if Bull Pup wasn't worrying about the late arrivals, nor would I.

Around 2 am I woke to the most terrible wailing argument. People were yelling, dogs barking and rocks hitting an iron roof. I sat on the side of the bed for a moment, listening and trying to take it all in. It sounded like someone had come into our camp with a load of grog. I was far from pleased.

I checked that Leisha was still sound asleep and secure, threw on my jeans, shirt and boots, and made my way to the back door. Not wanting to draw the people's attention to the house and have to mediate with a drunken group at this hour, I took only a weak torch. I could hear someone stumbling around on the cement pavers. Bull Pup started barking uncontrollably, and next thing I was confronted with a drunken, unkempt Aboriginal male entering my house from the back veranda.

'You wait at the back door,' I told him in a clear, strong voice.

He mumbled and cursed, coming forward, ignoring me completely. Bull Pup was going absolutely berserk but had somehow locked himself in the toilet just when I needed him most. The bad-tempered, drunken stranger just kept coming towards me. It was all the more frightening because I was unsure of his intentions. There were no men in the house, just me, my daughter and her nanny, Andrea. I could feel my body start to burn with aggression: this bastard had no respect for me or my family. There was no way he was going to invade my space.

Raising my right arm and pointing towards the veranda, I said very plainly, 'Get the hell out of here. Get out of my house.'

He kept on coming. Bull Pup's barking and my raised voice had woken Leisha and the nanny. My aggression grew as I heard Leisha's frightened voice calling, 'My Mummy, my Mummy!'

He kept on coming. I suddenly lost control – totally out of character, but I was overwhelmed by rage. As he entered the lounge room, I hit him for all I was worth with my right elbow. The blow sent him flying back against the fridge alcove. Then, before he had time to get to his senses, I hit him again and sent him staggering across the enclosed back veranda. My pulse racing, my temper running hot, I ran at him and pushed him right out the back door where he landed among my prize cycads.

I followed him out and waited for the right moment to brain him with a not-so-prized pot plant. Out of the darkness came other Aboriginal voices that I recognised as friendly. Silently the men moved into the lit-up area of the back veranda. Before I had any idea what was happening, they had the stranger by the legs and arms and carried him out into the black of the night.

'You all right, Missus?' asked Jack, my yard man. 'That little Leisha all right?'

'Yes, yes, thank you. Thank you for following him up.'

I let Bull Pup out of the toilet and closed the door, chiding him. 'You silly old bugger, locking yourself in the loo and missing all the excitement.'

I made a pannikin of tea and settled my girl back into bed before creeping outside, leaving Bull Pup in the homestead yard. I worked my way over to the station store, where I stood against the corrugated-iron wall. Eyes slowly adjusting to the black of night, I could see and hear people moving from the camp up to the rocky ridge that ran along to the homestead. Kero lamps were swinging in the dark. There was yelling and abuse, and women and children were crying and wailing. A full-on fight had broken out, with sticks and boomerangs flying everywhere. My stomach churned. I slowly let myself slide down against the wall, hoping not to be seen. I was worried for the old people, the women and the children. With my chin on my knees, staring out into the dark of the night, I watched and listened. If anyone was hurt I knew the camp people would come to the homestead for help. A boomerang whistled over my head and slammed into the shed. Old Alex was a champion with the weapon. Smiling to myself, I knew the drunks wouldn't hang around his camp tonight. The stronger elders must have been driving the drunks out of the camp.

Thunder had started to grumble in the valley and the night seemed to grow even blacker as the first heavy, cold spots of rain fell. Raising my weary face to the skies, I let the icy coolness trickle over my face.

'Send her down, Hughie,' I prayed as I crept back to the homestead. 'Please! Send her down and sober the bastards up!'

The rain poured down even heavier. Back home, I peeled off my damp clothes and let them drop in a pile on the floor. As soon as I hit the bed I fell into a dead sleep.

In the morning I was called to the back gate by Jack.

'Missus, Missus, the peoples want to speak with you,' he said.

I followed him to the gate where 30 to 40 people from the camp had gathered. There was total silence as they waited for me to speak. Everyone looked fresh, showered and sober. I still felt like hell and I hadn't even had a bloody drink. I looked around the circle.

'Who brought the grog into camp?'

Arguing broke out among them until an old woman grabbed hold of a man in his early thirties and dragged him into the centre.

'This one, Missus, you growl him.'

I knew this woman. She wasn't the sort to stand for any nonsense. She pushed the offender up to face me. 'Say sorry to Missus,' she ordered him. He apologised. I asked him to say sorry to the people. He did, showing such remorse he was unable to lift his gaze from his dusty boots.

'Don't ever bring grog into Louisa again,' I said, loud enough for all to hear. 'Every stockman gets two cans at night and the women and children get one can of cool drink, and that's it. We have a good and happy camp, but with grog it's fighting all night. Do you understand me?'

I was gazing at his sick and sorry state, willing the message to sink in.

'Yes, Missus,' he replied.

'Okay,' I said. 'Everyone have smoko now and we'll do the store rations later.'

The people drifted off towards camp, chattering and sounding a lot happier. The offender moved off alone. He'd been publicly shamed and it would be some time before he got over it.

Another hectic mustering season was coming to an end, the toughest one of all for Bob and me. As we worked the cattle through the dusty yards, I was not always as alert and nimble as I should have been. I was inadvertently putting my own life at risk, my judgment clouded by my grieving heart.

Bob's suffering was masked with deep, dark silences. His own faraway thoughts were evident in his sad eyes. At night he buried his agony by drinking himself to sleep. There was nothing I could say to help him. Nothing could heal the loss of Kelly. I battled to keep up my confident exterior. I had to be strong for my husband and daughter. Any tears I cried now were shed within the four walls of my bedroom.

One day at siesta time, I was resting my weary body and as usual wrestling with an overactive mind. Somehow I fell into a deep sleep. Suddenly, an urgent young voice woke me: Kelly's voice.

'Mummy, Mummy,' he was calling.

'Coming, Kelly, coming,' I cried, sitting bolt upright. My chest was pounding – there was such urgency in his young voice. I raced to the door. All of a sudden I realised what I was doing. My mind was spiralling out of control; my world had become surreal. I collapsed sobbing on the bed. It was obvious we all needed a break, me most of all.

I approached Bob with the idea of a family holiday in Perth, where we could visit my mother's sister Aunty Alvis on her farm at Mundijong.

'I don't need a break,' he snapped. It was obvious that he did need one, but I wasn't going to force it. Leisha and I flew to Perth without him. Aunty Alvis met us at the airport and drove us out to the farm. It was lovely to see her and put some distance between us and the place where we'd lost Kelly.

'I've got no idea what life has in store for me next,' I sighed. Aunty was a good listener and on the way back to the farm I poured out all my mixed-up emotions.

'You should go and see our psychic,' she said. It was the first time I'd ever thought about such a course, and I was curious.

'I'll come along with you,' Aunty added. 'She might do you some good, as long as you don't take it to heart.'

A few days later, with dear Aunty Alvis behind the wheel of her little car, we made our way along a narrow road bordered by freshly-harvested wheat rolled into haystacks. In other paddocks wild oats billowed in the breeze. How different it all was from our wild red cattle station! In the distance I could see a blue roof, shaded by a single jacaranda tree.

The farmhouse was old but lovingly maintained. I had a mountain of tangled questions running through my head and I needed answers. At this point I was desperate to try anything. I was often emotional, with anger, restlessness and explosive frustration all competing for space. I'd lost my self-confidence, and was worried that my marriage would not survive. The rug had been pulled roughly from under my feet and I was struggling to keep my balance. Bob was retreating behind his wall of silence and dark depression; there was often no communication between us at all.

Aunty and I were greeted at the blue front door by the card reader, a woman in her early thirties who had a floaty floral dress, bare feet and a mane of long, dark hair. I walked into the farmhouse filled with apprehension, feeling like a child, wanting to beg Aunty Alvis not to leave me alone with this stranger.

She led us down a passage of dull timber floorboards that creaked all the way to the vacant room where the reading was to take place. The room was filled with shafts of sunlight pouring in through a stained-glass window, although the air felt strangely cold. She sat down on the naked floorboards and beckoned for me to sit opposite her. I shivered. Her voice was soft and gentle. She seemed hesitant and didn't always look at me directly.

One at a time she laid the large wooden Tarot cards on the floor in front of me. The first card to appear was black, sullen and evil-looking. It screamed of death. I felt frightened and my heart pounded in my chest. Now I felt hot and flushed as the psychic hovered over the card, looking at me. I knew it was Kelly's death.

The next card depicted my suffering and the struggle Bob and I were having. One at a time, she laid out the chunky cards on the floor. It was hard to believe that this woman, someone I'd never met, could be so in tune with my life.

'There is another male in your life,' she said hesitantly. 'He is closer to your own age and he will make you laugh and feel yourself again. When he is near, the hurt will ease.'

I had no idea who she was talking about.

'But be warned,' she continued. 'Do not confuse this friendship with anything more than that. You are extremely vulnerable. Should this friendship develop, its only purpose would be to ease the hurt of your loss.'

She dealt another card, as filled with foreboding as the first. I wasn't to know then, but it signalled the death of my Aunty Grace, my Grandma Bond's sister, three weeks later.

I floated out of the card reading feeling detached, unemotional, even peaceful. Who could the mystery man be? I could only think of a couple of the bull-runners. Yet her warning had calmed me. Whatever happened would turn out all right. And the break from the station had helped us; Leisha and I had reconnected again. We returned feeling a lot better. If only Bob had agreed to take a break as well.

Ten months later, at the Halls Creek rodeo and ball, I was to receive first-hand proof of the power of the Tarot.

It was a beautiful full-moon night and I was very glad I'd managed to persuade Bob to attend. He hadn't wanted to go. Along for the ride were two teams of contract bull-runners, led by Jack from New South Wales and Morgan, a very smartly-dressed man from Queensland. Both men were good company and I was looking forward to the evening. As usual, all the men and women were beautifully dressed and the band was pumping out some toe-tapping music. Once all the trophies of buckles and ribbons had been presented, I was hoping to dance the night away.

The music started and I looked at Bob, hoping he would ask me up for the first number. He shook his head. I assumed it was physical pain that robbed him of his interest in me. He seemed quite content to have a beer or three, as usual. Morgan, the bull-runner staying at Louisa, was tall with steely broad shoulders, sunburnt, rugged good looks and an air of experience. He stepped up and asked Bob's permission to dance with me. I thought his manners were superb and I enjoyed being treated as a woman. It was certainly a contrast to the way Bob had been treating me.

We moved out onto the dance floor, joining all the other station couples gliding gracefully around the floor. My body seemed to soak up the melody floating around the room. Morgan's grip on my waist was firm. I felt free and happy, loving the music, loving the dance. As we moved about the floor, our eyes locked, both of us hit with a burning desire flowing from deep within our bodies. He pressed against me and I began to feel frightened by my raw emotions. At that moment I would have done anything he asked. This moment had an intensity I had never experienced before.

In a dream, we waltzed around the floor, lost in the crowd and savouring each blissful moment. Then out of the corner of my eye I noticed Bob. He was watching me with terrifying intensity, on his feet stalking me among the dancers. He ghosted through the crowd, an implacable blackness in his eyes.

'I can't dance anymore,' I whispered to Morgan. 'I must sit with Bob.'

Morgan's grip around my waist tightened as he held me for a few more seconds. At that moment I think we both felt an aching need to be loved, to be folded into each other and forget the rest of the world. Then he released me, bowed his head, tilted his Akubra and thanked me for the dance.

I returned to Bob with a pounding heart. It was difficult to reconcile what had just happened with our everyday life on the station. He felt like a stranger – never more so than in the weird way he had followed me onto the dance floor. I suggested we leave and go back to the motel where we were staying.

The following day I summoned Morgan to the homestead. I had trouble looking him squarely in the eyes, but had the strength to inform him I had transferred his bull-running contract to Kimberley Downs. A good bull-runner was needed there and I told him he should leave immediately.

After those few wonderful moments of sexual awakening, I realised that it was with Bob that my destiny lay, that the sexual desire I felt with Morgan was a kind of grief-fuelled madness. The way Bob had woven his way through the dancers, half-crouched, while I was with Morgan, hadn't left me. My place was with Bob. He was telling me, with his eyes, that I must never forget that. Through our history, and our grief, he had cast a kind of a frightening spell on me. I silently thanked the psychic for her foresight and wisdom. And I was glad to have received her warning, which had perhaps saved us from a very messy situation.

CHAPTER 13

Trouble in
the Camp

*B*ob had finally taken my advice and had gone for some time out on the Mango Farm near Broome. This left Michael, old Bluey and his wife Rita, Leisha and me and a camp of 40 to 50 Aboriginal people. We were all good company for each other in our unique ways.

I looked out at the sodden paddocks and leaden skies. No mail plane, no mail. The company was four months behind with our wages – again. Sometimes this made me angry, knowing the cattle numbers we had mustered for them.

Bob came home a worried man, suffering not only physical pain but deep depression over losing our boy. Again I tried to help him, but I was unable to reach him. His moods were deep and dark and his silences lasted for days as his anguish and agony translated into a churning turmoil in his gut. His suffering was tearing me apart. In three days' time, on 24 April 1982, it would be Kelly's sixth birthday. I had been obsessively counting every week since my boy had gone. Once a month I'd been taking the 1200 km round trip to lay native flowers on his grave in Broome. I sat in my bedroom, shaking uncontrollably, letting my tears flow. I had been holding on so tight, just to keep going. To be strong for Bob, Leisha and myself. I was afraid Bob might do away with himself. I cried until I fell into an exhausted sleep. It was as if the wet season was playing itself out inside me and in a funny way, just as in nature, it was necessary.

When the day came, Bob knew and I knew and the whole homestead felt the change, but nothing was said. I felt that to raise the thing we were obviously both thinking about would only tear Bob apart more.

In June 1982, there was a sign that the Australian Land and Cattle Co.'s troubles were affecting the station, when the Aboriginal stockmen from town refused to help draft, due to unpaid wages. The Perth office was late again with payment, and the boys were perfectly within their rights. Who wants to work for nothing? I promised the boys I would travel to Derby that same week and draw money from my personal account to pay them.

At the end of August, Dad called from Kilto Station to say he'd heard that the cattle stations could be going into receivership any day. Rumours had been circulating for months. I called the company accountant, who promised to send all wages and monies owing.

The old 'red-headed terror' and his devoted Rita were on a heavy drinking binge again. Home was a caravan balanced on the banks of the Mary River, shaded by beautiful white river gums. The trouble with old Blue was he never knew when enough was enough. If alcohol was in sight, he figured his job was to drink it. I decided it was time to run a check on him.

The caravan was a total bloody mess. Usually it was neat as a pin with everything in its place, just like the windmill work he did for me. The first thing I noticed was that he'd had a few disagreements with some of his appliances. Blue's flash new electrical jug was caught up out of his reach in the tree, the toaster was on its side out on the claypan flat and an electric frying pan (I didn't even own one) was over the bank alongside Blue's pride and joy, the portable red Honda electricity generator, which was caught up in the mud and flood debris three-quarters of the way down the riverbank.

I stood and gazed around the camp, thinking, my God, will they ever learn?

Both Mr and Mrs Blue were out cold, Mrs Blue in the deckchair with her skirt up around her waist in a most unladylike manner and Mr Blue unconscious in a swag, wearing a bright red pair of jocks. Seeing him in red jocks alone was enough to break the tension, cracking me up. I never realised Blue was so modern. I let them sleep and returned about four hours later to find Blue staggering around.

'You got hit by a cyclone, Blue?' I enquired, half-seriously.

'That effing power plant is buggered,' he answered. 'All that effing gear is buggered, it's not good, Missus.'

'Well,' I said. 'You're a silly old bastard, aren't you? Once you chucked out the power plant, nothing electrical would work, Blue.'

As I teased him, patting him on the shoulder, I saw something that was hard to believe. His sores were moving. More serious now, I asked him if I could take a look. Sure enough, his arm was teeming with activity of the maggot kind.

'For Christ's sake, Blue, you're bloody flyblown!' I said in shock. I tried to stay calm, remembering reading somewhere that maggots were used to clean out wounds during the war.

'Shower and get yourself up to the homestead, I'll clean those sores up,' I told him.

Blue duly showered and followed me to the house where I checked each very angry-looking sore and removed the maggots with tweezers, drowned them in Dettol and covered the sore with Betadine from the medical kit. Then I issued him with a large portion of beef and vegetable stew and told him to sober up.

* * *

When Bob was around the homestead I would strive for moments of joy, a break from all the sadness. After the incident with Blue and his appliances, Bob and I had a laugh. But the happiness never lasted long before he would drift away from me. I was finding this hurtful and confusing.

With funds always short in the company, and diesel running scarce for the power plant, Michael – a constant support to me – and I kept on chasing bulls. We would leave home with Leisha and Katie sitting up front in the truck beside me. With Michael in the lead, we headed out well before sunrise, hoping to catch rogues as they moseyed out in search of an early-morning feed in the sweet country. We knew there were five good-sized bulls hanging around at Dickie Plains, but each time we made a run for them, we would only down one. The others would head into the hills through breakaway gully country. So far the score was two down, three to go.

One morning, luck was with us. The bulls – two dark and one roan – had more on their minds than heading for the hills. Grazing with them was a 'bulling' cow, or a cow in season, and our three muscled-up quarries were fighting and shoving each other in an attempt to ride her. By the end of the day I imagined she would end up shell-shocked, her insides incapable of carrying a calf.

Leaving Leisha with Katie in the truck, I jumped into the buggy with Michael and we followed the plan we'd worked out. Working the cow away from the breakaway country and out onto the claypan flat, Michael put a rope over her head and tied her to a tree. Thinking they had evaded us again, the rogues stretched out and took sanctuary beyond the gullies.

Back in the truck, we moved on and managed to pick up three more bulls, then another two further up the plains. My stomach was telling me it was well and truly smoko time. We found a shady tree and Leisha quickly abandoned the truck for the buggy, where she sat up behind the steering wheel, pretending to chase bulls. Katie and I got a fire going and boiled the billy while Michael was checking a tyre on the truck.

'No hotplate, Missus,' Katie called.

We waited for the fire to die down, then moved the coals gently aside and cooked our steak and onions on the post-hole shovel. A pannikin of tea, a steak sandwich, and I could put my grief to one side. But when the working and eating was over, it would return, a familiar ache. As I stretched out on the ground, I watched the truck rock as the captured bulls settled themselves down.

On returning to the plains we left our truck under a shady tree some distance from our tethered cow. The three rogues were again showing some interest. I climbed back into the bull-buggy, a firm grip on the Jesus bar, as Michael swung in after the roan bull on the outer edge of the claypan. Around we went, spraying fine dust. The roan swung around as if to aim for the hills and Michael answered by coming up on his near side. The bull turned to hook the buggy and went down in a hurry. I strapped him, and away we went after the other two.

The next down in size was a dark, moody middleweight. He immediately decided to take a swing at us, hooking the side of the buggy with a mean-looking horn the size of a man's arm. He struggled to pull his horn out as he pounded along beside us, tonnes of beef in a fearsome race against the inevitable. We stopped and backed off, circled around him, and came in on his near side. The beast stretched out and started to gallop away. With his cap pulled down firmly over his sandy hair, my younger brother worked along with him. By now the rogue had had enough. As he swung to hook the buggy, Michael accelerated suddenly. Losing his balance, the rogue went down. Strap in hand, I hit the ground nearly as fast as he did, lapped the leather around him several times and buckled him up.

The third bull was lighter, more nimble and ready for a run. Michael accelerated to come up on his near side. There was no certainty that we'd get him as he stretched his well-toned body out. Tightening my grip on the Jesus bar, I wedged my legs firmly to take the weight as Michael slammed on the brakes and put the buggy into a spin. By now I was saturated in dust. I glanced toward Michael as he calmly manoeuvred the buggy into a wide swing around the breakaway and across a short creek. On the other side we came face to face with the nimble rogue. We positioned the buggy until we were on his near side. Exhausted, the bull turned to hook the buggy and we brought him down too, as gently as we could to minimise bruising.

Michael dropped me back at the truck and we loaded the three from the claypan flat, let the cow go and headed for home, happy and weary with a load of eight good bulls. I arranged with the company's Perth office to run 10 bulls to Broome, where the buyer, Gordon Bryce, would make the cheque payable to Shell Depot Derby. We could then load the drums of diesel and petrol we had ordered and return to Louisa. This was the way we kept the station operating.

After spelling the bulls in the yard, the plan was to travel to Broome in the cool of the night, as the days had become hotter and quite humid. I worked my way through the round yard, opening all the gates, planning on closing them on the first 10 bulls through.

Making sure I'd swung the round yard gate back properly, I climbed on the top rail with a firm grip on the oversize yard post. Michael could see that I was out of the way. I called him to push them up when he was ready.

I noticed that old Blue had arrived at the yard. He fell out of his Toyota, cursing and abusing it, half-cut again.

'I'll give you a hand, Missus,' he sang out, waving his arms. Too late, we heard the thundering of tonnes of galloping beef –

86 bulls rushed through the yard. I only wanted 10! The round yard was bursting at its sides, the gate somehow closed itself and the bulls were jam-packed on both sides. The old wooden yard was straining; I could hear the Cobb & Co.'s rattling. A rail cracked and the whole yard began shivering and shaking. Could we hold them, or would the yard give out altogether? Before I knew it, I had fallen in on top of the bulls. I was shocked, in total disbelief, but had no time to feel frightened.

Stretched out and face down across the mob, I knew I had to get out quick and not let myself slip down between those solid walls of muscle or I would be crushed to death. Lying across the bulls, stretching my body and fingers as far as I could, I strained to reach the weld mesh on the gate. The movement of the mob rippled outwards. I could almost grip the gate with my outstretched fingers, but then the surging mob carried me away. I was afraid to call for help, afraid that my cries would rally the bulls around harder, afraid that the old wooden yard would give up altogether. I was in and out of myself, as if this wasn't quite real. It seemed like forever, the longest minutes of my life. After the third or fourth attempt, my outstretched fingers reached the weld mesh and I gripped with every ounce of remaining strength. Somehow, I pulled myself across the bulls and arrived, shaking, on the top rail. I had got myself out of a lethal situation.

Shivering and dazed, I tried to take in the scene. Where was my brother? Mike hadn't even seen me fall in; he was too busy telling Blue to bugger off when the bulls rushed.

'Yumun! Yumun!'

Trying to focus, I could hear Alex's voice. Then I saw Alex, Ringer and Frank standing around me, looking very concerned.

'I'm okay,' I said. 'I must load the bulls.'

Michael was with me now, and I decided to let the men load the truck. I walked from the yard to get the head ropes ready to tie them head-to-tail once they were loaded. With the truck full, I climbed onto the crate and started tying. I threw the head rope over a set of strong horns and tied them off to the top rail, to prevent the beasts wrecking the truck and bruising each other.

I was going well, although I still felt light-headed as I moved from bull to bull. Working my way down the truck, I flipped the head rope over the massive horns of the second-last bull when the next rogue to be tied hit the back of the truck with a hell of a crash. The dried timber panelling splintered, and enough panels broke to give the bull a glimpse of freedom. I quickly shortened up and tied off. By now the whole truck was rocking, as the bulls all started to tug on their head ropes. Then came the loud crack of another panel as the last rogue made his break. I froze. Fear came over me. I felt cold, I could not move. The more the truck rocked, the tighter my grip on the top rail became. I could hear myself calling for Michael in a hoarse whisper, terrified that I might fall into the truck with the bulls. What came over me, I don't know. Maybe it was delayed shock. My dear brother and faithful stockmen were probably wishing I'd left some of the jobs for them. Michael had to prise my grip from the top rail, slowly help me down and place me in the buggy. Then he asked one of the stockmen to deliver me to the homestead. I went to the freezer, got myself a drink, and sat on the lawn staring at the stockyards. I'd never come so close to a serious, serious accident.

Luckily, Michael was able to repair the back panel for the trip to Broome. Once the bulls were loaded, old Alex came to check on me.

'We worry for you, Missus,' he offered in his quiet way.

'I know, old man, I'll be very careful,' I replied with tears in my eyes. Once again I opened the floodgates and had a good cry.

CHAPTER 14

Let It Rain

*E*arly 1983 brought the promise – or threat – of more rain.
I sat on the veranda, watching the dark thunderheads
beyond the cattle yards. The infectious laughter of the camp
children echoed as they played in the pools of water covering
the claypan flat. I knew that most of their blankets and clothes
were soaking wet from the heavy downfalls that had lasted
right through the wet season.

After each cloudburst, if we were lucky the sun would come
out and the old wooden cattle yard would burst into colour as
the camp women rushed to hang blankets and clothes out to dry.

'Missus, Missus,' called Katie. 'That Sandra got broken
this one.'

She pointed to her thigh bone. Holy hell, I thought, as I
raised myself from the lounge chair and hurried towards the
back gate where Leslie had arrived, carrying his six-year-old
daughter Sandra. She was screaming in pain.

'You should have sent for me,' I said quickly, glancing at
the bone protruding between her groin and knee. Tears were
rolling down her dear little face and she was screaming her
lungs out in sheer agony and fear. Sandra's high-pitched

suffering soon brought Michael and Bob to the back veranda. It wasn't something you could ignore.

We laid Sandra on a firm bed on the veranda. Since we were still in sched time, I grabbed the phone and gave the handle a really good crank. I stated the situation and was immediately put through to a Halls Creek doctor. While I was on the phone, Michael and Bob sawed down the wooden handles of two lawn rakes for splints. Sandra's dad sat by her side, trying to comfort her.

With the Flying Doctor kit open by my side, I listened to the doctor's instructions for drawing up the correct amount of morphine. Bob came to help, double-checking the dose, while Michael got the Ford ready for Sandra's evacuation to Halls Creek. I shuddered at having to inflict more pain on her with the uncomfortable trip, but knew it would bring her relief. We waited for her to settle with the morphine and moved her on our homemade stretcher to the back of the Ford. The police had informed us that the medical team were leaving Halls Creek immediately, coming towards us with a police escort.

By this time we'd almost forgotten that the roads between Halls Creek and Fitzroy Crossing had been closed for days. The creeks and rivers were up and down like yo-yos, and the roads were dangerous – boggy and very slippery. But this was an emergency and we had to get through somehow. The airstrip was out, so there was no other way but to plough onwards and meet somewhere in between. The distance to Halls Creeks was about 140 km, which could take an hour and a half in the dry season, but three or four hours, or more, in the wet.

With Sandra peacefully sleeping for the time being, we were able to concentrate on the task of delivering her safely. We wound our way down the track while the hail and rain pounded so heavily on the cab roof it drowned out our voices. I was filled with uncertainty: the night was pitch-black and the road a bloody disaster. Bob took the lead with the blue Toyota, Michael and I following in the Ford. We slipped and slid from one side of the road to the other but somehow progressed, in and out of swollen angry creeks that had never even existed before the rains.

I checked on Sandra and offered a little prayer as I sought a firm grip each time the vehicle slipped to the edge of the road. *Please God, help us get this little girl through tonight.*

We arrived at the Mary River. The only sign of the causeway was where the flood debris was banking up. In the vehicle's spotlights, the river churned past us, searching for an outlet for its tremendous foaming power.

After loading the tray of the Toyota with large rocks to hold it down in the floodwaters, Bob manoeuvred his way across. I checked on Sandra; now it was our turn. The rain hadn't eased up, and the flood was still rising.

Down into the murky waters we went, the water tugging at the vehicle. My grip on the wheel tightened. There was a sudden shock of cold water swirling around my feet, then a bubbling sound and a feeling of drifting . . . then relief as the tyres gripped the opposite bank. Yes! A massive sigh of relief as I opened the doors and released the floodwater from the cab. It had risen to cover my ankles.

Sandra was starting to murmur. It seemed like hours since we'd left the homestead. Patiently we ploughed along the road until we hit an unnamed creek which had turned into a swiftly flowing river. My heart sank – it was a raging torrent, even worse than the Mary. We had no choice but to stop. The rain had paused too. By placing a stick in the bank we could keep an eye on the water level as we waited, hoping to see the lights of the doctor and police on the other side. The mosquitoes were thick, and the bullfrogs were calling out to one another. Then, more heavy drops of rain started to fall.

Frankie, a family friend, holding me at the Fresh Water Rapid Creek camp.

Me, aged one.

Gran made these fancy-dress costumes for my brother Bruce (left) and me, Fresh Water Rapid Creek.

From left: my brothers Michael, Eric, Bruce and Darryl in the canoe that an old Aboriginal man from Yirrkala had given us.

Relaxing with my mum at our picnic spot at Melville Bay. I was about 16 when this photo was taken.

Nineteen years old and straight out of Arnhem Land.

With my beautiful boy Kelly on Napier Downs, 1976. He was just four months old.

With Bob on Oobagooma Station in 1971. We'd just been told by Monty, the station owner, that he wanted us to muster bloody donkeys for pet meat. We weren't amused!

On Blina Station with my girl crew, 1979. We were a happy bunch.

With Bob on Kilto Station, 1981. If I'd known we would lose Kelly only four months later, I'd never have left Kilto for Louisa Downs.

From left: Kelly, a friend and Leisha on Kilto homestead steps in 1980.

The homestead at Louisa Downs.

Looking up Christmas Creek on Bohemia Downs.

Top left: A four-year-old Leisha with stock camp damper on Bohemia Downs.

Top right: Old Blue, my windmill man, mechanic and jack-of-all-trades. He was a tough old bastard, but I couldn't help but love him.

Right: Alex Gordon, my very dear friend, always had that faraway look in his eyes. Alex guided me through my early years as manager on Louisa Downs and Bohemia Downs, and was there for me while Bob was away contracting.

My brother Michael, patiently watching while I strap a bull. 'Put some muscle into it, sis!'

My foot is holding the bull's nose down while Michael dehorns the beast.

Katie and Robby in front of the Louisa Downs' homestead.

Robby and I watch the children play in a spring on Bohemia Downs.

Rangy bullocks, old cattle yards and pretty skirts.

Sundown on Louisa saw the stockmen and their wives gathering after a hard day's mustering.

Bob in deep thought,
Louisa Downs.

Leisha (left), Kristy and
Robby waiting for the
cattle to be yarded at
Louisa Downs, 1985.

Jimmy Marshall was my right- and left-hand man. He stood by me through thick and thin.

Michael tangling with a scrubber bull.

A successful yarding on Louisa.

Yarding on sundown at Louisa Downs.

Robby and me by our man-made billabong on Kimberley Downs, the home of our 'pet' crocodile Dundee.

Leisha in a barrel race at the Turkey Creek rodeo. She won a buckle for this ride.

I loved the time Leisha and I spent together. Here we've just been for a late afternoon ride around Mount Marmion.

Robby following his mate to the airstrip on Kimberley Downs.

While he was away contract mustering, Bob would occasionally come home to Kimberley Downs to see if I needed a hand, 1989.

A yard full of cattle on Fairfield Station.

Enjoying life in the southern country of Western
Australia, 2006.

As the morphine injection wore off, Sandra's cries of pain were becoming louder, her little body trembling in fear. I wanted the doctor *now*.

Then the first set of lights appeared in the distance, followed by another set. In no time the doctor and police were on the opposite bank – but with this creek raging between us, we might as well have been miles apart. Sandra was starting to scream her lungs out and I tried to comfort her, rubbing her arm and assuring her that help was coming, knowing she would need more pain relief.

To the left of the crossing in the middle of the creek were some strong-looking gum saplings. We planned to get the wire rope across to the other side and hook it up there so that the doctor, with a firm grip on the rope, could work his way back across the river. There was no way a vehicle could cross.

Then, against Michael's and my wishes, Bob dashed into the river. One minute he had hold of the wire rope and the hook at its end, and the next he had slipped and gone under the rushing water. In the headlights, we saw him struggling as he surfaced downstream. I felt sick with fear, screaming out to him, but he didn't answer. He knew how dangerous this could be. Bob wasn't as agile as Michael or me, and I had a gut feeling that he had gone in with a death wish: if the river was to take someone tonight, he thought, let it be him.

Bob struggled back to the bank on our side and trudged up to us in silence. We still had to get someone across. Michael took hold of the wire rope with the hook and battled further upstream. Bob held our end of the rope, and I screamed at Michael not to let go. Outside the range of our headlights, visibility was nil, and I knew that if we lost anyone in these raging floodwaters, we'd never find them tonight. I kept the tension on the rope as Michael bobbed in the floodwaters, then felt massive relief to see him grip those saplings. The current had such strength now that mature gum trees were leaning right over.

Between the gums and the opposite bank the floodwaters were too deep for a vehicle to cross. We paid out enough slack for Michael to unroll the heavy wire rope and, after many attempts, he was able to get it to the opposite bank. The two vehicles were then hitched up, facing each other across the torrent. I backed up the Ford, which put tension on the rope, and Michael worked his way back across.

Sandra's screams of pain were now non-stop. I could see the brave doctor was anxious to attend his patient and, with the police's help, he strapped his medical bag to his back. He entered the raging river. The current grabbed him and pulled him under. He surfaced, only to be dragged down again. I was terrified. Then he surfaced again, but no sooner did he raise his head above the murky waters than he was pulled under again. We kept the tension on the wire rope as the doctor finally worked his way to our side, safe but exhausted.

He injected Sandra with some morphine, and we all waited another couple of hours, which seemed like an eternity, while the creek dropped.

Sandra was transferred to the ambulance; we turned around and worked our way back home. It had been a very long night. Some months later I had a phone call from the police and was asked if I would consider this rescue mission an act of bravery.

'No,' I said. 'This is a way of life!'

We expected risks, and Sandra's survival was at stake. There was something different about Bob's effort to get across the river, though. He wasn't acting out of bravery – more a mixture of self-destruction, grief, and a deep wish to take control again.

I kicked Bull Pup out from the toilet to make room for a vigorous attack on the bowl with a brush. Katie was busily flicking the straw broom over the back veranda to the music of Slim Dusty. Our clean-up was suddenly brought to a halt by Bull Pup's aggressive performance at the homestead gate.

'What's wrong, Katie?' I asked.

'Steve Hawke, Missus,' she answered and kept on sweeping, not worried that the dog might want to take the visitor's leg off.

'Who, Katie?' I asked again.

'That Steve Hawke fella, Missus.'

Troubled thoughts were racing through my mind. We had a very large camp of Aborigines and were not willing for outsiders to create unwarranted problems, as had happened at Noonkanbah. Restraining the dog, I greeted Steve and suggested he speak with Bob this time. It was nearly midday and I watched the two men as they walked out the back gate. Soon they had found a rocky outcrop where they could sit down in the fiery heat and talk. They remained there for several hours until Bob returned to the homestead and Steve left without a word.

'He's all right,' Bob said. 'He's trying to help the people get some land for a school. Some of them want to break away from the Louisa camp.'

Norm Cox and some families had been camping for some time in the area they wanted to call their own, near a rocky outcrop about 5 kilometres from the homestead. Neither Bob nor I could see any problem in their wanting a school. In fact, we thought it was an excellent idea that the children could be educated on the station. It wasn't a massive land claim; they simply wanted a few acres to build a school and community. Bob's only worry was that it would become a huge rubbish dump. We approached our company and in time the Aboriginal group were granted their land.

Noonkanbah had the only other school in the Kimberley where the Aborigines incorporated their own language in the daily lessons. Yiyili, the new school, would do likewise. It had to offer the children a better future than no schooling at all. The existing educational situation was to split families up and plonk their children in town schools, with mothers camped at ration camps on the edge of town while the fathers stayed working on station stock-camps. There were broken families Kimberley-wide. By asking for the land, and by getting it so peacefully, Norm Cox, Steve Hawke and Robin Dickinson, the school's first teacher, had set a precedent for the Kimberley. It also transformed our slightly wary attitude to Steve into a friendship.

One Tuesday in April 1983, Bob was on Kimberley Downs Station and I was left in charge at Louisa. That year the East Kimberley was receiving record rainfall – all roads were closed, and the rivers were running a banker. I can't say a long wet bothered me. I loved the cooler nights, with bullfrogs croaking and the wonderful sound of rain tumbling on the tin roof. Our red pindan earth had quenched its thirst a hundredfold, and was now producing luscious feed. Louisa was having its highest rainfall in its 30-year history.

The word from the camp was that the Mary had broken its banks. Or, to put it another way: 'Big floodwater coming this way, Missus!'

I sent one of the stockmen with a note to Bluey's camp, about a kilometre away on the flat, telling him to move to higher ground by the homestead or the windmill shed. I saw no sign of Blue and assumed that the river must have been dropping. Another possibility was that Blue didn't believe it would be a threat to his camp. Sometimes it was difficult to get through to the old bushman. I couldn't exactly order him to move his van. He had to want to do that for himself.

At 11 am, Katie ran into the homestead.

'Missus, that floodwater coming this way,' she said, pointing to the hill closest to the Aborigines' camp. There was still no sign of Blue. I asked the camp kids about him.

'Nah, nah, Missus,' they chorused.

'He might still be down that river, Missus,' one little girl volunteered.

My house girls returned to camp to rescue their belongings and help move the old people onto higher ground. Michael, Leisha and I jumped into the Toyota and headed towards Blue's camp.

Driving around the foot of the homestead hill, I gasped with shock at the sight of the rushing wake of brown frothing water racing towards the cattle yards and Aborigines' camp. What was once a crackling claypan flat between the Mary and the homestead was now a torrent of floodwater.

Not sure whether we should risk going further with Leisha, I decided to drive and search until the floodwater was halfway up the Toyota's door. Michael stood on the back searching for signs of life. With my hand firmly on the horn, which was starting to sound rather sick, I was hoping to draw Blue's or Rita's attention.

Goannas and snakes were swimming past us. I could not believe how quickly the floodwater had eroded the track. Down we went into a huge pothole which stopped the vehicle completely. My heart skipped a beat as the warm, murky floodwater washed in around my knees. Grabbing Leisha and hoisting her onto my shoulders, I got out of the car and worked my way through the pindan-coloured water full of lizards, spiders and spinifex particles, towards a gatepost that still had a few centimetres showing. The top strand of barbed wire was exposed – we could use it as a guide back towards the homestead.

I assured Michael I would be all right hanging onto this post while he ventured towards the windmill and pump shed – now half-underwater – to try to find Blue and Rita.

'Be careful, but please hurry,' I said as Michael headed off. The undertow of the red water was terribly powerful, tugging at my jeans and shirt. Ants and spiders wanted the last centimetres of dry gatepost as much as I did. My long hair had fallen down into the water, collecting spinifex particles which irritated my neck. With one arm gripping the gatepost, I held firmly onto Leisha's leg.

'Are you all right, girl?' I asked.

She never complained and took all the outback threw at her in her little stride. There was no sign of Michael; I grew anxious. The floodwaters had become deeper and stronger and we'd lost the barbed wire. Leisha and I started calling. Over the roar of the water I heard Michael answer. Looking his way, I could see three heads bobbing above the water. He yelled for me to move on up the fence. But neither Bluey nor Rita could swim, so I stayed put and as soon as Michael reached the fence, I grabbed Rita's arm and told her to slowly work her way along the fence, keeping a firm grip on the barbed wire, which was now well under water. Michael was more or less carrying old Blue. If he hadn't, I'm sure we would have lost him. It was dangerous and exhausting trying to keep Blue's and Rita's heads above water. Slowly we moved along the fence, pushing flood debris out of our way to keep a firm grip on the old barbed wire, which was cutting into my hands under the water. All the way, Leisha sat quietly on my shoulders. About 150 metres out from the homestead, I could see and hear the dogs barking excitedly; they would run into the water, get carried down with the current, get out and run back again. Then, along the ridge came my house girls, Katie, Alma and Jeannie. Tall, slim Katie came down into the floodwater and worked her way along the fence line, grabbed Leisha from my shoulders and worked her way back.

'Come on, Rita, keep going, not far now,' I said. It was a slow process. Rita was so small and frail, I had to push her whole body along, keeping a firm grip on the barbed wire. Snakes, goannas and spiders continued to float by in the swirl of water. 'Fair go,' I said out loud, slapping away a goanna who was desperate to use our heads and shoulders as a dry base.

I glanced ahead to see the stockmen and families running along the ridge towards us. Many came out into the murky waters to help. Finally on dry land, we slumped on the ground. I gave a thought to the faithful Toyota, now fully submerged except for the top of its cab. Then, with jelly legs I helped Blue and Rita further along the ridge to the homestead. My girls made a big pot of tea and we all sat and rested. As much as I enjoyed a solid wet season, there were limits!

By 1984, the company had gone into receivership. Kevin Meyer, the Receiver Manager, was by no means a cattleman, but was having a go.

Over the phone I had put a deal to Bob which I intended to lay on the table to Meyer. Bob had reservations, which infuriated me. He really hated change, but he grudgingly made the trip back from Kimberley Downs for the negotiations.

The evening before Meyer arrived, I had a rough contract written up. Bob and I would both resign from our job as manager. Bob would become a contract musterer. He could find work Kimberley-wide, or contract himself back to the station. I was looking for a way to get ahead. I had more faith in Bob than he did in himself now, but I knew what a good cattleman he was. I also thought that if his mind was pre-occupied with this new venture, it might help ease his pain and grief. The receiver could hire a new manager, or perhaps I could apply for the manager's position in my own right.

Bob came around to my way of thinking, and the gamble paid off. Kevin Meyer granted Bob the contract to muster the company's properties – Louisa, Bohemia, Kimberley and Napier Downs – and I was given the management position of both Louisa and Bohemia Downs.

I was very grateful for the opportunity. There were only two other women who managed properties in the Kimberley. One looked after 20,000 acres outside Derby, the other 600,000 acres near Fitzroy Crossing. I promised myself not to let the side down. For years I had wanted to break away from being an underling. Bob worried over dragging the family around the Kimberley chasing work, but the way we'd arranged it, we'd have a permanent base, and with him receiving 50 per cent of what we delivered to the meatworks, there was the potential to make much better money. If we both worked hard, the light would be really glowing at the end of the tunnel. Continuing solely on a manager's wage, this would have been difficult.

Our financial situation improved overnight. Bob did a muster on Roebuck Station outside Broome, and his share of that one muster was more than our wage for the whole of the previous year!

Bob was more or less based at the Mango Farm south of Broome now; it was a central place for the new business. Working apart, we seemed to be getting along better, and I knew that if I had a problem he was always there for me. In some ways I was relieved to be away from him, running the stations myself, without his temperamental behaviour and black, angry moods.

Leisha was now six years old. She was a healthy and happy child and wonderful company for me. But lately my beautiful, bubbly daughter had lost her spark and was sleeping a lot. I was becoming frantic. There was no pain, and she didn't have the flu. With no idea what could be wrong with her, I raced her to

Broome Hospital. A doctor raised the possibility of flu or a virus, but with Leisha feeling like a dead weight in my arms I was not entirely happy with this diagnosis; in fact I was terribly worried. I walked in silence towards the exit, thinking I'd take a plane to Perth for a second opinion.

Bobby Telford, the head nursing sister, called out to me to stop. She questioned me, then asked me to wait while she consulted with the doctor again. Within the hour, my darling girl was flown to Derby (which was the major local hospital at the time) by the Royal Flying Doctor aircraft, and was diagnosed with Murray Valley encephalitis, caught, they said, from a mosquito bite.

We were on tenterhooks, hoping and praying the encephalitis cells would not multiply. If they did, she might become fully or partially paralysed, or slip into a vegetative state.

Panicking and running on autopilot, I raced to the Mango Farm to inform Bob, grabbed some clothes and arrived back in Derby in record time. I was shocked to see my little girl in a semi-coma. It brought back memories of Kelly, she had so many tubes connected to her body. Why I did this I will never know, but I asked the nurses – who in turn had to get permission from the doctor – to disconnect the tubes. This was probably not a smart move, but I was adamant, and they consented. I felt that Leisha, who had never been parted from me, needed the closeness of my body more than she needed what was in the tubes. I lifted her floppy little body from the cot and laid her on my stomach on a hospital bed. In happier times, when she would need comfort, this was where she would like to curl up, always on my tummy with her face snuggled into my shoulder.

I willed her to get better. I prayed in silence. We slept, I believe, for eight hours and both woke at the same time. The hospital staff never had to reconnect her to the tubes, and were amazed at the speed of her recovery. They didn't even need to administer more medicine.

More tests were done, including a lumbar puncture, to see if the positive cells had multiplied: they had not. Leisha and I lay alone, day after day. I was fired with a single-minded determination not to lose her. I *knew* she would be all right: I have no other way of describing my certainty. On the fifth day, after she'd steadily recovered and the doctors had consented to let her come home, I loaded the Ford with stores, plug tobacco, frozen bread and cool drink, and Leisha and I headed back to Louisa. I was profoundly happy to have her well again and by my side.

'Missus, Missus!' called Alma.

'What's wrong, Alma?' I asked.

'That old man, that old man,' she said, pointing with her chin but not saying his name. We had many older men on Louisa, so without knowing who she was talking about I dutifully followed her down the hill to the camp.

At the camp I was met with total silence, just a lazy breeze through the cattle yards gently scattering some leaves. I went over to Alex, who was sitting on a flour drum. He stood up to greet me. I took his hand and whispered quietly: 'What's wrong, old man?'

'This way, Yumun.'

The camp people were staying out of sight in the shadows of their corrugated-iron huts and bow-shed humpies. The 20 or so inbred, hairless dogs were quiet for once as I carefully made my way under low awnings, around open fireplaces, dodging hanging billy cans and sleeping dogs till we reached the old man's camp. Knowing that all eyes from the shadows were on me, I looked at Joe, the oldest man in the Louisa camp, lying on his stretcher bed. I walked across the well-swept dirt floor towards him. Two blue-eyed dogs sat by his bed, watching. I moved closer to check the old man's pulse.

'Old man, old man,' I whispered, my eyes filled with tears. I pulled the old grey swag blanket up over his body and paused for a minute to gain my composure. A little ray of sunlight had forced its way through the rust holes of the humpy and was throwing gently moving patterns over his body.

I later estimated that Joe Nipperiappi was between 90 and 100 when he died. He had never been to town. His people had first followed the station mustering camp for the scraps of beef and damper left behind, and it was the same trails which had finally led them into the Louisa Downs Station from the O'Donnell Valley.

As I slowly wove my way out of camp, people emerged from the shadows of their humpies, looking to me for an answer.

'Old man finished,' I said softly. 'He was a very old man, his body very tired, old man finished now.'

The camp people wanted the body buried at the station. I agreed, as long as I could get permission. Why bury him in a town when he had never visited one? On the edge of the rocky plateau 100 metres from the homestead was the grave of the white man Frank Cox, who'd founded Louisa Station. The Aboriginal people and I decided we would bury old Joe next to him.

I called Welfare in Halls Creek and asked would they obtain permission for me to bury the old fella on the station. The police and Welfare were most helpful, and a light aircraft was arranged to take the deceased to the Fitzroy Crossing morgue.

I marked out the area and filled a 44-gallon drum with water to dampen the ground. It would be hard going with only a crowbar and shovel for tools. Working in the early morning and in the cool of the evening, we took it in turns loosening the rocky ground with the crowbar and shovelling out the grave. Five days later, we had finished.

Aboriginal people had gathered at Louisa from stations and communities near and far. Ringer, Frank and young Eric, three of the stockmen, went out and butchered a killer, which gave us sufficient beef to share around. It was Saturday 25 February 1984, when a plane burst out of the clouds, circled the homestead and landed with the body, back from the morgue. In the blue Toyota, I drove the coffin around the old wooden cattle yard to the burial site. Because the Aboriginal people wanted this burial, I suggested one of them conduct the service. Coolibah Quilty proceeded to give the most beautiful and moving sermon, followed by hymns sung by Norm Cox's girls, who had voices like angels.

Somehow I found myself balanced on the rim of the grave, the only white person, rocking gently with the mass of mourning people, terrified that I might fall in. Then I heard Coolibah say what a good person I was, and 'the sorry they feel for Missus, and the sorry they feel for Kelly boy'. With the mention of dear Kelly's name the painful memories came flooding back. I let the tears wash my face, knowing that although I felt sorry for the loss of the old man, it was Kelly I was crying for.

Around this time I discovered some very positive news. I was pregnant again and was quite sure I was carrying a boy whose name would be Robert Kelly, Robby. Bob came back to the station to hear the news, and pulled me onto his knee, where I sat with the biggest smile ever. We were both over the moon. It had been three years since we'd lost our boy, and deep down we hoped this would help heal our grief and bring us closer together.

It had been two years now since Bob started contracting and I'd begun managing on my own. Not much had changed, except I didn't have to consult Bob before making decisions. Bob told me I was doing a good job, and I was pleased he'd come back to contract for me. Leisha and I were doing fine, but we always looked forward to Daddy coming home.

Our chopper pilots, Ken and Bob, arrived ready for a muster in the area between Pond Spring and Me No Savvy. I had to drive into Halls Creek in the truck to pick up flour and rations, and also to bail out Chatterbox, one of my stockmen, and any others who had decided to join him for a short stay, not exactly a free one, in Her Majesty's quarters in Halls Creek. There were sore heads and huge smiles all round.

The chopper muster went smoothly, or as smoothly as it possibly could, considering that at least two-thirds of these cattle were pure rogues and had never had contact with man. Descendants of cattle that were first driven into this country, they'd multiplied healthily, taking up residence in the outlying areas of valleys and rugged ranges. If we could outsmart them, and yard them, they meant dollars on the hoof.

Even though the country had just come through a good wet season, with plenty of feed and young, tender spinifex, the 700 head the choppers had in hand had stirred up great billowing clouds of dust as they filed down our hessian-covered wings into the portable yard. The soundtrack to this spectacle was the clashing of horns as the dominant bulls tried to force their way though the mob, and the constant call of cows trying to track their weaner offspring.

The cattle troughs were hooked up to the water tanker, so with a bellyful of water the cattle might start to settle. We could then jump into the buggies and head for the homestead.

We had the right helicopter pilots. Skogy had given flying away. He'd lost an arm in a freak car accident when a semi-trailer's loose rope had wrapped itself around his elbow while it overtook him. Bob and Ken were bringing in larger numbers of cattle, and quicker, than mounted stockmen. Helicopter mustering was cheaper and much more efficient, and if the cattle were handled right from beginning to end there was very little bruising. I felt sadness as I thought about the future of the horse-plant musters and the future of the Aboriginal stockmen. I shuddered to imagine the damage this would do to their families. With helicopter mustering, we hired six men compared to a team of eight or 10 stockmen on horseback. Progress was putting Aboriginal stockmen out of work, leaving many lying around their camps or hanging out in towns. But I also understood the need for progress: the stations couldn't remain viable otherwise.

I was highly pleased with the muster, estimating we had achieved about 700 head yarded plus more than 50 good bulls. I watched closely as two of the larger bulls muscled their way through the yard, bellowing and locking horns in a show of authority. You could hear the *brrrrr, brrrrr* of the big fella as he kept locking horns and shoving the smaller brindle one about the yard. We worried about the massive horns and the bruising and holes they might punch in the other cattle. Gangrene set in quickly in this country.

Down in the yard, Bob disconnected the hose from the cattle trough. Michael moved the water tanker closer to the yard to get extra slack in the hose, turned up the pressure on the water pump, then hit the bulls with as much pressure as he had. But it didn't seem to be working.

By now the dominant bull had shoved the brindle onto the yard panels. Grey dust rose above the mob. The portable yard was moving with the force of the fighting bulls and we had good reason to be worried. At that very moment the big fella charged at the brindle, missed and picked up the portable yard panel with a horn. The panel lifted off the hinges, and suddenly tonnes of beef were racing for freedom. There was an immense thundering mixed with the cries of calves, flesh clashing with flesh. Bob and his right-hand man, Browny, jumped into their bull-buggies and drove directly into the missing yard panel with engines revving amid the blinding dust. With visibility nil, they were risking their lives. Fierce determination to keep as many of these cattle in the yard as possible was written on Bob's face.

My stomach churning with fear and anger, I sat with eyes fixed on the scene. For a moment it was all confusion, a stubborn man and a thick wall of dust. Then magically, the cattle stopped spewing from the enclosure and I could see Bob's and Browny's silhouettes in the grey bulldust as they pulled the yard panels together again. We estimated our loss at approximately 100 head. Sometimes my dear husband frustrated me with the risks he took, especially since our family was growing. But I knew how he hated anything to beat him. Bob came home to Louisa to do this muster for two days with us, then had to leave . . . to keep mustering!

Leisha's cousins from Broome had already arrived. Her many playmates from Yiyili and the station camp were there too, letting fly with squeals of laughter as they played chase and tag around the back lawn. Bob too was back on Louisa for his girl's seventh birthday and was sitting with his pannikin of tea on the back veranda talking to Alex and Ringer about musters, helicopters and horse plants. I had succeeded in keeping Leisha's doll cake hidden from her in the coolroom. It would shortly take two of us to carry the cake out.

Leisha's eyes were glued to her dad and me as we steadily moved across the lawn, carrying the large cardboard box from the coolroom. Placing it on the table on the veranda, we gently lifted the box from the cake. There were screams of excitement all around, but not a word from our girl. She just stood and stared at the cake in amazement.

'Happy Birthday,' we sang. Leisha walked slowly around her cake, gently touching, poking and feeling to see if this beautiful doll was edible. The doll cake, just like the ones I'd had as a child, was nearly as tall as she was!

My pregnancy had gone without a hitch. I was eight months along and big, although not as large as I was with Leisha, who'd weighed nine and half pounds at birth. All I wanted was to produce a healthy boy, a brother for our girl and a son for Bob.

It was time to wait patiently for the wet season to start. Huge red dust storms would be seen in the distant desert. Leisha and I would watch the storm for days as it rolled towards the homestead. Once the wall of red dust hit the front horse paddock, we'd run like hell into the house and lock it up. It didn't matter how hard we tried to block every tiny hole, with towels rolled up and jammed under doors, sheets and blankets over bedding, and windows – when the storm had passed we'd need a road sweeper to find our way out. Louisa's average 350-millimetre rainfall meant every drop was a blessing. The first storms would have the cattle stormchasing, and waiting on green pick – the first green shoots of grass. Leisha would be running around all covered in red mud, or flat-out making mud pies with her mates. Once the initial groundwork was completed, the big thunderheads would roll in and give us the works. The torrential rains would bathe the countryside, leaving it clean and fresh. Then the heat and humidity would ease and we would start to appreciate the wet season as the surrounding countryside burst into life.

CHAPTER 15

New Life, New Challenges

*T*he trip into town from the station felt long and uncomfortable. My feet were swollen, as if I'd eaten too much watermelon. I was booked into theatre at 8 am on Tuesday 28 November 1984, and I couldn't wait. I'd already been informed it would have to be another caesarean. It seemed unfair that I couldn't experience natural childbirth, but there was no choice.

Prepared and gowned, lying uncomfortably on the hard theatre trolley, I told the nurses to write Robert (Robby) Kelly on the name plate on the baby's cot. Perhaps, thinking I was desperate to have another boy, they were humouring me. There was silence, and one of the nurses asked if I had any girls' names, 'just in case'.

'No!'

I was adamant I was having a boy. They wheeled me into the cold, stainless steel, sterile theatre. As the mask was placed over my nose and mouth, I began to shiver. I remember being asked what sex I thought my baby would be. It seemed the theatre staff were laying bets. After that, the blackness came quickly and pleasantly.

In no time at all the darkness was lifting and I could hear excited voices. Someone close by whispered, 'You have your son, Sheryl.'

Someone else scolded that person; maybe they wanted Bob to tell me. I felt terrible pain in my lower abdomen. Still sedated heavily, I couldn't speak; deep choking sobs and tears of joy escaped, mixed with pure happiness, and then blackness again.

I woke several hours later to see Bob, Leisha and the Irish nun in charge of maternity admiring our beautiful new addition. At seven and a half pounds (3.4 kilograms), Robby was the spitting image of our beloved Kelly. We were so lucky and so blessed! I walked from the hospital with our new precious cargo snuggled lovingly in my arms, blissfully happy. I lifted my gaze from baby to an immaculately-restored early model Mercedes Benz, white with huge rolling mudguards and large gleaming chrome grille. I hesitated, admiring its beauty for a moment, and turned to Bob.

'Isn't it a beauty?' I said. He placed my hospital bag on the back seat.

'It's yours. Thought you might like it,' he said in his bushie drawl.

'It's for you, Mummy,' Leisha chorused loudly, skipping excitedly around the car.

'It's beautiful, just beautiful, I feel so lucky,' I enthused, walking around the car with our baby in my arms. I'm an old-fashioned girl at heart and had always loved the early model Mercedes. But I'd never imagined Bob would ever see any sense in me owning one. This beautiful, fully-restored Merc was a loving gift from the heart from my husband and daughter. How Leisha kept this secret between herself and Daddy, God only knows.

* * *

Louisa was a hive of activity. The stockmen had erected the portable yard, and the bull-buggies, cattle trucks and water truck were ready to go. I woke around 3 am to the distant call of a dingo, a matter of concern since my bull terrier bitch was on heat. She was a brazen harlot at these times and I needed to check on her. My movement disturbed Robby, but there was a lot to do. After breastfeeding I would change and settle him before starting breakfast for the stockmen and pilots. My life ran on routine while Robby was small. But there were days I would feel absolutely shell-shocked and exhausted, wondering if I could keep up the pace. A long-time mate, Jimmy Marshall, joined me in the kitchen and proceeded to put together the lunchtime tucker box and billy cans for the stockmen. Breakfast was over and there was still no sign of sunrise. The peacefulness of the night was rudely broken as two choppers burst off the ground, sending dust and spinifex flying. The chopping sound faded in the distance as they headed for the plains to begin the day's muster.

The big news was that the Premier was arriving, to confer on a new arrangement for sharing land with the Aboriginal people. Across the country, there were legal moves afoot to ascertain Aboriginal people's rights to land. I'd sent a message to the camp: 'The Premier fella is coming to Louisa. When the planes circle the house come up and sit on the homestead lawn. Maybe you might want to ask this boss fella something.'

I sent a stockman out in a buggy to check out the airstrip and clear it of horses. All the camp dogs and my bull terrier had to be chained up. We couldn't possibly have the dogs disgrace us by latching onto the city folks' long town pants!

I said to Katie and Alma, 'Let's make a chocolate cake for this boss fella; he's the boss of this Western Australia country, Labor boss. They're coming for a big smoko.'

There were the usual last-minute dramas. Would you believe I burned the bloody cake and ended up with a restoration job on my hands? That meant cutting off the top, turning it upside down and smothering it in very thick chocolate frosting. Also, some of the dining room chairs were a bit dicky. If you sat on them with your weight distributed to the good legs, things were okay. But I had never had the leisure to test all the chairs.

'Them gardiar [white] men coming, Missus!' called Katie, her long skinny legs striding out towards the kitchen to check on the kettles.

Two aircraft circled the homestead and landed. West Australian Premier Brian Burke emerged first, then Kevin Skipworth, Tom Stevens and Ernie Bridge, all members of parliament, and then two others. The party walked up the path and into the lounge, where they found seats around the table. Katie and I made tea in the huge pot. The visitors seemed terribly quiet for a group of men and I had the feeling some were slightly uneasy. Maybe they had never used a pannikin to drink from before, or maybe their concentrated looks came from trying to ride the wonky chairs.

With as much aplomb as I could muster, I proceeded to pour tea, then feverishly passed around the restored chocolate cake before the heat had the frosting dribbling down the sides and all over our distinguished guests.

To eat his cake quickly, Premier Burke went to move his chair in closer to the table. Oops – his chair gave way. He put up a tremendous fight to keep it intact, but the chair got the better of him and he went arse-up. Head down, I scurried to the kitchen, unable to contain my laughter. Katie and Alma both had their heads on the benches trying to hold themselves together.

'Come on, Katie!' I urged. 'These people are distinguished guests.' It must have been the way I rolled my eyes to the heavens – laughter got the better of her and she crumpled to the floor.

'Get up, Katie!' I hissed.

'Nah, too weak,' she replied, still shuddering with laughter.

I pulled myself together, went out and apologised to the Premier, for what I don't know, and said: 'Most chairs are like that around here, you've just got to learn to ride 'em.'

The Premier spoke to the 40 or so Aboriginal people on the back lawn. His government wanted to restructure the Kimberley cattle industry, he said. Existing properties would be broken up into smaller holdings. There were 'too many multinational companies using the stations as a tax dodge,' he said. His government wanted to improve the way the land was worked, to make it more productive.

We'd already heard rumours that the government wanted to resume all of the Australian Land & Cattle Co.'s properties and give them to the Aboriginal people. Another rumour suggested that the Burke government was looking at our neighbouring properties, Go Go, Cherubun and Christmas Creek, to purchase and split into smaller holdings to give all cattlemen in the Kimberley an opportunity to have a go independently.

Bob and I had heard about this already, so it was easy for us to understand – but not so for the rest of the Premier's audience. After waving the distinguished guests goodbye, I turned to the Aboriginal group and asked: 'Did you understand any of that?'

'Nah, nothing,' came the reply.

Wednesday 24 April 1985 would have been Kelly's ninth birthday; so Bob drank himself to sleep at the dining table. I found him with his head resting on his arms. My insides ached. I hesitated, taking in the sorry sight, unsure of what to do if I roused him. Would he abuse me and tell me to just leave him be, or come quietly? I shook him gently. His clothes were covered in dust from the cattle yards and his odour hung heavily in the air. His eyes were dark and mournful as he raised them. I dissolved into tears. Kneeling down and wrapping my arms around him, I wept, letting free my bundle of grief. Kelly's birthdays were the days we suffered most, reliving that terrible, unforgettable accident. There was no response from Bob, not even an arm thrown around me. He was as hard as an empty shell.

In July of that year, we had a visit from a new Receiver Manager, Peter Melsom. Later that evening, Bob, Peter and I sat on the veranda negotiating a plan to work the stations out of receivership. Was it possible for us to work together, for Peter to clear all company debts on the way through, while meeting expenses, and the station come out in one piece?

The answer was yes. We had mustered all the company's properties and had a rough idea of cattle numbers. Peter was upfront, admitting he knew absolutely nothing about cattle – he didn't even have a clue what a steer was.

'It's a mickey minus balls,' I said. 'A mickey is a young bull with balls.'

I remained as Peter's manager, with Bob as his contractor. So began an excellent 10-year working relationship.

In mid-July, my first cousin Mary asked if I'd take her son Guy for two weeks over the school holidays. There hadn't been a lot of communication between Mary and me over the years, but if Guy wanted to spend time with me on the station that was fine.

Guy, 14 years of age, was an active smoker and knew a few more tricks than I did. I flatly refused to supply him cigarettes, so he broke into my bedroom and helped himself to the Log Cabin tobacco. I wasn't pleased – this was the only tobacco theft in all my years on stations. I may have felt better if he'd been a stranger, but he was family!

One evening while Guy was with us, I noticed a huge fire burning down by the Aborigines' camp. Every so often I heard a small explosion. This surely had something to do with the fact that my stock of pressure-pack toilet spray had been disappearing rapidly. As luck had it, Bob and Browny were at the station. When Browny heard the explosion, he jumped in the buggy and caught Guy red-handed teaching the young Aboriginal boys how to make magic.

I spent the following days trying to phone Mary, but to no avail. I needed to send Guy back, or to talk about how to deal with him. A week later, I lifted my head from the evening dishes at the sink to see fireballs glowing all over the hill between the homestead and the camp. Realising the house was far too quiet, I started yelling for Leisha. I ran into the darkness with torch in hand, and found her; she'd followed Guy outside. Then I sat down to wait for him.

He walked in from the dark shadows, all front, not a shred of remorse. To provoke me further, he carried a boombox blaring horrible, distorted music. My blood boiled. I grabbed him by both shoulders.

'What did you think you were doing?'

'Nothing,' was all he could say. Grabbing both of his hands, I rubbed them in his face.

'What were you doing with my diesel fuel?' I asked.

'Nothing.'

This little bugger had tried to make petrol bombs, using diesel instead of petrol. Thank God. Had he known more about bomb-making, he could have killed Leisha, the camp children, and himself. By this point I'd had an absolute gutful.

Mary had disappeared into thin air and didn't seem to be coming back. We heard that she'd taken off with a truck driver, but didn't know for sure. I called Mary's mother, my Aunty Merle, a severe migraine sufferer who had been left with Guy's two sisters, Del and Kristy.

Since my finances were more secure than Aunty Merle's, I suggested that I try to keep the children together by taking the two girls as well. But they would have to live on the station. She sent them from Dampier, roughly midway between Perth and Louisa. The plan was then to fly all three children to Broome, where they could enjoy a week at our log cabin and all the fun of the Pearl Festival.

Guy was 14, Del 11 and little bewildered Kristy four. Within an hour of their reunion, fights had started between Guy and Del. I already understood why cousin Mary had disappeared! The obscene, abusive language and the damage to my house had me wanting to pull my bloody hair out and disappear too. They hadn't an ounce of respect for each other, or anyone else for that matter.

This was not good. I worried for my own two, who had never witnessed anything like this. Robby was only one year old.

I sat Mary's children down and laid it on the line.

'I want you all to understand that if you don't shape up, you will be shipped out. I'm not your mother; I'm trying to keep you all together as a family. This is your only chance.'

After a few sullen moments between the older two, it was on again. Guy antagonised the girls by trying to flush Leisha's pet joey down the toilet. I'd had enough. I contacted the Department of Welfare's head man in Kununurra.

'How many spare bedrooms do you have at your house?' I began. He was speechless. I repeated my question.

'How many spare bedrooms do you have, sir? There is no bullshit attached to this. I'm sending you a couple of abandoned children.'

He flew to the station within days. After a round-table discussion, Del and Guy made it clear they wished to return to the city. There was no way I was going to let little Kristy be shunted in and out of foster homes. She was a lost, wistful little soul, clinging to her security blanket day and night. I simply wished for her to be happy and secure, and if her mother couldn't supply this, I could. Many family members and friends told me not to get involved. Even though I had two young children of my own, a household and a cattle station to manage, I could not bear see this girl go without. A little love and care cost nothing.

The older children became state wards and I became Kristy's guardian. I had tried, with the older two, but they were beyond my help. Bob never complained, bless him, and he put up with my rescue efforts like the good man he was.

Over time Kristy came out of her shell. With a child's innate love for animals, she joined Leisha feeding the poddy calves and riding the ponies around the backyard in the afternoon. She had moments of sadness, sitting with her thumb in her mouth, thinking her own thoughts, curtained behind her thick mane of honey-coloured hair, but her face would light up when Leisha took her out to play or look after the animals. I couldn't help but love her; she fitted into our family as if she were our own.

Late one afternoon Bob suggested Leisha and I go for a run out towards Three Mile in the buggy with him.

'We can check the bull numbers,' he said. 'May be worth a run to fill the last truckload for the season.'

We didn't find many until we came upon a lone rogue crossing a barren flat. Bob accelerated. Sensing something uncontrolled in Bob's aggression, I grabbed Leisha with my right arm, the other hand in a death grip on the Jesus bar. I started yelling at Bob: '*Not with Leisha!*' Screaming, begging: '*Please, not with Leisha!*' My heart galloping and my breathing shallow, I was full of outrage and disbelief.

'Let the bull go!!!' I screamed. 'Let the bastard go, Bob!'

As I screamed, the wind whipped saliva from my mouth. Bob made no facial movement to acknowledge me, just total dark concentration and determination. He was a wild animal mesmerised by his prey.

The massive black rogue would probably be the largest, most aggressive bull we'd run that season. He had a huge hump and an enormous set of horns with deadly tips. I'd seen maddened bulls like this simply hook and drop the guts out of a horse. His appearance was overwhelming me. I shoved Leisha under the dash and secured her between my calf muscles, my legs wedged to hold me in place. Afraid for my daughter's life, my palms sweaty, I tightened my grip on the Jesus bar, realising we had no choice but to ride this out. I felt like I didn't understand Bob at all. Sometimes I didn't know who he was.

Bob threw the buggy into a skid, sending up clouds of dust and gravel as he worked to dodge giant antbeds and work the loner around the flat. Just as Bob thought he had the big bugger lined up to go down, it swung around to hook us, narrowly missing me and tearing the back of my seat apart with his razor-sharp horn.

Wind whipped my face and hair and carried my screams off with the dust. Bob maintained his speed, roused all the more. The buggy flew forward into a spin. Bob gave a gentle push under the beast's ribs as it attempted another attack on the buggy and down it went, simple as that. With strap in hand I was ready to go. In spite of myself, this was one job I would enjoy.

'Stay with Leisha!' Bob demanded. He grabbed my bull strap to secure the enraged animal. It was all muscle and fury now, with the strength to lift the buggy up and down like a yo-yo. Bob had only walked from the tail to the head of the beast when it pushed the buggy off, the strap still loose, and got to its feet, a tonne of might and muscle. We were in trouble, big trouble. Bob stood, motionless. One move and he would certainly be dead. His gammy arm and hand, without an ounce of feeling, had let him down badly. The loner twitched its muscular body in rage, its piercing black eyes darting at us. It was important for us to stay calm and quiet. We also had to do something, quickly.

I slowly inched my way to the driver's side of the buggy, still with a firm grip on Leisha, keeping her safely by my side. Bob remained motionless.

'Hang on very tightly,' I whispered to Leisha. I moved slowly, as if in a trance, engaged the four-wheel drive, then found second gear. Every fibre in my body was stretched to breaking point, knowing I had to hit the bull hard and fast to save Bob's and our own lives.

'Ready,' I whispered to Leisha. By now the bull was tossing, snorting and throwing his head and shoulders about, stamping his feet, making agitated swishes of his tail. He'd had enough? Well, so had I.

With the clutch half-out, my right foot pressed the accelerator pedal to the metal. Dust and gravel exploded from the spinning wheels. Down went the monster with a thump, sending bulldust up all around.

Bob made a mad dash to the buggy; I slipped back across to the Jesus bar, still gripping Leisha, who had shown no fear throughout the drama. Letting the bull up, Bob lapped him around again, came up on the near side, put him down and securely tied him, no mistakes. My bull-headed husband had caught his bull!

Afterwards I confronted him. This had been a stupid thing to do. I was absolutely furious with him for putting our daughter's life at risk. 'It was too bloody close!' I shouted. Typically, he had no answer. He rolled his cigarette and walked off, finding something else to do.

Alex had escaped to the back lawn for some peace and quiet. Asking Katie to make smoko, I took two pannikins and joined Alex. I liked to sit and talk to this old man; he was an important part of my life. As an elder, Alex never liked the younger ones to call me by name. He would come forward and correct them.

'Yumun,' he would say – 'Missus Boss.'

Squatting under the jacaranda tree, our talk came around to Alex's early days on Bohemia and Louisa, about the white managers and some of the horrifying treatment dished out to Aboriginal people. This old man didn't drink and he never lied to me, so I believed what he said.

He told me I was 'a good Yumun, not like them before'.

'What did they do, old man?' I quizzed him, thirsty for Kimberley history.

'Him bad, Yumun, him bad,' he whispered, head bowed.

'Tell me, old man, it was a long time ago,' I gently questioned. 'What did he do?'

'That gardiar boss,' nodding his head in the direction of Bohemia. 'He want one boy's woman. That gardiar manager send that stockman to fixem that fence in morning,' he quietly continued, scratching the ground with a twig.

'Then what?'

'Not long gardiar boss follow him on horse,' his voice low. 'He had a gun.'

We were sitting cross-legged on the ground. Alex lifted his head and looked at me with sad eyes full of misery.

'Only gardiar fella come back, Yumun.'

Battling to keep my emotions together, I looked into his clouded, sad eyes.

'Poor Yumun,' old Alex whispered.

I felt that Alex was sorry he'd told me the story; he hadn't wanted it to make me sad. But I really wanted to know more.

'How many people?' I asked.

'Plenty, Yumun, plenty,' he answered, ever so softly.

'Where did he put these people?' I wanted to know it all.

'Deep hole, long way, those hills.' The old man pointed with his chin in the Bohemia direction.

I couldn't believe it. I felt sick to the stomach. It wasn't the first story I'd heard. In the early days, some white managers treated Aboriginal people worse than mongrel dogs. When we stood up, I put my hands on Alex's weary shoulders and gave them a squeeze. I shook my head, saying nothing, as I turned towards the coolroom to collect his beef ration for the day. I was thinking, Let's leave it behind, let's leave it in the past and move on. I'd had so much pain, I couldn't handle any more.

The next Sunday was picnic day for women and children, and we made a pilgrimage to Old Bohemia Downs. With the guidance of the elder women, I tracked in and around rocky outcrops, across the claypan, dodging antbeds, down and through shallow creeks towards the range, until we were suddenly at the homestead. Here were the remnants of years gone by, stone placed upon stone, the walls of a once-sturdy building. The goat pen was still standing, empty now, of course. I gazed into the distance, still troubled by the whereabouts of the 'deep hole' Alex had mentioned. It disgusted me to think a white manager handed out such deplorable treatment to unfortunate stockmen to satisfy his own lust.

* * *

One Monday in September 1985, I woke at 1.30 am. The night was a black one, with a light fog and the air damp. I felt lethargic, but it was time for another ration run. I tenderly secured my three sleeping children – Leisha, Robby and Kristy – to the front seat of the Ford. They never murmured or complained about such privations; they seemed to understand. Such dear children, I thought. How I loved them.

Without taking my eyes from the road, I drove from Louisa towards Fitzroy Crossing, stopping several times, honking to wake up cattle bedded for warmth on the blacktop. But south of Plum Plains I was afflicted by every driver's worst nightmare: I fell asleep at the wheel. Over the verge we sailed, ending in a heavy thump. I woke in shock, disoriented, with the vehicle still travelling at great speed. The trunks of ghost gums were flashing by and there were some very solid antbeds looming. My heart pounding to choking point, I offered a quick prayer to my God and put every ounce of skill and strength I had into pulling up safely.

The first thing I did was check the children. Although they were strapped in, we had been bounced around heavily. Their beautiful, scared, sleepy eyes were looking to me for reassurance. Tucking them in again, I tried to be reassuring. 'It's okay, go back to sleep now, Mummy will fix it.' I was speaking with more confidence than I felt.

The realisation set in: it was freezing cold and my teeth were chattering, and all I could see in my headlights were the ghost gums against the blackness. Unsure of my bearings, my mind still fuzzy, I checked the Ford for any leakage of fuel or water. It was all right. Tired and shivering, I couldn't seem to locate the road. Eventually, I crossed my arms over the steering wheel and slept.

I had driven in and out of Derby town every fortnight for five years. This was a warning. I was becoming tired, with too much driving.

Two days later I woke from a deep afternoon sleep to a heavy pounding on my bedroom door.

'Missus, Missus,' hollered Katie, against a background of noise and confusion.

'What's wrong?' I answered wearily.

'One boy stole Mallick's bull-buggy.'

'Which way have they gone, Katie?' I hurriedly pulled on my boots. She pointed her chin past the old wooden cattle yards.

'Three Mile?' I asked.

'Ya, ya.'

At the back door, Jack, my yard man, was pacing.

'It's Jeffrey in that buggy, Yumun,' he said. Jeffrey, Jack and Alma's boy, was my Kelly's old playmate. The memory of Kelly's death flashed through me. I raced to the linen cupboard and retrieved two clean sheets – why, I don't know.

'Katie, you mind the kids!' I yelled. 'Jack, come with me. I may need help.' As it turned out, this wasn't a good call.

My gut told me this was urgent. I drove the Ford to the Aborigines' camp and yelled for help. Three stockmen jumped onto my vehicle. I shuddered as I drove through the gateway, past the site of Kelly's accident. No-one had any idea of Jeffrey's intention, and we followed the buggy tracks zigzagging across the dusty road – signs of an unsure driver – then through a turn-off down a decrepit fence line. We tracked him for 7 more kilometres, arriving at a steep, sandy creek. The Ford, without four-wheel drive capacity, had to be left behind. Grabbing the sheets, I yelled for someone to bring the waterbag and set out running.

It was 2 pm, a shimmering hot day, and my head and heart were pounding from exhaustion. I stopped, sure I could see the buggy on the far side of the claypan. Using my shirt sleeve to wipe the perspiration from my eyes, I paused to get my bearings. The heat bored down ferociously. This was an illusion. We were looking upriver and into the sun; were my eyes playing tricks on me?

Turning, I motioned Jack and the boys to follow. We tracked the buggy around the outskirts of the yellow claypan. Two hundred metres out I spotted it, balanced on its side.

When we got there, Jack and the boys began crying uncontrollably, wailing, bashing themselves with rocks to bring on the drawing of blood, agonising over what they had predicted. I checked young Jeffrey's pulse, but he was gone, pinned under the buggy. Moving quickly, I checked Lenny, the 16-year-old who had been driving. He was still huddled under the buggy, in shock – with good reason, as he was probably in line for a payback for causing the death of his friend.

Making sure Lenny hadn't broken any bones, I pulled him out and made him comfortable under a tree.

Some of the others were still wailing and bashing themselves.

'Stop it, stop it!' I screamed at them. 'You must help me lift the buggy a little bit and pull Jeffrey out.'

We couldn't leave him there, but the accident had terrified them. They were crying hysterically and shaking in their shoes. I was running on pure adrenaline. Taking Jack by the shoulders, I begged him.

'Pull yourself together, please, pull yourself together. I need your help.' I was determined to pull Jeffrey out from under the buggy. Since the wheel jack was buggered, the only way was to lift the vehicle. It had to be one good lift, or we risked dropping it and cutting the body in half. I couldn't live with that. I looked at Jack.

'When I say pull, I mean pull the boy all the way out,' I said clearly. Somehow we found the strength to lift the buggy an inch or two, enough to get this dear boy out. Two bubbles popped out in the vein in my right arm, but we did it.

Wrapping young Jeffrey in a white sheet, I placed him in his father's arms.

'Nurse him, old man,' I said. 'Nurse him.' Jack rocked backward and forward, lost in his grief, chanting his mournful grief song.

When word flashed around the homestead, 200 mourners gathered. Lenny, who came from Fitzroy, needed to be hidden. The Flying Doctor arrived and took him away. The police and the public health nursing sister were informed, and came to collect the body. Leisha's shock and tears at the sight of the corpse's exposed foot saddened me terribly. I should have covered Jeffrey better.

I was sitting alone on the back veranda reflecting upon the tragic event when Jack walked in from the shadows and sat by me. There was no need for words. Now we had both lost sons on Louisa. They were mates, and now they were both gone. What a waste.

'Yumun,' Jack's voice was ever so soft. 'Payback him fix up.'

This news set my pulse racing. My emotions were all over the place now, but I let him explain. From his culture, this age-old law still carried enormous significance. It seemed harsh to my ears, but it was their way.

'Jack,' I whispered. 'Can I ask something of you? Let our white law test this boy first. Please let the white law test this boy first up. If you're not happy, then I know nothing.'

I knew Jack respected me, as I did him, and we left it at that. I measured out the burial plot, and filled the drums with water to dampen the ground. The following morning, we dug the grave with crowbar and shovel.

The autopsy completed, the body was returned home. An emotionally-charged crowd, all swaying trance-like, watched as the coffin was lowered. Bob hadn't returned to the station for Jeffrey's burial; though we never put it into words, we both knew he couldn't have handled it. As soon as Kelly's name was mentioned, I felt the warm tears begin to flow all over again. This was serious mourning: a wailing mob, the throb of deeper voices, traditional bloodletting.

'Burial finished, everybody, burial finished,' I said at last, emotionally exhausted. I wove through the throng of people towards the homestead. I'd made a decision. As deeply as I cared for everyone here, who had looked after me in my darkest days, the time had come for me to move on. I had three young children who needed me strong in body and mind, and not going to pieces, or falling asleep at the wheel. I could not bury any more young people on Louisa.

CHAPTER 16

Mango Farm

O ur move to Mango Farm became a life change. The big
family safety net of Louisa was replaced by formal classes
at school in Broome and town life for the children. The girls
began modelling and dancing lessons. I revelled in the luxury
of my own home, filled with exquisite Italian furnishings and a
wardrobe of Carla Zampatti and Christian Dior clothes. What
a contrast to Louisa it was, although once the novelty of all this
affluence had worn off, I found that I could take it or leave it.

The money had come from Bob's contracting, which was,
as I'd foreseen, tremendously successful. We acquired three
more 10-acre blocks outside Broome and successfully grew
Townsville lucerne. Watching the crops mature made me
happier than anything. In the shed by the house our plant and
machinery stood shining and ready, rebuilt and mended for the
coming mustering season.

While my girls were at school, I had lots of time to con-
template life. One day I was making a fresh cup of tea and
thinking how much I missed Katie and Alma, who had done so
much to help me keep my sanity in Louisa. A soft scraping
sound, like sandpaper moving across slate tiles, came from

where Robby was playing with his toys on the lounge-room floor. Then I heard an explosion as something bulky crashed into the window.

That made me jump! I dropped the crystal sugar bowl and shards went flying. One pierced the main artery in my ankle, sending bright red blood spurting over cupboards and walls, but I couldn't worry about that now. What if Robby had fallen through the window? I bound my wound with a tea towel and hobbled around to the lounge where I was confronted with the largest king brown snake I'd ever seen. I grabbed Robby up off the floor and urgently checked him for puncture wounds. By now I'd forgotten about my problem, and blood was spraying the furniture. The place was beginning to look like the scene of a massacre.

I had to sit down and re-tie the tea towel. Robby was bawling but my eyes never left the snake, which had stretched itself out along a wall in the breezeway. I guess it was a cool place to hang out.

We sat eyeballing each other while I tried to stem the blood. I hopped out to the workshop with Robby on my hip. Starting to feel dizzy, I had to stop to rest. It was blazing hot as usual and the distance between house and shed seemed like miles.

Soon I spotted Browny, Bob's leading man, working on the dozer out on the farm. Sitting Robby down on the burning ground, I called for help, but the noise from the machine drowned me out. Browny never lifted his head. Robby was wailing at the sight of so much blood or perhaps his little bum was burning on the superheated pindan. I lifted him onto my hip but had to sit down again as my vision clouded. Cupping my hand over the wound, I waved the blood-soaked tea towel and called again. Browny spotted us, did a double-take and in no time we were heading for Broome Hospital.

While I was being treated, the snake was killed – there was no choice. It turned out that the initial explosion, causing me to drop the sugar bowl, was caused by a kite-hawk flying into the window. When I returned home later that day, I cleaned up the blood, my own and the snake's. But I have to admit, the place never felt the same after that.

In April 1986, we heard that the Burke government was getting what it wanted: the Australian Land & Cattle Co.'s properties were being resumed by the Lands Department. The company geared up to take the State government to court. First it took out a full-page advertisement in the *West Australian* newspaper to alert the country that the Burke government was trying to pass legislation to regain land without appropriate compensation. The government argued that the cattle stations were run-down, and the Australian Land & Cattle Co. had had crippling debts ever since its Camballin dam and sorghum-farming plans went bobbing down the Fitzroy River. Julian Grill, the Minister for Agriculture, said no TB testing of cattle had ever been done on the properties. This wasn't the case: Bob had done the first TB tests at Mariana Bore in May 1974. There were eight positives, but the government hadn't extended the testing regime as it should have. TB is an infectious disease of cattle and humans caused by a micro-organism which manifests itself in different parts of the body. Testing for TB meant two rounds of mustering a year, 30 days apart. If a positive TB result was returned on the second test, that paddock of cattle had to be sold and sent to the meatworks, where further testing would be done. It was a hard, but clean and safe way to go before planning to restock.

Eventually the government and company reached a settlement: the company would sell Bohemia and Louisa for redevelopment, and keep Kimberley and Napier Downs and the cattle. Head Office offered me the manager's job on Kimberley and Napier Downs, and Bob was offered the contract mustering.

Bob suggested I view Kimberley Downs before taking the manager's position. I was keen already. After three months in Broome, we couldn't get out fast enough. I was lost in town; I had everything, but it meant nothing. Ever since the brown snake incident, I'd been uneasy in the house. After the initial excitement, the children felt the same about Broome. Leisha didn't like going to school on the bus, and had got into a fight with a boy after he pulled her skirt up. Besides, she lived for horses, which were out on the station. We weren't built for town life.

Bob and I journeyed to Kimberley Downs. Paint was peeling off the buildings and there was a general air of neglect. I walked around the sheds and homestead, the men's quarters and the kitchen. The company hadn't spent one cent on repairs and improvements while fighting the government. Inside the homestead there was nothing, not even a chair. It was so depressing.

I sat down against a veranda post. Not a word passed between us. With little company funds, could I pull this together? Even more than the homestead, I was worried about the condition of the bores, mill, tanks, dams and fences. This would be an enormous job. Bob's hard-edged voice broke the silence.

'Give yourself six months. If you can't show signs of pulling it together, get out.' Forthright and blunt: Bob's usual style. His rough way of laying things out always got my back up and goaded me into a decision. This would be my challenge. Bob knew I needed more in my life than the Mango Farm. But still, I hadn't seen Kimberley Downs for six years and its dilapidation shocked me.

'I'll take the position – I can do it,' I answered.

The decision made, I was ready. Usually my taste for big tests meant hard work and heartache, but I couldn't help giving this one a go.

The company negotiated a loan with the ANZ Bank. Could the station repay it and survive? 'Yes, the dollars are on the hoof,' was our answer. It had become a kind of mantra, that phrase.

It was time for action. I hired men to whitewash the walls inside and out, no frills. We hired a lovely Thursday Islander, Beccy, as cook. Sandy, a woman who was living with one of the stockmen, would be a nanny and governess for the children. Three fencing teams were needed for repairing, replacing and erecting new fences. We worked hand in hand on the TB program with the Derby office of the Agriculture department.

Soon we were on a roll, with hard work and happy faces. We had hired hands in the men's quarters, women in the converted old Kimberley Downs schoolhouse, and my family in the 'big house'. All meals were taken together, with no airs and graces. The children ran around the homestead playing, excited to be back in the bush. We had more staff here, a little community nestled in the valley, surrounded by Homestead Creek and Mount Marmion. Robby had just turned two, big sister Leisha was nine and Kristy seven, the 'mother hens' keeping a watchful eye on their little brother. I shot seven snakes in the first week, including one we found in our toilet while Robby was in there. I blew off the snake's head, pellets ricocheting from the porcelain pedestal to the corrugated iron walls in a deafening blast which left a huge hole in the wall.

Jimmy Marshall, an Aboriginal fellow, became my right-hand man. My brother Michael had left us to run the power plants on Balgo Station on the Tanami Desert. Having fallen in love with Janine, a Broome local who would become his wife, Michael was looking for an independent future. Jimmy was, like Michael, a jack-of-all-trades – he knew about bores, fencing, welding and mechanics. He was a little old for ringing on horseback – or mustering as a stockman – but the knowledge was there. Jim had been around Bob's camps for 30-odd years, and now he was in mine.

The bores were in terrible condition. Jim was doing a wonderful job manufacturing parts, but the water tanks were rusting away. We patched them with fibreglass, or hessian and tar, or even, in one case, with some antbed that Jim broke up and packed down like a poultice.

The challenge turned out far bigger than expected, but I knew there was a light at the end of the tunnel. Bob returned home between his musters on Millijiddee Station for the Aboriginal owners there. He suffered worsening back pain now, and would sit for hours smoking quietly, lost in his own world. He was nearly 60, but seemed much older judging by the pain written on his face. Still, the children brought a smile to his face as he watched their antics about the homestead.

CHAPTER 17

Killer on the Loose

S oon after we moved to Kimberley Downs, a crazed marksman was on the loose in the area. Joseph Schwab had been stalking and killing people in the Victoria River district of the Northern Territory and the Pentecost River region of the Kimberley. It was worrying, since Bob and his team were off doing the last roundup on Louisa and Bohemia.

We were out of stores on Kimberley Downs and in need of parts. Before leaving, I made enquiries; the general opinion was that Schwab had left the area in his Toyota Hilux. Of our people, Bill and Sean were out on the mill run, Sandy, our nanny/governess, was with the children at the homestead, Jack, Alma and their family from Louisa were in the camp, and Beccy, my Thursday Islander cook, was with me.

'Be aware of any Hilux with a bull terrier,' I warned everyone before heading out to do some shopping. Apparently a bull terrier had gone missing after Schwab's horrific execution of picnickers on the Pentecost River north of Napier Downs, only a day's travel away.

* * *

The Gibb River Road was rough and corrugated. As always, the Toyota had a tendency to chug and choke, usually due to an obstruction in the fuel tank. The truck would slow, the blockage would clear itself and we would regain speed. 'My God, Bec, we don't need fuel worries today,' I said. I felt frustrated and was now uneasy about the trip. As the Toyota cleared itself, I drove at breakneck speed towards Derby. At the Meeda turn-off I came across a Hilux, seemingly lost. Surely not, I thought. Anxious and fearful, worried for my children and staff, I wanted to turn back to the station. Instead I continued to Derby, shopped like a crazy woman and threw the stuff in the back as quickly as possible.

'Any news on the killer?' I asked the fuel attendant at Rick Jane's garage in town.

'I think they got him,' he answered vaguely. Why I didn't go to the police station to report my sighting of the Hilux I will never know.

Kimberley Downs's front gate was 50 metres off the Gibb River Road. I swung into a skidding halt. Someone had padlocked the gate behind him and was travelling at high speed towards the homestead, leaving a wake of red pindan dust.

I couldn't believe what I was seeing. It seemed unreal. I went cold. Sick to the pit of my stomach, I had the most terrible fear that this was Schwab.

'It's locked, Sheryl,' came Bec's dejected voice from the gate. I trembled with fury and fear as I rummaged through the toolbox and found bolt-cutters.

We had the padlock severed within minutes. 'Hurry, Bec!' I yelled, jamming the Toyota into second gear for a quick take-off. 'I'll ram this bastard.'

Accelerator flat to the floor, I chased the red dust, gaining ground on the vehicle. Heading towards the next gate, I realised the dust had diminished.

'Bec,' I said, 'that vehicle has turned off towards Boundary Bore.' We flew towards the homestead. Pulling the vehicle around and reversing up against the freezer, I heard the kitchen phone ring.

'Sheryl, phone. It's the Derby police,' yelled Bill, my windmill man.

'Have they caught the killer?' I asked the sergeant. He didn't answer, but advised me that a Hilux, with wide tyres and a bull terrier in the back, had been sighted in our area.

'Do not approach the vehicle under any circumstances,' he said.

'Is it the killer?'

He repeated the warning: 'Do not approach this vehicle.'

We ate dinner with an eye on the entrance to Kimberley Downs. My children were frightened and nervous. Robby didn't fully understand the situation, but clung fearfully to my side. The staff were moving about on eggshells. Jack and Alma came up from the camp to sit close by. My gut was a tangled mess, although I remained composed as I spoke to my staff. I worried for my children's safety. I knew we were sitting ducks for a marksman, and the homestead and buildings could not be secured.

'If any of you wish to leave for Derby, then do so,' I said. 'A truckload of horses is due within the hour. As you all know, I have thousands of head of cattle relying on pumps to keep the water up to them, so I must remain. Those that remain with me roll your swags; once the horses are unloaded we'll go outback to Tullock's Bore and camp.' This was a safer bet than staying at the homestead.

All the staff remained with me. The evening was pitch-black, no breeze, a light scattering of stars. Headlights showed on the rocky ridge above the entrance to the homestead. We froze in fear. A hush came over us all as we stood with ears straining to hear if it was a truck or a Hilux.

'Truck, Missus, truck,' said Jack with his eyes wide, catching his breath after a run through the blackness. He had taken it upon himself to keep watch from the stables. Good old Jack, he always looked after us!

After we had unloaded the horses, the fearful state of the truck driver became evident. 'Can I use the phone?' he asked, running towards the homestead. The driver had been informed on his truck radio that Schwab had been sighted in the area. We said we'd escort him through the two sets of gates to the Gibb River Road.

Three Toyotas set out, escorting the truck, each with a front passenger riding shotgun. We were all terrified. With the truck on the road, we drove to Tullock's Bore and set ourselves up to spot any lights. During the restless night, I woke to the cry, 'Missus, Missus!' Heart and pulse pounding, we were frightened to death of a cab light in one of the vehicles.

There was huge relief when golden rays of sunrise came bouncing across the yellow claypan. We crawled along the dusty two-wheel track towards Homestead Creek and stopped. Sean and Bill, my windmill men, courageously crept on ahead to check all buildings. I was afraid that Schwab could have stolen into the station under cover of night and was holed up in one of the buildings, his sights trained on any one of us.

Later that day I took the children and all the staff – about a dozen of us, no-one left behind – along the Lennard River via Rarragee to Napier Downs, where Jimmy's parents, old Johnny and Rita Marshall, were the caretakers. From behind the range came the ringing of two high-powered gunshots. I was frightened, but also angry that Schwab had us on the run like this. Jack sat by the old wooden cattle yards keeping a watchful eye on the station entrance and the Napier Range.

The boys worked in the shed while I splashed some whitewash around the homestead to keep myself occupied.

At mid-morning the following day, Bob arrived from Louisa. Without telling me, Bob had contacted the Fitzroy police and offered to fly at his own expense to try to locate this maniac. The police advised strongly against this. Schwab was believed to be carrying an arsenal capable of shooting down a plane.

Without knowing it, on his way home Bob had passed within 200 metres of Schwab. As we travelled back from Napier to Kimberley Downs, I alerted Bob to some fresh tracks which did not belong to a station vehicle. The tyres were wide. When we arrived at Kimberley, the top gate on the airstrip paddock had been left open and the star picket flattened: someone had left in a hell of a hurry.

It wasn't clear if someone had been in the homestead, but a chair had been positioned behind overflowing hanging ferns on the veranda, providing a panoramic view of the buildings. On a table beside it were kitchen butcher knives and old-style hand shears.

Schwab was spotted on Plum Plain, south-east of where we were, the following day by the pilot Peter Leutenegger, who was heli-mustering horses for the Fitzroy Rodeo. Peter alerted the authorities, and Schwab made the fatal mistake of taking on Western Australia's top tactical response squad. Surrounded on Plum Plain, he answered their demand to surrender with a torrent of gunfire, and was shot dead. We were left with some frightening unanswered questions. Had the vehicle we had seen on the station, tearing up the track towards Boundary Bore, been Schwab's? Had he been in the homestead, sitting on the chair with knives and shears at the ready? There would never be a way of finding out for sure.

CHAPTER 18

My Girls

*B*y 1987 Leisha and Kristy could ride, no doubt about that. Leisha was 10 and Kristy eight. The girls were good mates and looked alike. They didn't receive their first saddles until proving their proficiency by galloping bareback to Bob. Their favourite after-school pastime was racing each other up and down rocky ridges, jumping deep gullies and crossing hazardous creeks. Strongly competitive, they were riding better every day.

I'd spent most of the day checking bores on the east side of the property. Arriving at the homestead, I stopped at the stables and noticed Leisha's horse, Lucky, was missing. Jud, my nephew, the station's horse-breaker and Kimberley Saddle Bronc champion, pulled a buggy up beside me with Leisha looking dishevelled, dusty and tear-stained in the passenger seat. Jud's offsider was riding Leisha's horse.

Having earnt an early mark from school, Leisha had saddled Lucky and, unable to remember where she last took off her riding boots, rode through Homestead Gap and around Melody's paddock. As she paused at a trough for water, her horse reared up and shied away from a brown snake. Lucky took the bit in its teeth, and the girth slipped. With the saddle sliding off to the left, Leisha leaned to her right. The next terrifying moment her foot slipped through the stirrup right up to her knee and, tangled in the saddle, she swung out to the right of the panicky horse, which took off and hit the fence line. Leisha narrowly missed being torn up on the barbed wire, saved only by her grip on a handful of horse mane – but there was more to come.

Jud, working on the fence line, hollered to his offsider: 'She's hung up!' Swinging their buggy around, he approached the galloping horse. Leisha, seeing the homestead gate shut ahead of her, had visions of the grey attempting a jump. From the buggy roaring alongside, Jud fearlessly leaped across to the galloping grey, simultaneously wrapping his arms around his cousin. The grey didn't miss a beat, gathering itself to clear the gate. Pulling Leisha, the saddle and the girth, Jud went to ground, taking the brunt of the fall. The grey slammed into the gate. As a veil of bulldust rose around her, Leisha sat up in shock, her trembling body sore and bruised.

Jud patted her on the back. 'You all right, Bub?' he asked with a short nervous laugh.

Bob came in from the stock-camp, having heard of Leisha's horse accident.

'Hello, Daddy,' she called as she limped towards the kitchen veranda, happy to see her father home.

'What happened?' Bob demanded bluntly, looking as if he'd had a thundercloud hanging over his head for a week.

She looked at him in shock, unable to believe the harsh way he was speaking to her. He never gave her time to answer. As she stumbled to find the right words to explain her stupidity for riding in sandshoes, he blasted her again.

'You know better – you're a McCorry,' he said. Then he got himself a pannikin of tea and sat glaring into the distance.

Leisha was vulnerable after the fall; a little emotional support would have helped. When I questioned his ruthlessness, Bob said we were expected to get it right the first time. Looking back on this, I wonder if he was reacting out of the fear of losing another child. At moments like this, it can't have been far from his mind.

The station had begun attracting media coverage. Copies of stories in the *West Australian* and the *Western Mail* magazine were sent to the station from as far afield as Melbourne and Brisbane. I was attracting attention as a woman managing a big outback cattle station. I was pleased that my boss, the Receiver Manager Peter Melsom, had enough faith in me to give me a go. We had a big job to do and this was a big operation and I was keen to give it my best shot. But I was embarrassed by the attention. I felt it wasn't really a big deal; it was a job I loved and I was lucky to have it. It was sheer hard work and I loved it. But I hoped the stories might prompt other women working in the male-dominated cattle industry to hang in and have a go.

As the stories hit the newspapers and magazines, Bob became sombre and reclusive, leaving me feeling isolated and very lonely. I felt most distant from him after the *Western Mail* magazine put me on the cover, with the title 'Cattle Queen. Station Manager, Sheryl McCorry.' The inside caption read in big letters: 'No bull, she's boss.' The girls saved several copies of the magazine to show Daddy. At least the kids were proud of Mummy, I thought. When Bob returned from work that day, the girls raced out and put the magazines on the veranda table. They were full of excited chatter and wanted him to take notice. Bob never even glanced at them, simply shoved them off to the side, and ignored all of us. I continued my daily work as if nothing bothered me. But it certainly hurt, since I had always placed Bob on a pedestal. I wondered if he was becoming insecure in our marriage. Was the age difference worrying him? Not all his parts worked as well as they had in the early days, but I married him expecting this and was fully prepared to accept it without reproach. This was the 'For better or worse' part of our marriage vows. He needn't have worried. All my life I had worked with men and been treated with respect. I never had the inclination to drift, and, aside from that one dance with Morgan at the ball years ago, the thought never entered my mind.

Or maybe his insecurity was professional rather than personal. Bob had always insisted that I was to familiarise myself completely with the Kimberley cattle game, an opportunity I grabbed with both hands. Bob assumed that I would outlive him, and would need this knowledge to support the children and myself. I always saw myself as his apprentice. I wondered if this idea of my becoming the 'master', as I was being painted in the magazines, was making for an uncomfortable reversal.

At Easter 1988, we took advantage of a glorious day for a picnic. The weather was hot and humid, and we needed more rain, but there was no sign of the hoped-for thunderheads. Beccy, Sandy, the children and I planned a trip to Rarragee Billabongs, then to Lennard River for a swim. Billy cans and tucker box loaded, we took the bumpy two-wheel track through Melody's paddock. Wild ducks lifted in unison and circled as we approached the billabong, exposing a sea of shining green lilypads and thousands of magnificent blue waterlilies standing in all their splendour. We parked in the shade of two cabbage gums. How could their leaves remain so glossy while the surrounding earth was crying out for rain? It was a miracle of lushness.

The billy simmered on hot coals. The aroma of smoke competed with the eucalyptus scent. I cut flowers for the house. Beccy and the children collected bulbs as she gave them a lesson in bush tucker. The ducks returned, their webbed feet outstretched. Landing with aplomb, they waddled blithely in and out of the camp, quacking their heads off.

I sat on a groundsheet, pannikin of tea in hand, appreciating the peaceful beauty and wildlife. I had quiet moments of grief and sadness – it had been seven years since Kelly died and I still thought of him every day – but the joy of Robby, Leisha and Kristy helped leaven the sadness.

'Look Mum,' Robby called. 'Look here!'

I left the billabong and walked towards the children on a sandy ridge. I knew exactly what they were doing. Their heads tilted back, they were popping huge white bardi grubs into their mouths. I had terrible visions of these big, creamy grubs crawling around the children's stomachs. I convinced the children to cook them in the fading coals. But Beccy assured me they were 'all right'.

With the windows down, the cool breeze flowed through the vehicle as we travelled towards Police Camp Bore. I heard the shrill of a flock of brolgas before sighting them. We stopped and sat mesmerised by 15 to 20 of these lithe creatures dancing, heads high, wings spread wide, magnificently circling the claypan flat. The children sat in wonderment, watching silently. We moved on, checking Police Camp mill and tank before arriving at the Lennard River where we were greeted by the sight of our stockmen throwing somersaults from the bridge. I immediately banned the girls from following suit!

We swam for several hours, enjoying the crystal-clear water. But our peaceful afternoon was broken by a terrifying clap of thunder, too close for comfort. We saw mountainous thunderheads moving across the ridge above us. I screamed: 'Out of the water!'

Lifting Robby by his armpits, I rushed in knee-deep water towards the bank. There was a flash of lightning and a simultaneous burst of thunder, leaving Robby and me short of breath, as if we'd been whacked in the chest. Scrambling over the bank, unsure of what had happened, I felt dry and raw in the throat. It appeared that we'd been struck by lightning.

With the children safely in the car, we left for the homestead. As we crossed Bullock Paddock flat the sky turned from mauve to deep dark purple. The heavens opened up, hailing golfballs. Unbelievable but true! We tracked home through the paddock, holding out our Akubras to collect the ice. It was the beginning of our 'knock 'em down' rain: the last rains of the season, windy and wild, mowing down the tall spear grass so we could start the mustering season. The lightning strike was a message: time to get to work again. Nature's logic is impeccable.

CHAPTER 19

Sadness and Solace

*F*or a long time Bob had been unwell. Aside from his spine degenerating rapidly from wear and tear caused by years spent in the saddle droving, he now had internal bleeding from an ulcer and was occasionally vomiting blood. He also had pancreatic problems, and his doctor had informed him that the vertebrae in his neck were not far from severing his main artery. It might only take a knock, fall or jar of some kind to kill him. It was unlike Bob to consult a doctor, but he did so under pressure from me. He was that poorly. I begged Bob to let Browny take control of the mustering. I worried that Bob's heavy workload was taking its toll, but my words fell on deaf ears. His constant suffering made him moody, driving him to that dark solitary place in his mind where he grew angry and defiant.

I called his doctor and begged him to help. Bob was furious with me. I doubted that he wanted any help at all.

But in spite of his pig-headedness, I loved this rugged old cattleman of mine. His back was really bent and he walked bow-legged from years in the saddle. I simply wanted to help him handle his grief and pain.

It was early 1988 and Robby was now three-and-a-half. His favourite pastime was playing with his trucks under the canopy of the huge rain tree that shaded the kitchen veranda. Robby never got to spend much time with his dad in these early years. I always felt that Bob was frightened something terrible might happen to him.

I arrived at the homestead late one afternoon after clocking the kilometres of a new fence forming Telegraph Dam paddock, to find Kristy lying on the couch, noticeably unwell: quiet, pale and lethargic.

'What's wrong, love?' I asked her. Any other day this would most certainly have been horse-riding time.

'Pains, Mum,' she said, pointing to her lower abdomen. Appendix! The pain would generate and decline, then gnaw at her again. I contacted Derby Hospital and spoke with a nursing sister. Kristy was promptly admitted to the children's ward.

'Doctor, would you check her for appendicitis?' I asked before leaving the hospital. 'We live a long way out of town.'

The doctor seemed to think it was just some childhood bug. I'm no doctor, but I could see it was more than that. I tucked Kristy into bed, kissing her goodbye, uncomfortable leaving her there without some conclusive diagnosis. She looked pale and sick. Reassuring my girl, I said, 'Mum will be back in the morning to check on you.'

I returned to Kimberley Downs. The next day there was no improvement in Kristy. In fact she looked worse, and the doctor was still vague. Working on a mother's intuition, I said I wanted to take her to Perth. Shock clouded the doctor's face. He hadn't a clue what the problem was. I wanted to move fast, and to his credit he gave me his support.

At the same time, I was worried about having left Robby in the care of Sandy, Leisha and Beccy. He was only little and not used to being away from his Mum. Bob also returned to

Kimberley Downs. I had never left my children for any length of time before, but this was an emergency.

By the time of our departure, Kristy was deteriorating rapidly. The hospital delegated a nurse, with tubes and bottles hooked to the stretcher, and Kristy was delivered by ambulance to the aircraft. I flew with her, frightened and stressed, with panicky urgency. After what seemed like many, many hours, my mind nearly blown away with flashes of Kelly's emergency and the worry of great distances, we eventually arrived at Princess Margaret Hospital for Children.

I waited patiently for a doctor to examine Kristy. The nurse from Derby Hospital had vanished into thin air. I was suddenly all alone, fighting an uphill battle. I kept hounding the nurses' station to find a doctor. Thirty minutes later one walked into another cubicle and went to walk out again.

'Excuse me, doctor,' I said, thinking, *There is no way you are leaving now, mate*. 'I need five minutes of your time, please. It's imperative you look at Kristy now.' I'd come from the Kimberley, for God's sake! If I'd had to barricade the door to keep the doctor in, I would have.

After a quick examination the doctor arranged for emergency theatre. What seemed like hours later, my stomach churning, I was relieved to see the orderlies push Kristy towards her room. The doctor's diagnosis was peritonitis. Seven months earlier he had attended another little girl with the same complaint and similar age, and he picked it up immediately.

Lying in bed, Kristy looked small and fragile, with many terrifying-looking tubes connected to her. My dear Aunt Merle, Kristy's grandmother, arrived. I didn't know where Kristy's mother, Mary, was, and was too distraught to find out. But I knew how much Kristy loved her grandmother. Merle and I comforted each other over the many long days and nights we spent by Kristy's side.

Back at the station, it took her six months to fully recuperate. She lost so much weight through her ordeal, her body was just skin and bone. But with lots of tender love and care, she started to gain some strength and to smile again.

While I was in Perth, Bob had started mustering Kimberley Downs again. When he was out mustering or drafting the cattle during the day, the children were in the good hands of Sandy, their governess-nanny. Leisha and Robby were happy to have Daddy around the house and would sit on his lap or hang off his arms every chance they had. He tried to be the best Daddy he could. But there was one instance, while I was in Perth, that hurt me deeply.

After a hard day's mustering, Bob, the stockmen, the Department of Agriculture boys and the vets all got on the grog at the homestead. Sandy saw the children to bed, then went to bed herself. About 2 am, Robby started to sleepwalk. He was missing me terribly. Somehow he found his way out of the bedroom. Out the front door, he climbed down the homestead steps into the blackness, and walked down past the old schoolhouse. Then Beccy who had a room in the single men's quarters, was woken by the sound of someone dragging their feet on the gravel by her bedroom window. Beccy jumped out of bed, grabbed a torch and went out in the dark to investigate. By this time Robby was heading for the gate to the homestead house paddock, nearly 100 metres further on. Beccy was unable to believe her eyes to see a little blond boy wandering around in the dark by himself. Beccy called to Robby softly and led him back to the homestead. By the time Beccy banged on the front door to wake Bob, she was very upset. Bob was shocked at his own behaviour: he'd passed out after his bender while his own son was sleepwalking. Anything might have happened to him. Unperturbed, Robby got tucked into bed and slept the rest of the night away. Bob didn't sleep at all, instead sitting at the foot of his son's bed keeping an eye on him and reproaching himself for his thoughtlessness.

The choppers had landed after a good day's muster. Bob was home from the cattle yard, showered and looking fresh, his health problems giving him some respite for the moment. In his blunt manner, although with a cheeky smile, he suggested I make a pot of tea and meet with him on the veranda. There was evidently a problem he needed to discuss. I had woken unhappy. That day was my birthday, and he seemed to have forgotten.

Waiting impatiently on the veranda, I kept flicking a ball of newspaper from pannikin to pannikin, until it missed the pannikin and went under the table. Bob came out, and I noticed his anxious look as he retrieved the ball and plonked it down in front of me.

'Happy birthday – it's for you,' he said.

I unravelled the ball of paper, finding a seven-carat aquamarine ring encircled with diamonds. It was extraordinarily beautiful.

Bob was a plain-spoken man and never over-generous with praise. He had his own special way of making me feel privileged. I wore that ring while I worked, though after covering it in black oil from the jack pump I decided to put it away for special occasions.

My dream was to purchase a cattle station of our own in the Kimberley, but Bob would not borrow funds, even though the contract mustering was proving so lucrative. I saved and tied up every spare dollar we had, placing large sums on term deposit with the ANZ Bank in Derby, taking advantage of the high interest rates at the time. Bob never gave a damn, or questioned me, about money; he had 100 per cent faith in my ability to manage our investments and resources. He didn't mind as long as we had sufficient funds to put food on the table, clothes on our backs and a roof over our heads – and the occasional gift for me. This was his simple philosophy.

He treated the children well, never denying them anything. At that time Kristy and Leisha were winning barrel races (timed events where the horses galloped around a track marked by barrels) and 'All Round Cow Girl' titles Kimberley-wide. I was so very proud of them. I persuaded Bob to attend several rodeos and watch the girls ride, hoping he would show appreciation for the long hours and hard work the girls put into their horses. But the trips were a punishment for his weary old body and he found it hard to muster enthusiasm. Thankfully Leisha and Kristy understood Bob's struggle with his pain. They knew that having Daddy with us wasn't something to be taken for granted; it was a special sacrifice on his part which would intensify the happiness for us all.

We were making good progress with the fencing and TB eradication programs, but I also knew that if we slipped up it would open the door for the government to have another go at trying to resume the stations. On Kimberley Downs we continued with two rounds of mustering a year. If a positive TB result was returned on the second test, that paddock of cattle had to be sold. This happened to us once, costing us a couple of hundred head.

I was alone in the shed one day when out of the blue a wild storm came roaring through the gap between Mount Marmion and Homestead Hill. Pushing balls of spinifex, tarps and drums, it ripped bonnets from trucks and buggies on its way towards the shed. Sheets of torn corrugated iron came with it.

Little Robby ran through the shed door, crying with arms outstretched: 'I was worried about you, Mummy!' There was no time for fear. I thanked God my boy was safe. We crouched behind the power plant. I could feel his little body trembling against mine. The next instant Leisha, who was 12, arrived, crying as the wind hurled her about. I raced out and grabbed her; we fought the wind and took cover with Robby.

We watched, petrified, as the torn and twisted metal from cars and shed roofs went spiralling high into the sky. The noise was deafening. Eventually, after only five violent minutes or so but seemingly much longer, we ventured out. Twisted sheets of iron stretched out across the station for a kilometre towards the ridge. The buildings in a direct line with the gap were destroyed. Old-timers had warned me to beware of any storms that came directly through the gap, and they were right!

'Mum, Mummy!' I heard the raised voices of the children as they came running towards me. 'There's a crocodile in our billabong!'

Laughing, believing they were pulling my leg, I paid no heed. Des Higgins, the owner of Waterbank Station, had excavated the billabong for me for the price of a pannikin of tea. It was now very beautiful and filled with flowering blue waterlilies, surrounded by bottlebrush, golden wattle and the sharp leaf of pandanus – so beautiful, it attracted all manner of creatures.

I knew that Bob had found a 1.5 metre freshwater crocodile stretched out under a cattle trough, looking terribly thin and dehydrated, and now the kids were telling me that he'd put it in our billabong. I didn't believe them, and brushed them away. Big mistake. Admiring the lilies several weeks later, I glanced up to see a crocodile slowly move up out of the water to the opposite bank and settle to soak up the morning sun.

Next store run, I bought a sign that said, 'No Swimming – Crocodile' and attached it to the boab tree close by. No visitor ever believed the sign was for real.

'Dundee' took up residence and remained for many years, free to roam. He took a holiday during the wet season when all the rivers were up and running, and returned once Homestead Creek dropped.

Our pet would scare the living daylights out of old Jim in the workshop and once, enjoying the cool cement base of the shower recess, sent one of the men running partly-clothed from the ablution block. Liz, our newly-hired Pommy cook, often took fright, screaming blue murder when she saw Dundee. I considered relocating our crazed crocodile to the Lennard River, but soon after that Liz nearly electrocuted herself by washing an electric handbeater in the kitchen sink while it was switched on, and she up and left.

Dundee remained king of his billabong and kept us on our toes – never more so than when Robby fell off a wattle branch into the water with the croc. The water was freezing cold and Robby scrambled out at record speed. After he arrived at the house, shivering, his eyes the sizes of saucers, he told his father: 'I walked on water, Dad. I'll never do that again.'

Bob had completed a mustering contract at Millijiddee, an outstation of Noonkanbah. He was back at Kimberley Downs, and I waited patiently for him to sit down with a pannikin of tea before breaking the news.

'I bought Kilto Station,' I said.

Bob looked at me, eyes wide with disbelief.

'I have, honestly. We're now the owners of Kilto Station.'

Although the property belonged to the same company I worked for, it was through town gossip that I found out it was on the market. Unable to make contact with Bob on Millijiddee, I'd faxed off a tender. I hadn't given it any more thought until several weeks later I received the phone call from the Perth

office. Kilto was ours! My plan was that we'd develop it for ourselves at the end of each Kimberley Downs mustering season.

Bob didn't express his feelings in words – in fact, he never
said anything, but he showed his pleasure in a typical Bob way.
On breaks from mustering, he went off to Kilto to work enthusiastically on the station. This was how I knew he approved.

Sandy, the girls' governess, and Craig, one of Bob's stockmen, had
been living together as a couple for some time. On Craig's return
from Millijiddee, they decided to tie the knot in Derby town,
much to the pleasure of us all. Between many helpful hands in the
kitchen, we produced a wedding dinner suitable for a station
marriage. The girls decorated the kitchen veranda with balloons
and colourful homemade streamers and tinsel cut from Alfoil.

With the help of Narda, our new cook, Leisha short-
sheeted the marriage bed and secured my condamine and
camel bell to the mattress springs. On retiring for the night,
Sandy and Craig apparently enjoyed the bells so much they
kept the remainder of the station staff, including the dogs,
awake all night with the continuous clanging and the slow
dong-dong. The bells would start, the dogs would start, and
the whole station would start yelling at ungodly hours. I'd
never been so pleased to see piccaninny daylight smile over
Homestead Hill.

All were red and bleary-eyed over breakfast. The finger
was pointed at me; with tongue in cheek I confessed it was my
idea and my bells and I'd do the same for any of them who
wished to marry on the station. One thing we all agreed on:
Sandy and Craig were off to a great start! The following year,
Sandy and Craig became the proud parents of a beautiful baby
girl, whom they named Kelly after our son. I was sure my bells
had had a hand in her conception!

* * *

We battled on through wet and dry, keeping Kimberley Downs running on the smell of an oily rag while it remained in receivership. If the rains came late, the dams bogged and we lost cattle. I dragged survivors out of the mud myself, just as I patched tanks and fixed fences and harangued head office for funds. Bob's year was filled with contract mustering jobs and then working on Kilto. I ran Kimberley Downs independently. At times it seemed our lives were running in parallel, and I grew so tired, not only from work but from carrying the worry of Bob's battle with his grief over Kelly, his pain and moodiness, on top of everything else, sometimes I wondered what was the point of it all.

But the bush would always offer up moments of salvation. One hot humid day, about a hundred in the waterbag, not a breath of air, even the odd bird having fallen out of the sky, I was sitting in the shade of an ancient boab feeling that I couldn't keep going. I spotted an amazing sight: two large golden-brown serpents, raised from the ground and swaying in harmony.

All my life living in the bush I had never witnessed two fully-grown king browns perform a mating dance: a most impressive performance as they swayed in a gentle rhythm, slowly closing the distance until they were entwined. It was things like this that gave me back my strength and determination to go on.

The children were my other source of strength. Robby, now six, would help me with outside jobs, following me around to slit open the bagged 20-kilo blocks of mineral supplements I was laying out for the cattle. One day at Mariana Bore, Robby yelled out 'Look out, Mum!', warning me that I was about to be nailed by an aggressive mickey bull. If it hadn't been for my little offsider I could easily have ended up on the ground, a flattened out mum!

Leisha and Kristy were always helpful with the horses and stables, and one day I rewarded them with a trip to the limestone range that ran the full length of Napier Downs. We stopped near a place where, many years ago, a Flying Doctor aircraft returning from a mercy flight to Mount House Station had crashed, killing all on board. My thoughts drifted to my beloved Kelly, the outback and the great distances. Could we have saved him if we'd lived closer to town?

'Come on, Mum, we can't see anything here,' the children urged, dispelling my sombre thoughts.

We were heading for one of my favourite places, a nest of caves containing what had been described as a religious vision. We picked our way across the buggar buggar blacksoil plains, going easy on the Toyota to minimise damage. The plains were rough, scattered with hundreds of tough ant mounds and treacherous holes. We got out and climbed a 7-metre rise to a hidden cave's opening, camouflaged behind a sturdy bauhinia bush. We ate the picnic lunch in one of our secret spots, a welcome cool breeze flowing from within the caves. We gazed back across the plains towards Kimberley Downs. Everything was covered in brown spear grass and willowy floodweed bent from the knock 'em down rains. In the distance we could see the treeline of the Lennard River. A rangy bull was busily pushing his little herd of cows further afield. I thought of Kelly again, how I missed him terribly, and of Bob's grief and the dark places it had taken him. Then I glanced towards the children, and their happy laughter reminded me how lucky I was.

We advanced into Lake Cave. Its deep cavities were filled with clear, pure water, which gave off a chill, and the rock had a luminous crystalline shimmer. We found stalagmites and stalactites, even bats. The children were curious. If you stopped with torches off and looked towards the glow of daylight coming from the entrance, you could see a striking impression of the Virgin Mary. I'm not a religious person, but I marvelled at the likeness and had photographed it many times.

I asked the children: did this rock formation remind them of anything at all?

'No, just a rock, Mum.'

Bless me, Father, I thought, but I have tried. Having found great comfort over the years from Father Lawrence, who had propped me up, telling me to 'believe in myself', I'd had him to the homestead one day to talk to the children. He had tried untiringly to educate the children and me on some of the Bible's teachings, but our sit-down took a farcical turn when Robby leaned towards me and asked urgently: 'Mum, is this Jesus fella like that Father Christmas fella?'

There wasn't much Father Lawrence could say after that.

We retraced our steps out of this beautiful place, leaving it untouched, as it should be. Further along the range I liked to check that the many human skulls were left in peace. On my return after six years away managing Louisa and Bohemia, I had noticed that eight skulls had disappeared, others were broken and only pieces remained in a particular cave. This upset me. What demented person would want a human skull on the mantel or in the storeroom? I decided the only way to keep skulls, Aboriginal art and artefacts safe was to stop all visitors to this range, which I did while I was manager. I believed there were something like eight different tribes who once lived along this range. Those skulls were their only known remains.

Much later in the day, after I'd shown the children some Aboriginal art and an unusual water supply, the sun gently settled west of the ancient range, throwing its shadows across the plain towards the river. The children and I, bone-weary, were looking forward to returning to the homestead.

CHAPTER 20

Trust in Them

*I*t hardly seemed like 10 years since we'd lost our dear son. On the anniversary of Kelly's death, we always went to his grave in Broome. This day in 1991, I laid fresh flowers for my darling boy and Bob spent the day clearing the grass from the grave. Robby was seven now, and I felt I needed to explain that his older brother was buried here. There were questions about Kelly and questions about Daddy, and as I told Robby about it all I shed many tears.

Bob, meanwhile, sat alone by the graveside, a heart-wrenching sight. When we went back to the station he did what he always did on this day: he drank himself to sleep. He was a quiet drunk. Inconspicuously, he had started to drink more and more, in his steady and private way. He seemed in more pain than ever and sometimes just sat doubled-over, holding his stomach and saying nothing, preferring to be left in a world of his own.

As Bob's health and moods deteriorated, children were truly my consolation: mine and others', caucasian and indigenous. I couldn't get enough of children's company, so I offered to

246

look after young people who were troubled or trying to find their way in life. I had a motto: 'We pull together to survive.' To explain this to some of them I would collect a bunch of twigs, and liken them to people. Then I'd hold the bunch in one hand and demonstrate how hard it was to break, compared with how easy it was to break one twig on its own.

Just as Bob had placed trust in me, I placed trust in the children. In 1991 I was looking after Bert, a 16-year-old boy from Mingenew, a wheatbelt town. Bert had arrived via the Welfare people in Derby: a volatile and angry young man unwilling to accept anyone into his world. I'd made it clear to him that I was the boss of this outfit, I carried no passengers, and I tolerated no bullshit. I'd made Bert a deal. Welfare was paying him a pittance to be out of Derby and on the station. I gave him three weeks to prove to me he could work. If he did, I would pay him a respectable salary. Bert worked hard in the camp, and as his confidence improved he took up rodeo riding, competing in the most dangerous events. He wasn't a bad kid by any means; he only needed someone to show they had faith in him.

That same year, the Welfare office in Perth called, asking if I was in a position to take Del, Kristy's sister, again. Del had turned 16. From my understanding, foster children at that age were moved into group housing. Del, who had stepped out of line, was in trouble. Could I help?

In a round-table conference, my children said they rather liked the idea of having Del around again. When she returned to me on Kimberley Downs, I sat her down, laid the rules on the line and gave her the choice of work or study. She chose to study under Sandy. But the first month's lessons were a waste of time. Del dedicated herself to putting Sandy through the wringer. Luckily Sandy was made of sterner stuff. After reading Del's first report, I fired it from one end of the kitchen table to the other where it stopped directly in front of her chest. As I'd done with Bert, I made a deal with her. If she tried to improve her grades I would give her a pure Arab gelding, a horse of her very own. The horse in question was called Kidman, and she'd had her eye on him since she'd arrived.

This proved the best deal ever. Del's grades went to straight As and Bs. She just needed some kind of incentive. Together she and Kidman won many trophies and ribbons, and eventually Del moved out and grew into a responsible adult.

It wasn't as if my attempts to guide troubled young people were always an unqualified success. When Beccy, homesick, returned to her family on Thursday Island, I hired a new cook. Mary was tall, honey-blonde and very attractive – model material. My first question had been why a girl like her had accepted a job to cook in the outback. 'A change,' was her answer.

Two weeks after Mary started, the whole station cleared out to the Fitzroy Rodeo, except for Sandy, Leisha and me. Mary stayed too, saying she wished to settle in. Before returning to the homestead from an evening walk around the horse paddock, Sandy, Leisha and I came across a sight that sent my blood cold. Leisha stood shivering, with her hands clenched. 'Surely not!' she repeated over and over. There were remnants of some kind of mayhem: scattered on the ground were two empty whisky bottles, hair combs, and what was once a packet of cigarettes now in shreds. More frighteningly, there was also our razor-sharp Green Rivers butcher's knife, often used for boning out killers, near what looked to be the claw marks of a crazed and disoriented animal. But I could soon see that the claw marks were human. Returning to the station, I immediately went to Mary's room. My mind was a can of worms, churning, questioning: 'Why?'

I called her name as I slowly climbed the steps to her room. When she heard me, she tried to run away.

'Front up to it, Mary,' I urged rather harshly. 'Look at me!' I held both her shoulders. 'The butcher's knife, Mary,' I said. 'What were you going to do with the butcher's knife?'

She sobbed her heart out, eventually telling me, 'I heard voices in my head telling me to kill myself.'

'No, Mary,' I said. 'You're strong – stronger than those voices.'

Thank God in the dark of night she'd been unable to find the butcher's knife that lay partly hidden in the bulldust. The marks were where she had been clawing in the dust to find it. At times I have cursed the bulldust, but that night I blessed it. I called a female doctor friend and explained the circumstances. She advised the children and me not to allow ourselves to be cornered in a room with Mary. I noticed that some of Mary's mail came from a well-known psychiatric institution. Her usual medication had made her tired and sleepy, she had stopped taking it, and the devastating scene we had witnessed was the outcome.

I had her walk twice a day with me and talk. At times she cried in anger: 'You are tougher than my counsellor!' Back on her medication, Mary was happy. In the four or five months she was with us on Kimberley Downs, she never tried to kill herself again. Later we found out that Mary was schizophrenic, which was never helped by a bout of secret drinking.

My own girls were growing into young women, which brought a whole new glut of worries. One Turkey Creek Rodeo week, while Leisha and Kristy went off I remained behind on Kimberley Downs with Bob. He had been prescribed a low dose of morphine every day to help with his pain. I worried myself sick wondering what was at the root of it all. Three days together without any action about the station would do us both good, though, and I planned to rest.

I tried, but I couldn't stop fretting about Leisha and Kristy, who were, I heard, soon caught up in all the excitement, the competition, and the fun of meeting up with friends their own age. Desperate with a mother's anxiety, I had my own means of keeping tabs on things. One night, while all the crowd were drinking at the bow-shed bar at the rodeo, the Turkey Creek police paddy wagon pulled up. Tommy, an Aboriginal boy who'd grown up on the station, stepped out, dressed in his full police uniform. The sight of a cop and the police wagon sent the crowd scattering. There was immediate silence, then a whispering:

'Shit, it's the cops!'

'Who's in trouble?'

'Cripes, Leisha, he's looking at you!'

Standing all alone at the bar, Leisha might have been panicking until she recognised Tommy, who walked directly up to her and asked: 'Have you called your mother?'

Tommy gave her a lift a few miles into Turkey Creek to call me, then returned her to the rodeo. Tommy threatened to put her in the back of the paddy wagon if she didn't call me immediately after the rodeo!

In a way, it was a proud moment: I'd looked after Tommy when he was a wayward little boy who'd come to me from Derby Welfare, and now he was looking out for my girls.

CHAPTER 21

The Darkest Dawn

*J*uly 1992 saw the beginning of a very painful period in my life, a time I still have difficulty understanding.

A black cloud had started to drift over our happy and beautiful life. It was to be the worst time since losing our beloved Kelly.

I had been surviving in a fluctuating marriage, ever since the grief of losing Kelly had come close to killing Bob. I went on willingly, because I had a strong and happy young family to look after and a husband who needed me and, I thought, loved me in his own mysterious way.

This day in July, I was at Kimberley Downs and Bob was at Kilto. The phone rang shrilly, breaking the peace of the homestead surrounds. I bounded towards the house.

On the line was a family friend, the mother of Fiona, a girl we usually took with us to the Fitzroy Rodeo. Fiona was another of the youngsters I had brought under my wing. A very confused and disturbed 16-year-old, she seemed to be battling some emotional problems.

Fiona had something to tell me, her mother said. As I waited, my brain hammered with maddening thoughts.

'You haven't picked me up,' Fiona whimpered angrily. 'Why haven't you picked me up?'

That day I would normally have picked her up and driven her back to Kimberley Downs to take her with staff and family to the Fitzroy Rodeo. This time, though, I hadn't included her on purpose. I was tired of taking responsibility for her and her wild ways. A lot of lonely young stockmen headed in for the rodeos, and I wasn't sure I had eyes in the back of my head to check that she wasn't wandering off with one of them.

I mumbled an excuse, and then she said she had something to tell me. I asked her to tell me on the phone, but she said there was much more to it. She needed to talk to me face to face. Organising Sandy to watch the children, I jumped into the new Mercedes, one of Bob's unpredictable gifts bestowed on me during a trip to Perth, and headed for Fiona's house, about two hours away. I was so angry and confused for not being told the problem over the phone, I came close to rolling the Merc.

As I drove, I thought about some other things I knew about Fiona. It wasn't just the anxiety over watching her that had stopped me taking her to the rodeo. Once I had found many letters from Fiona hidden in Leisha's untidy dressing table drawers. Reading and re-reading their contents had absolutely floored me. I don't know why, but possibly because they were exposing some truths I'd long suspected, I photo-copied the letters. They sickened me to the pit of my stomach. I knew I was invading Leisha's and Fiona's privacy, and didn't want them to know, but I was too overwhelmed by shock and anger to let it drop.

In one letter the writer confessed to having sex with someone after a drinking binge, but in her bleary haze she couldn't remember if there were more men. Her utmost fear was that she might be pregnant. Coming across this heart-wrenching but disturbing bundle of personal confidences was a mother's nightmare. Written by a 16-year-old to my younger, 14-year-old daughter, it was unforgivable. Fiona and Leisha were as close as young girl friends could be, sharing confidences and girly stories. Fiona was a lovely girl, but seemed very lost and lonely. This was the reason I'd let her visit as often as she did. But I didn't want her behaviour to affect Leisha.

Walking confidently into her family's home, I found her in the kitchen with her parents. I asked her gently, 'What's wrong?'

There was some fumbling but no answer.

'Are you pregnant, darling?'

I thought surely we could help her. To be pregnant wasn't a death sentence. Her father withdrew to the back lawn and I was left sitting with Fiona and her mother. The feeling of watching a play came over me. I was standing on the perimeter looking in, my mouth dry, my heart hurting against my chest wall. This was surreal. She was the star attraction with her nervous – or was it stupid? – smile. Surely if something was so important, she couldn't think it funny?

Her mother urged her to spill the beans. I was tired. I had travelled a long way. I needed to know.

On hearing her words, I felt total disbelief. My body was now burning, my blood raging. I shook my head slowly in denial. I rose, trembling, and walked steadily out of their house towards the Merc, down what seemed a long, dark, winding tunnel. Everything else was a blur. I closed the car door and drove with a very heavy heart towards Kilto to find Bob.

Crying one minute, angry the next, I drove erratically. I desperately needed Bob to level with me. Fiona hadn't been to the police herself yet, as far as I knew, but she had spoken to a counsellor who had made a complaint.

I knew Fiona frequently bothered Bob at the Mango Farm while he was working there. Both of her parents worked, and she was often home alone. He'd told me many months earlier that she would visit him after school, and he would send her home. Then she would return again, complaining every time that she felt sick. After phoning one of her parents to tell them where she was, Bob would let her remain, though I'd warned him to be tougher with her. His humaneness could turn out to be his own worst enemy.

Driving frantically, seeing nothing, I wheeled the Merc around the sandy bend onto the two-wheel track leading to the Kilto homestead, careening to a halt in the heavy sand bog at the house paddock gate. It was 2.30 pm and stinking hot. Bob had heard the vehicle. He was walking slowly down the fence line towards me: one stooped, agonising step after another. He looked so sick, his pindan-covered clothes just hanging off his frame, and much older than his 63 years.

My mind in turmoil, body aching with anger, tears mixing with perspiration flowing down my face, I frantically tried to rock the heavy Mercedes back and forward in the fierce afternoon sun to free it from the sandy bog.

The closer Bob came, the more emotional I grew. With heaving chest and uncontrolled sobbing, I released my frustrations by thumping the steering wheel of my beautiful vehicle, my foot flat to the floor sending sand flying into the air, only digging a deeper hole and, finally, bellying it.

Bob's worried look grew intense. He hadn't seen me in such a state since losing our son. With his arm around me, my anguish subsided as we walked slowly through the wall of heat towards the homestead.

My composure returning, I relayed the dreadful news. I told him plainly that Fiona had accused him of indecent assault.

'You are supposed to have touched her several times,' I said fiercely.

Bob had heard me threatening many times to gut-shoot anyone who interfered with my children. Taken by surprise, he was struggling to make sense of what I'd said.

'Try to think back,' I begged him. 'Please, think!'

By now I was fanatical, tears streaming again down my face.

Bob said, 'If I had at any time, it was certainly not intentional.' He would go to the police station first thing in the morning to find out what this was all about. I wanted to believe him, but I was confused. What had he meant by 'not intentional'? I didn't know, and didn't press him. He seemed vacant – not really knowing himself what he meant.

Bob plodded off down the paddock to check the water supply to the cattle yard and dig the Merc out of the bog. I sat alone with a pannikin of strong coffee on the back veranda, confused and full of resentment towards everyone involved. I remembered a day, many months earlier, when Fiona arrived at the station to spend the weekend, as she often had over the years.

Bob had parked the Toyota by the big house, taking his travel bag in one hand and briefcase in the other. He moved to the veranda in his slow way, placing the bags down, while our children waited impatiently to welcome him home. They, and I, were out of luck. Fiona bustled forward and wrapped both her arms around him. Taken aback, I was cross with her and with Bob for letting it happen. I'd walked unhappily towards the cook house, needing to think for a while, and Leisha and Kristy came running and crying: 'Mummy, Fiona won't let us near Daddy.'

This was a red rag to a bull. Outraged, I spun on my heels, telling the girls to follow me as I hurried back to the veranda.

Fiona was still holding him. Fronting them head-on, I laid it on the line.

'The children need their father too!'

I told Fiona to let go of Bob, enabling the children a chance to hug him after not having seen their father for several weeks. I silently interrogated Bob's dark eyes. I loathed him for his weakness, not showing the strength of character to untangle himself from this sticky situation.

Now, back on Kilto, gazing down to my empty pannikin as the evening chill replaced the mugginess of the long day, that day's suffering returned. Bob had gone to sleep in our bed. Unable to eat, I went and lay curled up beside him in a shivering foetal position until fatigue took over for a couple of hours. Attempting to talk to Bob seemed pointless. I could feel him on a hair-trigger, ready to explode against me if I confronted him.

But the next morning I was up early, emotions still churning in the pit of my stomach. I needed answers. In the kitchen, I again questioned my husband: 'Did you touch her? Think back!'

He wouldn't say anything; he wouldn't even look at me. He was a vacuum, sucking all the emotion out of me into the open. It ended with me screaming and emotionally out of control. I denounced him for being blind, stupid and too weak. I collapsed to the floor in inconsolable sobbing, blaming myself for not having put an end to Fiona's visits.

Bob helped me to my feet. I searched his vacant eyes for answers. Finding no response, I dropped my gaze. His tight grip was bruising my shoulders, his gammy hand and dead arm insensitive. He moved his hand from my shoulder to my chin, forcing me to look at him again.

'You must accept whatever is thrown at me,' he said, releasing me from his arms.

I cried uncontrollably once more, screaming, 'No, No!' and shaking my head from side to side.

Sternly he repeated: 'You will accept.'

My torture turned from tears to confusion. My mind was caught in a massive cobweb. I was furious beyond belief. *Accept?* Why should I accept anything if he'd done nothing wrong?

Bob left for the police station; I waited at Kilto. He was told that there were no charges at this point, but he would have to come back to the courthouse later to be charged with indecent assault. It didn't make a lot of sense to him but he did as he was told and returned to Kilto.

'Charged with what?' I demanded. 'When? Where?' How many times?' I wanted to know. I was angry that he wouldn't answer me. He seemed to disappear into that deep sealed-off place. My tears and tantrums followed, and of course he was confused and still trying to draft this mess in his own mind.

I called Brian Singleton, QC, a friend of many in the Kimberley, and asked him for help. Singleton arranged to find out exactly what they were charging Bob with. My confusion and exasperation were greater than Bob's. I felt he didn't really care what happened to him; he didn't care whether he went to jail or not. He was a sick man and on morphine, still caught in his need to be strong and silent. I needed him to talk, to reason with me. I needed to know something. It was as if I was paddling our canoe upstream all alone in darkness.

During this time friends from Derby and Broome visited to show their support. Others distanced themselves from us. The hurt and anguish I suffered from this alone is indescribable. To point a finger at the accused was one thing, but to shake it at the children or myself was another.

The time came to sit Leisha down and I tried, without crying, to explain the circumstances that now surrounded her father. I told her how this was a nasty and awkward situation, with heavy repercussions for him. Most people, I told her, would believe any rumour; a few of those people would transfer the heavy cloud from Bob to enclose us, his family.

I asked her: 'Has Daddy ever touched you in a way you felt wrong?'

Leisha's answer was quick and aggressive. 'Don't be so stupid, Mum, Daddy's not like that.'

That was the end of the conversation.

I had become an emotional wreck and was not sleeping well on the nights Bob was home at Kimberley Downs. He sat on the foot of our bed one evening.

'You don't trust me around the children anymore,' he said solemnly. 'You don't sleep until I'm asleep.'

This was probably the longest sentence he had uttered in weeks. A realisation ran through my body: I had hurt him. I had begun to think Bob was impossible to hurt, that he felt nothing. Yet, looking into his black eyes, I was still unable to find the answers I was looking for.

'I'm so sorry, but no,' I whispered. Then, letting fly tearfully, I cried: 'You're an adult, for God's sake, you should know better!'

I rolled over in the bed and turned my back on him.

'I don't trust anyone anymore,' I said, and broke down, sobbing my heart out. He never touched me. He sat on the side of the bed with his face in his hands.

He was right: I didn't trust him. I loved him deeply and had always trusted him fully, but these allegations had wiped my trust away. I had become a human lioness and my only real concern was shielding my cubs from all the innuendoes around us.

The following week I arranged an appointment for Bob with the best psychologist I could find in Perth. I was becoming frantic in my desperate need for answers, or reasons.

I travelled with him to Perth and patiently sat out his appointment in the waiting room, only to be left sitting there as he
walked out past me, his black eyes expressionless. This was his
first and last visit to a psychologist.

The wheels of justice turn slowly at the best of times, but it was
excruciating for us to wait months and months for the police
to work up the charges against Bob and take the matter to
court. And yet, somehow, life still went on. During this time
I recognised the fierce determination shining through in my
dear Leisha. Kristy and Robby, on the other hand, were still
little children. I thought I was keeping my family cocooned in
warmth and love, but as I fell apart fate somehow handed that
role to my 14-year-old, Leisha.

Sandy and Narda, our cook, kept Leisha on the rodeo
circuit. With the hardened rodeo crowd behind her she walked
with her head held high and never bowed to the humiliation or
innuendo surrounding her father. She rode the rodeo circuit
like never before. Between herself and her horse's outstanding
endurance she won 11 championship buckles. She also took
out Kimberley Rodeo Circuit title for All-Round Cowgirl for
the second year running, while still only a junior competitor,
an achievement that drew our focus during this miserable time.
I knew I had a leader in the family, a daughter of whom I was
supremely proud.

I kept running the bores and mills. There was no end to
the problems, with columns rusting, pumps full of mud, tanks
leaking, wind drought and much more. Day and night I was
either carting water with Bob's tanker or offsiding Jimmy on
pulling a bore, or dropping the pump further down a hole in
search of water. Jim was an honest, caring and extremely hardworking man. I'm sure no other man would have battled along
by my side, using and reusing old bore columns, joiners and

jack pumps that had really seen better days. Even when we were both covered head to toe in heavy, black, coarse sump oil while pulling the jack pump off Boundary Bore he never complained. Many men would not have stuck around and put their heart into their job like Jim did. At a time of my greatest need, Jimmy's dedication was a constant reminder of how good and true a man could be.

CHAPTER 22

Life Goes On

The build-up to the court case brought massive stress and illness. Bob, peeing blood constantly, became too sick to either run Kilto or remain at Kimberley Downs. The local hospital transferred him to Sir Charles Gairdner Hospital in Perth. Robby and I flew to his bedside. He had been operated on and was haemorrhaging, at death's door.

His prostate and pancreas problems were getting on top of him, though he wouldn't tell me precisely what was wrong. When I asked him, he'd fob me off. I felt as if I didn't exist. Many, many get-well messages arrived for Bob. He showed no interest in any of them.

I sold the Mango Farm, my way of disconnecting us from memories of Fiona visiting Bob. Alone, I tried to manage Kimberley and Napier Downs, Kilto and our contracting business. I was becoming so worn-out trying to keep everything together, spending all day offsiding Jim, then racing to Kilto to check on the waters, arriving back at Kimberley Downs at three o'clock the following morning, I came close to chucking in the towel. I wondered what the hell I was doing. Then my children would run towards me, happy and full of laughter and stories about their day, and I would push my worries to the back of my mind and go on. I always knew I would keep walking towards that dim light at the end of the tunnel, and would not give up.

Robby was eight years old and in the past few months had started to wake with nightmares. He had never suffered from a lack of confidence, and I was sure this change was brought on by the stress in the household. Crying and screaming, 'Mum, Mummy!' complete with mumbling and gurgling sounds, his tossing and wrestling scared us all. I would fly out of bed with heart pounding and rock him in my warm embrace, assuring him that Mummy was here and would never leave him. Sometimes it would take me minutes, the longest minutes in my entire life, to calm him down.

When Bob came home to Kimberley Downs from hospital, he offered no support to either one of us. This was terribly confusing and hurtful, as Bob had never shown any unkindness towards the girls or Robby in the past. When Robby had a nightmare, Bob would lift his pain-filled body from the bed and yell, outraged at his own son. This, of course, caused me to retaliate. Once, while calming my son at some ungodly hour, I told Bob to put a sock in it or not bother coming home at all. When he was well enough, he returned alone to Kilto.

When I ask myself how I remained with Bob during this time, I have a simple answer: I was too busy working. Running the stations, there was always work and another work-related crisis around the corner. Work served as a constant distraction from my pain. If I had had nothing to do but sit around and dwell on our problems, things would surely have taken a very different course.

One day Leisha had completed her school lessons early and was accompanying me as my 'bore run' offsider. I relished quiet times with Leisha, as her strength and energy made me forget my troubles with Bob.

My heart sank on arrival at the Telegraph Dam. The heat was intense and the glare brought tears to the eyes as it shimmered from the mudflat to the surrounding banks. The flies and native bees hammered us in search of the salty moisture. In the middle of the black pit of steamy mud were two wild horses bogged to their huge fear-stricken eyeballs. As one of them battled to gain a footing, the other would sink down further, almost submerged and struggling to stay alive.

The fence around the dam was still secure, although the top wire showed signs of strain and horse hair. Turning towards Leisha, I noted dark beads of perspiration on her forehead. I knew I would have to choose my words carefully.

'Love, they are wild horses, they run outback with the mob between Mariana, No. 67 and Davies bores,' I volunteered gently.

'We must save them, Mum,' came Leisha's anxious reply, anticipating what I was going to suggest.

I could see the tears in her eyes. Leisha didn't need to be told that if Daddy were here he would shoot them first and then drag out the carcasses. I rummaged through the Toyota, hoping to find a bull strap or car tube that would substitute as a collar. We were out of luck. It was a case of pull them out, pull their heads off, or shoot them. But we'd give them a chance. An eagle circling above let out a cry and somehow, I don't think he was wishing me luck.

Leisha grabbed one end of the rope and made a noose as she waded in waist-deep mud towards the bogged animals. As the brumbies lashed about violently, she dropped a loop over the one that was closer to her.

Within split seconds of my turning my back to hook the rope to the vehicle, the silence was broken by Leisha's blood-curdling screams. The distressed animal had a death grip on Leisha's cheek and was shaking her savagely from side to side like a rag doll. I grabbed a lump of wood and moved in. But before I got to her, Leisha regained her footing in the mud. She gave the animal an almighty punch in the head and it let go.

Leisha' s tough exterior couldn't fool me. She was in a lot of pain, her cheek black and covered in blood. At this point I felt like pulling the horse's bloody head off and wondered why we had bothered at all. With the rope around the brumby's neck, I hooked on with the vehicle and pulled it towards the bank. No matter how violent I felt towards that horse, I prayed I wouldn't behead it in my daughter's presence.

Without any more mishaps, we rescued the other brumby too.

We were fatigued but happy, giving each other muddy hugs of relief. We felt good, between the two of us, for having accomplished a difficult job under trying conditions.

Leisha carried the terrible imprint from her rescue mission for the next six months, until the bite mark eventually faded.

CHAPTER 23

The Court Case

*B*y late 1992, things were looking good for the TB eradication program and I felt some satisfaction over a job well done. I'd updated the station maps, and marked all new fences, paddocks and bores. I now had enough separate paddocks to rotate – I was successfully managing the only million-plus-acre property that was 100 per cent boundary-fenced. I was proud that I'd achieved all this while my entire life seemed to be falling apart.

The police notified Singleton three days prior to the court case that it would be best for Bob to plead guilty, to avoid putting Fiona on the stand. In return, they would charge Bob with indecent assault but not scratch around for more accounts. Singleton put this to us in his motel room. After leaving, I turned around on Bob and said, 'Is there any more?'

I needed to know for the children's sake and my own sanity. He then opened up for the first time. He admitted to once rubbing Fiona's stomach for a few fleeting minutes when she arrived at the Mango Farm after school crying with severe stomach pain. He said that when he was in his Toyota with her, Fiona would never remain seated on the passenger seat, always moving over to squeeze right up by his side. He admitted to one other incident: he had got out of the driver's seat to close a gate on the station, and when he got back in, Fiona had moved over into his seat, and a touch of madness overcame him. He placed his head on her chest for a few seconds. He said there was no more to tell me.

I swung around on him, angry and frustrated, thinking, *How bloody stupid could a person be?* Very firmly and quietly, I said, 'Remember you were supposed to be the adult, for Christ's sake.'

I did believe him. I believed that that was all that happened. Bob wasn't a romantic or sexual man, and I took his word for it. And yet, my emotions running amok, I was upset and in tears again. Words could not describe my pain and frustration. I felt sorry for all concerned in this cyclonic mess, but most of all for my children, the innocent victims.

Then came Bob's day in court, the second most terrible day of our life after losing our son. I parked the Toyota outside the courthouse, asking Leisha, Robby and Kristy to remain there until after the verdict.

To say I was in a distraught state is an understatement; my nerves were truly shredded and I was upset to the point of being sick. Bob showed no emotion whatsoever. We entered the packed courtroom and I noticed many of Bob's supporters, but also some others who were there simply to gloat. There were also half-a-dozen ringers and contractors up on a cattle-duffing charge.

Balanced on the edge of my seat in the courtroom, I was strung as tight as a good top wire on a fence line. When his turn came, I leaned forward to hear Bob's words. Without hesitation he stood and spoke in a loud, harsh voice: 'Guilty, Your Honour'.

The judge set no jail sentence. Bob was landed a fine of $5,000. As he left, he stumbled slightly. Leisha, who had burst out of the car, pushed her way through the crowded court-room. Taking her father by the hand, she led him away. I slowly rose from my seat. Some low types verbally harassed me. Confused, angry and shaken, I left the court, my heart cut to shreds.

Unable to stand another day of anguish, I needed peace, space and time away from the humiliation. The day after the court case, we left Kilto. I drove the family, including Bob, all over Queensland with no destination in mind, trying to find peace and freedom from the past for us all. Leisha, Kristy and Robby were delighted and cheerful; it was an adventure, with new towns, new motels, all new scenery and beautiful weather.

Bob showed no interest at all. He may as well have been a zombie. He was detaching himself from us, falling into his well-known pit of deep, dark despondency. I drove through Camooweal, Normanton, Atherton, Palm Cove, down through Hughenden, Longreach and as far as Holbrook in New South Wales. Bob might as well have stayed at home.

He took up smoking in the enclosed car, something he never usually did. The children and I suffered, particularly Leisha, who had asthma. Our family holiday soon had the edge of an unhappy ordeal. Bob, somehow full of resentment towards me, would not talk to me. He was still angry at me for wanting him to contest the case. I saw him as being innocent of indecent assault – why had he pleaded guilty? I would not do as he'd told me; I would not *accept*.

In Holbrook, we met up with a friend who had once been a head stockman. We were all sitting around a park table, talking and managing a laugh over old times, surrounded by rolling green paddocks and vineyards, the air crisp and clean. For a short time I felt the pressure lift from my body. Then I raised my eyes towards Bob's – they were expressionless and burning black with anger at me. I felt deflated again. Needing to vent his frustration somewhere, he'd settled on me. I tried to understand him, but he wouldn't let me in. As we returned to the station, I kept offering encouragement to the children, to keep them smiling. But my veneer of the tough, coping, outback woman was wearing bloody thin.

CHAPTER 24

Fairfield

The three or four years after the court case seem, looking back, to have been a constant treadmill of work – work on the stations, and work to find a fresh start for Bob. The unrelenting effort took a toll on my health too. After suffering chronic blood loss I had a hysterectomy in Perth, during which I haemorrhaged quite severely. I remember a frenzy of post-operative drama filtered through hazy shadows as I moved in and out of consciousness. Though I recovered, I later began to suffer exhaustion and joint pain, and tested positive for the Ross River virus and another three mosquito-borne viruses. I didn't regain full health for years after Bob's court case.

After our driving trip, Bob continued to descend into his zombie-like state. His body would go through the motions – he would drive around the bores on Kilto, start and check engines, look at the solar pumps and inspect the cattle, and then, if all was well, return to Kimberley Downs – but his mind was elsewhere. Increasingly he sat on the homestead veranda for hours on end, saying nothing. Even the children were having trouble trying to get his attention. Once, when I asked him why he was unhappy, he slammed down his pannikin with such ferocity that the table jumped and the condiments rattled. I watched him storm off, feeling stupid for having asked. It was obvious, wasn't it? He was in deep pain. I couldn't help seeing my growing independence as hammering further nails into his sense of helplessness. When our TB eradication program was coming to a successful end, and I told the company secretary in a phone call that I preferred mustering up the last stray bulls with the buggy and truck rather than destroy them, Bob shouted wildly, 'Shoot them, shoot them.' The secretary told Bob we would do it my way. He told Bob in no uncertain terms: 'Sheryl is still the manager.'

I did not know if it was me the woman, his wife, his children's mother, or me the station manager and owner – once his eager young apprentice but no longer – that he needed to vent his anger upon. I walked away, shed my silent tears, but ultimately remained in a state of total bewilderment. I more than anyone else understood the suffering his body was going through, yet surely in a life filled with pain there comes a time when one must accept help gracefully?

I often wondered where it would end. Just before the court case, Bob had pronounced his wish to leave the children and me and disappear by himself into Queensland. I made the decision to sell the Mercedes and bought a new Toyota tray-back for him and put a canopy on the back, outfitting it with long-range fuel and water tanks in case he was going to go off for a long journey. Over the last couple of years I'd had a constant feeling that the responsibility of a wife and family was becoming too much for Bob, that the pressure was smoth-ering him. He had always called himself a 'bagman'. He was a loner, and I felt he would be happier with just himself and a swag, so to speak. At first I was frightened he might have planned to shoot himself in the middle of the outback. I tried to shut out those dreadful thoughts. And anyway, he never took the trip.

I was always looking for a fresh start. At one point I suggested buying Kimberley Downs for ourselves, but he responded with a scornful, loud, 'What?' Then he stared at me hard, with that dark unreadable look I was growing to hate so much. I'd managed the property for seven years now. Was that what he resented? My success? Unable to find any more words, he ended up completely ignoring me, sitting on the veranda drinking a pannikin of tea, rolling one cigarette after the other, gazing toward the horizon. At this point I didn't really have a marriage; it was more a silent battlefield, with pot shots exploding every now and then.

It seemed long ago now, but I had loved the man I'd worked with on Oobagooma Station, and deep down I still loved *that* man: that kind and gentle cattleman who had made me feel so safe. I was not ready to give up on our marriage yet. I could still see a future for the children and myself with Bob. But I needed to get him to come out from under that black cloak that was smothering him to death.

Life on an outback station can't be overtaken by domestic drama. The real world was always ready to raise its head, in one way or another. We had a scare when a python took up residence in our bathroom, announcing its presence by whacking me while I took a shower. Another time, when we were beset by a shrieking flock of cockatoos, I excited Robby by taking out a shotgun.

'You gunna shoot them, Mum?' he asked, full of enthusiasm and looking for adventure.

I had to disappoint him. 'No, Mummy doesn't shoot birds, I only want to scare them away.'

Robby had both hands firmly over his ears as I fired into

the air and away from the trees. There was instant silence from the cockies as they lifted high, circled the homestead and landed above us again.

'There,' I said to Robby, 'I never shot one.'

At that moment a cockatoo landed with wings folded right between Robby's feet, dead. Thinking of it now, that bird was far too stiff to be freshly shot. Too hard, too dead, no pellet marks. My stockmen were sitting at the smoko table only a few feet behind me. I'd like to know which one of them threw the dead bird!

Life certainly wouldn't be dull after the Mabo case in 1993, when the High Court of Australia ruled that native title was recognised at common law. There was a lot of disquiet in the Kimberley, with pastoralists and graziers fearing widespread Aboriginal land claims. I got caught up in the post-Mabo environment when, seeking another fresh start for Bob and the family, I bought Fairfield Station. Fairfield was a neighbouring cattle station in the hands of liquidators, a half-million-acre cattle run that had fascinated me since as far back as 1969, when I'd visited the property with my first husband, Chuck. There was something about it I'd loved at first sight – a small house in a beautiful valley surrounded by mountain ranges, and beyond them some lovely plains.

With some trepidation I invited Bob to look over the property. Instead he suggested, offhandedly, that I do it myself. I was looking for a way to give him direction in life, as had happened when I'd bought Kilto. Gruff though he was, Bob was also showing his total faith in me. Strange though it may sound, that faith had survived and prospered during our turmoil. I was a woman, but this hard, silent cattleman trusted me with his life.

I put down a $40,000 deposit on Fairfield, planning to turn the property into a steer depot with an eye on the market for shipping steers to Asia. Almost immediately, I heard of three

Aboriginal land claims on the property. This did not leave me jumping with jubilation, I have to say. Naturally I was trying to distinguish 'land claim' from 'land grab'. Most rural landholders saw them as one and the same. A lot of station people were sceptical, and I was too: an older indigenous friend had told me he was going to claim land at a certain place on Meeda Station. 'That good place for picnic, Missus,' he innocently said. Both he and I knew he had no connection with that particular area. Was he testing me? I didn't know. It may have been a joke.

I called Elders, the selling agent, and made it clear that we still wished to purchase Fairfield. Bob and I would attempt to sort through these land claims with the people ourselves. To my relief, he was showing signs of interest and enthusiasm again.

But this wilted when the land claims began to get bogged down in arguments among competing tribes, and we didn't know if the sale would proceed smoothly or be held up forever in a land claim court. More and more, Bob was asking if it was all worth it.

The dispute was resolved in an astonishing way: I told two Aboriginal elders that if I could not buy Fairfield Station, I would move the family away from the Kimberley and find a property somewhere else. They went off to get all the tribal leaders together, and the result of their meeting was that they all suddenly withdrew their claims to Fairfield, leaving the property ready for us to take possession. I felt enormous appreciation and gratitude towards these people. They must have wanted us to stay in the country. Heartbreakingly, though, Bob couldn't bring the same commitment and generosity to the venture.

I clearly remember one of our last nights on Kimberley Downs, in September 1993. Bob had already moved across to Fairfield ahead of us. The children and I were sitting quietly on the homestead veranda one evening, all deep in thought. Robby wondered if Bull Pup's grave on Homestead Hill would be all right after we'd gone. Kristy hoped she had all her horse gear, which seemed to be her only worry. Leisha sat quietly while I shed a private tear.

I gazed towards the white corrugated-iron huts beyond the stables thinking that only six years ago these were Aboriginal camps. Alma and Jack had lived there. This time of the evening, children would have been playing, their happy laughter echoing through the valley, entwined with the playful barking of the camp dogs. I could almost sense the misty haze and aroma of the many camp fires as the women cooked for the stockmen. As the beautiful blues and pinks blended in the evening sky, I saw the dark silhouette of the wheel where the Aboriginal boys once turned out tough greenhide ropes.

Near the wheel was the old schoolhouse, renamed the 'honeymoon quarters' after Sandy and Craig were married and made it their home. Next to it was the cook house with the palms and beautiful shade trees I'd planted – so open to the elements but we all loved it.

Later, as I showered and looked for little pythons, I smiled and thought of the many delights they brought to our lives. I tried to ignore the large holes behind the toilet and laundry and throughout the homestead, battle scars from my many encounters with less friendly reptiles.

Lying in bed I remembered when Kimberley Downs carried 20,000 head of cattle with hardly a decent fence. Now there were working bores that my windmill men had resurrected to keep the water up to the cattle, and a workshop with Kimberley Downs painted boldly on the roof.

As I drifted peacefully towards sleep, I felt blessed to have been surrounded with excellent staff and family to attack the challenges and opportunities together. I felt proud and content. I have to admit that I was also enjoying a moment of freedom from the tension caused by Bob's presence. When I was away from him, I could feel that moment's peace by myself, and it seemed more precious and pure.

One day at Fairfield, Robby had something on his mind. Sitting close to his father on the veranda, he said softly: 'Dad, Kelly has died, and Bandit [one of our dogs] has died, and Susie [another one of our dogs] has died. They're all dead, Dad,' With a slightly worried look, he continued: 'Who will be next, Dad?'

I could tell he was worried about his father. Bob refused to see any doctor, even though he was in constant pain. Bob told Robby that we were only here for a certain time, before we were taken from the earth again. Robby was satisfied with this answer – he just wanted to know that his dad wasn't about to be taken away. But Bob had already left us; I just hadn't realised it yet. I'd wanted Fairfield for the family, after the trauma we'd gone through. It could present a new beginning for Bob, a property we could all work together, enthusiastically and proprietorially. But I was banging my head against a brick wall. He was no help during the move, even when, hot and exhausted, I had arrived with the last of many truckloads. When I got out of the truck and walked up to the house, wanting nothing more than the warmth of my husband's arms around me, he thrust me aside, never speaking a word, walking around me as if I didn't exist. His dark look was fixed somewhere in the distance. Horrified and astounded, I shivered in the gentle spirit breeze, wondering why I bothered. That rebuff was the revelatory moment for me, the first time I saw that our marriage might truly be coming to an end.

We only spent a year at Fairfield, a brevity that still wrenches me with pain. Bob went from bad to worse. While I was away for a few nights in Perth, he went through all of my personal possessions. He had become paranoid, and confessed on one of his drunken nights that he had had me tailed by a private eye while I was in Perth – he said the detective was in the motel room next to mine! Whether this was true or not I don't know. I was worried that he was losing his marbles.

I shook my head and said, 'After all we've been through, you do this to me.' As usual, Bob had nothing to say.

Why did I stay? As a wife and mother, having just purchased a cattle station of our own, I lived in hope that this situation would turn around and I'd have the old Bob back.

I announced I was taking a walk before sundown, alone. I climbed through the paddock fences, working my way towards the airstrip, in search of silence and tranquillity. Walking north towards the claypan, my overwrought mind repeatedly churning over my anguish, I could see nothing, feel nothing – only sorrow. I needed these walks to get away from what was quickly becoming my homestead of sheer hell. I had never been so distraught in my entire life; I was really battling, and trying to make sense of things.

Looking towards the end of the airstrip, I noticed a small gilgai – a depression in the ground – filled with water from the rains and surrounded by grass. Three dingoes were hunting frogs and lizards while others lounged close by. Then a touch on my arm. With my nerves stretched to near breaking point, I swung around screaming in fear. Robby got such a fright and we both burst into tears. I felt awful when I noticed the confused and worried look in his blue eyes. With my arm around my distraught son we turned towards the homestead.

Bob's strange attitude was affecting Robby terribly. His father was no longer communicating with him. This made me both angry and unhappy, and I would try to comfort Robby all the more.

Looking up I had noticed that my screams attracted another two dingoes from the far side of the airstrip. The first three abandoned their hunting around the waterhole and I was now fearful for my son's safety, noting five very large dingoes were slowly and fearlessly slinking towards us.

I searched frantically for a weapon, a rock or a lump of wood. Refusing to turn my back, I grabbed a piece of timber and prompted Robby to walk a little quicker while I frantically swung at the two forward dogs. I hated the way they were half crouched and never took their yellow eyes from mine. As they kept coming I kept swinging while Robby walked ahead of me towards the homestead, trying not to show fear.

Picking up the throb of the power plant the dingoes backed off, and we were left to clamber through the horse paddock fences, then home. That evening we told Bob. He couldn't have cared less.

Life wasn't all doom and gloom on Fairfield. I put in great effort trying to shield the children from our stressful situation. They and I had many happy and exciting days investigating the beautiful springs that flowed freely from the great Oscar Range. Wire Spring in particular was a place of solace. I visited often, searching for lost peace. There was a spring that seemed to pop right out of the rock, cascading down from one perfectly rounded granite pool to the next, so clear and clean with the constant flushing from the spring that no algae or weed grew there. Close by, an enormous fig tree provided shade for an all-day picnic, a perfect spot for the children and me.

But while there were moments of happiness and even laughter with the children, each night Bob drank himself into oblivion. After only a few months on Fairfield, Bob said he wanted us to sell the station and Robby was suffering from nightmares again.

CHAPTER 25

The End of a Marriage

*I*t was an unusual day for March, overcast and cloudy, more like winter. Worried that the three creek crossings in Delta paddock were flood-damaged, Bob and I drove as far as we possibly could and then walked the remaining distance into the paddock.

The Kimberley had had a good wet season, rivers still running, roads churned up and the buggar buggar country too boggy to move around on. I followed Bob down the fence line dragging a broken wire, which constantly caught on the mounds of grass growing in the heavy black soil. He was not speaking to me again, his mood deep and dark as he walked ahead under his black cloud.

As I followed, dragging the wire, I tripped on a mound in the buggar buggar and fell into the quagmire of oozing soil, my arms sinking to my elbows. I lay there, shocked and helpless from the fall. Bob kept walking, without missing a beat. Any decent person would have stopped and checked on a dog if it was stuck fast in the hungry mud like I was. What would it take to get a word of kindness out of him? This jolt was the final wake-up call I needed to believe in myself and regain the self-respect that I'd once carried so proudly. No more excuses. Bob was no longer the man I'd married some 20 years earlier.

I'd had a gutful. His cocktail of medication and alcohol was enough to destroy the average person's sanity. If things kept going as they were, his deterioration would surely destroy me and in turn the children. This man that I loved so dearly with all my heart had hurt and humiliated me more than I ever imagined possible. The children would be emotionally scarred for life if I didn't do something now. Bob would not leave the property or take a holiday by himself, as he had often threatened to do, so I finally realised that the only way out was to give up everything I had worked so hard for and everything that meant so much to me. I knew this was the right move.

I gathered the children around me and said Robby and I had to move to Derby. We would come back out to help on the weekends until we sold Fairfield. Leisha and Kristy knew I didn't want to sell it, and weren't too keen on moving into town, so they stayed for the time being. Their horses were at Fairfield, and they knew no other life – nor did I for that matter – and of course they also loved their father.

Leaving my dreams behind, feeling quite numb, I moved into a duplex with Sister Pat of the Catholic Church in Derby. Robby moved with me. Within days Leisha left Fairfield, unable to handle Bob's black moods. Kristy followed soon after, moving to the small township of Camballin where she had other family. Bob took it upon himself to give away many of my personal possessions: two new sewing machines, a beautiful Italian table, a bucket of garnets I'd collected, and more. He even sold, or gave away, a caravan I'd bought to take to rodeos. I'd go out there to pick something up, and it would be gone. But I was too hurt to get to the bottom of it.

My bright spark was Robby. He loved schooling in a class atmosphere and having mates his own age. Once he was off the station and away from heartache, he bloomed.

I was battling mixed emotions living in the town and suffered enormous grief over leaving the station. But Bob was out of control. Loaded with stores and fencing material, Robby and I arrived at the station one weekend to be greeted by a shocking sight. I tearfully rescued my treasured photos and paintings, all attacked with an axe and discarded in the rubbish tip among the trees near the track leading to the homestead. Afraid for our safety, I hid them behind the shed, but not before noticing my favourite, a poster-sized portrait of Bob and me from our Oobagooma days. He had chopped himself to pieces with the axe!

Yet several hours later, on his return from a bore run, all hot and tired, his body noticeably racked with pain, he insisted on cooking for me and treating me like a queen. He served the food and made me tea like a servile waiter. When I went to put the kettle on, he jumped up to do it for me.

I was so confused. One moment he would be the man I knew, and the next a bitter, nasty, calculating madman. I lost any semblance of trust in him. He was a stranger to me.

In the last weeks at Fairfield, his delirious mood swings only got worse. He handled the sale of one of our company businesses, yet not a cent from this deal was ever returned to the company account. He had been receiving the proceeds in cash payments behind my back. For a man who didn't spend money and had never been interested in it, this was quite a shock. I don't believe he had any plans for it, unless he was worried that I might dud him on the sale and was insuring himself pre-emptively. It was so uncharacteristic of him – but no more uncharacteristic than the wild acts of generosity that were happening at the same time. He bought me an $8,000 emerald bracelet, and tried to splurge more on jewellery until I stopped him. Truly, I was so numb by now I could hardly raise the energy to be angry.

I made one last effort. I wasn't going to let go of everything without a fight.

Robby and I returned to Fairfield one weekend, to work alongside his father as we always did. We had checked the mills. I was cleaning a trough that was spring-fed from the Oscar Range, located at the foot of the escarpment on a rugged mound of dirt covered with craggy white gums.

Bob sat in the Toyota watching me, half-concentrating as he rolled a tailormade in the palm of his hand.

'Bob,' I hesitantly began. 'Are you positive you want out of Fairfield?'

His head was on a slight angle, his eyes suddenly wary. I stopped cleaning and stood to look at him, making eye contact. He continued rolling the tobacco at the same steady pace, showing total disregard to my question.

'I have a bank loan, a five-year budget and program worked out,' I said. 'If you don't want the station, then please sell me your half share.'

I still dreamed of running Fairfield as a steer depot for the export market. Regaining what little composure I had left, my head ready to explode with anger, I placed the bung in the trough and turned again to Bob with my arms reaching out, palms facing the heavens.

An unreadable darkness covered his eyes. As a sardonic smile crossed his vacant face, he shook his head. He was not a man to change his mind.

'Why, why, Bob? Just give me a reason. For God's sake, you must have a *reason*!'

My lifelong dream was shattered. He may as well have kicked me in the guts. Bob knew I could make Fairfield work, but he refused to give me a fair go.

That evening Bob cooked roast beef and vegetables. He drank more than his fair share of beer. As I stood to leave the table, he asked me to sit down again.

'Well, what's happening?' he said.

'Surely we can get it together,' I said.

In an offhand way, he said: 'What about a divorce?'

I looked straight into his eyes, which were hesitant. 'Is that what you really want?'

After another long hesitation, he said: 'Yes.'

'Do you trust me to do the paperwork, so the lawyers don't rip us off?' I said.

'Yes.'

And that was that.

Before I climbed into bed that night, he placed a small rug on the floor by my side.

'So your feet don't touch the cold lino in the morning,' he said. His movements were stiff as he tried to straighten the rug on the floor. A kind gesture but impossible to reconcile with the Bob I had come to know. I felt like crying with exasperation. He had chosen this moment, now that we'd agreed to divorce, to show such small acts of kindness.

The following week I discussed the outcome of the property sale with the children, then told them about the divorce. Leisha and Robby made it very plain they didn't want me to fight for the station on their behalf. In fact they wanted to be as far away from Fairfield as they could. They understood that Daddy was not well, and I was afraid of his threats.

* * *

The divorce papers were ready to sign in the middle of the big wet season of 1994–95.

Jack, our trusted friend, also a Justice of the Peace in Derby, travelled with me along the Gibb River Road to meet with Bob. Bob arrived via chopper, piloted by another friend. There on the muddy banks of flooded Mount North Creek we signed the legal documents.

'Don't be sad,' Bob offered. 'It's only a piece of paper.'

I felt both relieved and bewildered by it all, and returned to Derby to my little flat.

In 1995, after I'd been unable to get Bob to agree to selling me his half-share, Fairfield was sold to the Aboriginal people who had kindly waived their land claims in favour of us at the beginning of the saga. With the property on the market, their land claims were reinstated and Fairfield subsequently became theirs with our blessing. Bob could never give me a reason why he hadn't let me buy it. Deep down, I think he was afraid I might make a success of it.

CHAPTER 26

Long Yard

*I*n the year following our divorce, Bob and I were to travel in different directions across Australia in search of peace. Having left school, Leisha moved to Townsville, and Bob roamed around Queensland, wandering from place to place until he stayed with her for a while. Always close until that last year at Fairfield, they reconciled. I stayed in Derby for a while and then took Robby down to the south-west of Western Australia, searching for a small block with some cattle. Bob and I kept in contact for the children's sake with the odd letter. His were sometimes apologetic, at other times a tangled mess and out of this world with incoherence. I hoped that somewhere in his travels he would find a cure for his pain and learn to be at peace with his mind. Before leaving Derby I studied meditation and counselling with the West Australian Ministry of Justice and also found time to listen to Robby and his schoolmates read aloud during class. To see a beautiful smile come over a child's face was well worth it.

In late 1995 and 1996 Bob and I both bought properties 18 kilometres apart in the Great Southern, near Albany in

Western Australia. I bought the Shiralee, a 230-acre farm –
barely a horse paddock! – and Bob bought Sleepy Hollow,
a 160-acre property. There we endeavoured to start afresh.
Although living on separate farms, we knew about each
other's usefulness and knowledge. Cautiously, we offered to
help out with each other's cattle. Sometimes I visited him just
to see that he was all right. I'd take him shopping, because
his driving was wobbly. After a while, we found we could
go for little picnics in the country. After everything that
had happened, I felt responsible for him. He was an elderly
man, and the father of my children. There was a bond I
couldn't – and didn't want to – break. If it hadn't been for
Bob, the cold would have surely driven me home to the
Kimberley.

With my visits to his farm, helping each other as we had in
years long gone in the simple pleasures of shopping, fencing
and cattle work, we regained some of the respect that we'd
once had for each other. Having lunch out together once a
week, something we'd never experienced as a couple, brought
much contentment and gladness to us both. I was very for-
giving, it's true, but I knew there was something wrong with
him – his grief, his bodily sickness and pain – that was responsible for the worst things he'd done. It seemed to me now that
a measure of the real Bob, the one I had known at Oobagooma,
was re-emerging.

Still ambitious and in need of more stimulation, we went
to look over a large neighbouring cattle property of a few
thousand acres, Crystal Brook, with full intentions to buy it.
I was ready to buy land again and get back into the cattle game.
This would be my way of moving on from the past, but I could
not move on from Bob. I felt that buying land together, and
consolidating what we had, would set things up for the
children so that they might have a future on the land. Two

weeks later, near the end of 1998, I noticed a sudden and drastic decline in Bob's health.

I'd had suspicions when he brought me two magnificent rose bushes and said, 'If anything ever happens to me, don't become sad – sit and look at these roses with a cup of tea and think of the good times.'

I was visiting him every day, bringing him food and checking on his wellbeing. He was old and sick, but when I found him unconscious on the bathroom floor of his house, it was still a shock. Deep down, I knew he was a terribly unwell man – but not the dying kind, for he had suffered pain as long as I could remember.

Leisha arranged an appointment with a top specialist in Perth while I organised a charter flight from Albany to have Bob there on time. An afternoon of tests and visits yielded the fateful news: he only had a month to live. He had advanced cancer of the pancreas and the liver.

Dazed and heartbroken, I travelled with Robby to St John of God Hospital and slept by Bob's bed until the end, nine days after the diagnosis, on Leisha's twenty-first birthday. She came too, so the three of us were there for him.

The room was filled with yellow roses, my gift to him. A grey cloud filled the space, and the evening sunrays bounced off a crystal vase on the windowsill. I saw flickers of light moving across his worn-out body.

For a fleeting moment my thoughts returned to the old Aboriginal man, Joe Nipperappi, whom I'd buried on Louisa all those years ago – the same loneliness, but a long distance away. Death was returning, bringing its heavy freight of sadness.

We performed one final ritual: the children and I knew it was time to put Daddy's boots on. Bob had always said he must 'die with his boots on'.

I sat holding his hand, then my breath tensed as he opened his eyes, which were now seemingly peaceful.

His final words, mouthed in a barely audible rasp, were: 'I love you.'

You tough old bastard, McCorry. It took you a whole lifetime to whisper those three simple words.

Epilogue

Since Bob died in 1998, I have remained in the Great Southern region of Western Australia. The veranda from which I view the Porongurup Ranges and relive the past is only a few thousand kilometres from the stations Bob and I bought more than a decade ago. The Kimberley is a long way away, yet I feel it as a constant presence in my heart and in my blood.

The cold winds continue to blow in the winter months, causing me to stop at times and wonder why I don't return to the north. I think, once again, of Bob. When he was trying to cheer me up against those winds and against that temptation in his last years, he said: 'The past is gone, Sheryl, you don't go back. What have you got to prove by going back?'

Bob never went back.

As significant as what he said, towards the end, was the fact that he was talking to me at all after so many years of deep, thickening silence. We had come to a hesitant peace, for the children's sake as well as our own. It would be wrong to say Bob and I were fully reconciled. That could never happen after some of the things he had done. But we could be friends, and friendly, to each other. After all, Bob was always, even in our darkest hours, the person who had had more faith in me than anyone else in my life. Bob placed total trust in me. Yes, I placed him on a pedestal; but so, in his way, did he lift me.

After he died, I fell in an emotional heap that lasted many months. Robby, only 13, was a source of great strength, even as he was battling with his own feelings of unfinished business with his father. We all suffered. Leisha partied hard, trying in vain to drown her sorrows, while Kristy, who had just entered the workforce, was seesawing with raw emotions. All of this had built up in the previous few years, and was let loose by Bob's passing.

In an emotionally vulnerable state, I took possession of both farms, the Shiralee and Sleepy Hollow. Later I did fulfil part of my dream, which was to buy and sell young steers for the export market. I regained my enjoyment in life bit by bit, boosted by the mateship of growing and selling cattle. I even had a short but passionate affair. The children came and worked with me, and often we talked about that old story of the bundle of sticks which, as long as they hold together, cannot be broken. Thank God I didn't chuck in the towel.

Once my grief settled, I found that my spirit was still strong. I met and married Ron Beacham, the owner of the Cable Beach Caravan Park in Broome and a farmer. But two days before our marriage, I was diagnosed with breast cancer. I had no choice but to have immediate surgery. I elected to have a lumpectomy, with further treatment after the wedding. The chaos upended my children's lives, and Leisha refused to leave my bedside in hospital. Then, as I was recuperating, she, Robby and Kristy looked after me on the farm.

Fifty-eight this year, I am reasonably happy and healthy. I move between Broome, where Ron's work is, and cattle farms at Carbunup River and Narrikup here in view of Mount Barker. My visits to the cancer clinic are down to once a year.

Weeks after the court case, Fiona told Leisha and me that the complaint against Bob was taken out of her hands and blown out of all proportion. That was 14 years ago now. We are all very close – Fiona, her parents, and my family. There is no anger or animosity, only love, between us. The girls are as close as ever.

Five years after her father's death, Leisha married and produced two beautiful sons. She is now single, 30 years old, and devoted to her two strong boys, Brock and Cohen. Her fighting spirit is well and truly back, and she has recently begun to compete in rodeos again.

Kristy, now 28, has remained single and her love of horses is as strong as ever. She worked as a track rider for Bart Cummings in Sydney and Melbourne for a while and has returned to live in the south-west of Western Australia. She still works with thoroughbreds.

Robby, 21, has teamed up with Tara, his girlfriend, and they are currently working for my husband, Robby's step-father, at Cable Beach Caravan Park. The land is very much in Robby's blood and he will return to it one day.

My parents, now in their eighties, live in peaceful Northampton, north of Geraldton. They try to keep off the beaten track. Thank you; Mum and Dad, for your many trips to Louisa. Your love and advice helped keep me going.

My four brothers and their families all own properties around Broome. They enjoy sundowners at sunset and of course the fishing. We are still close and see each other at various times through the year.

Michael, my youngest brother, works for a mining company at Turkey Creek, between Wyndham and Halls Creek in outback Western Australia. He married Janine, who visited him on Louisa Downs all those years ago, and they have three children.

Jamesey, who caught bulls for us on Napier Downs in the 1970s, built up a cattle station of his own. Sadly, he was killed recently in a chopper accident on his property.

Shawn Murphy, who answered my distressed radio call when Kelly died and courageously flew into Louisa after dark, was killed while heli-mustering cattle in Gascoyne, Western Australia, in the 1980s.

Bluey and Rita left Louisa when we did, and moved into a retirement home in Derby, where they both passed on.

Jimmy Marshall returned to Derby, where his family were based, and he still lives there today. I still keep in contact with that fine man and his family.

Katie, who worked by my side at Louisa, is still there and calls me regularly, bringing me up to date on her part of the Kimberley and its people.

So many of my dear Aboriginal friends who helped guide me and stood by me during the saddest times of my life have now passed on, but always by my side are my wonderful and courageous children. Thank you, Leisha, Robby and Kristy. Extra special love to you, Leisha and Robby, for your un-wavering strength in sharing your home with so many people over the years. It was tough at times, I know. Thank you for your stoic support while I wrote this memoir. Your cries of, 'You can do it, Mum!' kept me going. This is for you.

Acknowledgments

I'd like to say a big thank you to Pan Macmillan for its gamble in taking on a bushie's story of life in the Kimberley. Thanks go to Alex Craig for her faith in the outback; her belief inspired me to make this book the best it could be. Thank you also to Malcolm Knox for helping me bring it all together, and to Catherine Day.

Thank you also to Peter Melsom. Your trust was my strength in those difficult times.

Finally, thank you to my family – you know who you are – for your ongoing encouragement and support.